The Observant Walker

Also by John Wright

A Natural History of the Hedgerow

The Forager's Calendar: A Seasonal Guide to Nature's Wild Harvests

A Spotter's Guide to Countryside Mysteries

The
Observant
Walker

Wild Food, Nature and Hidden
Treasures on the Pathways of Britain

John Wright

P

PROFILE BOOKS

First published in Great Britain in 2023 by
Profile Books Ltd
29 Cloth Fair
London
EC1A 7JQ

www.profilebooks.com

Copyright © John Wright, 2023

Designed by James Alexander

1 3 5 7 9 10 8 6 4 2

Printed and bound in Great Britain by
Clays Ltd, Elcograf S.p.A.

A CIP catalogue record for this book is available from the
British Library.

ISBN 978 1 78816 687 4
eISBN 978 1 78283 797 8

For Edith

Introduction

In May 2021 my wife and I set off on one of the least adventurous adventures ever recorded. It was from Fulham to Marble Arch in London. Apart from the traffic, it was not dangerous, and at barely four miles it was certainly not arduous, with coffee shops and pubs along the way making it nothing more than a leisurely walk, a springtime day out in a sunny London. What was different was that our plan was to pay attention to our surroundings in a way that people rarely do when walking in a city – or, indeed, anywhere. Rather than a bit of window-shopping, a visit to the barber's or the post office, we instead looked closely at the herbaceous plants and the trees, at every lichen and every insect that crossed our path.

Our London stroll was the first of eight walks we would take all over Britain, their aim being to look closely at the things that make each terrain unique and interesting, and to name, examine and describe those things, those *organisms*, that are passed by as commonplace yet unknown, of no superficial interest, but which are nevertheless profoundly fascinating once considered with an observant eye.

I led my first wild food foray in 1992 and have taken between twenty-five and forty every year since. That makes about a thousand forays and perhaps fifteen thousand people who have been kind enough to join me. The aim of all my forays is, of course, to teach people how to recognise plants, fungi and seaweeds, to show them the edible species and the poisonous species, as well as explaining various related subjects, such as the law of foraging and conservation. However, I have always wanted them to be much more than that, to open people's eyes to the glories around them, even if they nestle in the cracks of a London pavement.

So, if we find a fungus, I will tell them what it is, how to recognise it and if it will make for a pleasant supper or a frantic trip to A&E. But I might also explain its relationship to other fungi, relate the story of the creatures within it that they see only as maggots destined to ruin their tea, describe how the spores are formed and explain the barely credible process by which they are ejected into the air. For a plant, and again in addition to its suitability as food, I will answer such questions as what the incongruous red sphere on one of its leaves is and what it is for, why a plant is found here and not over there, what the striking orange pustules on some of its leaves are and how the plant distributes its seeds. It is these intricacies that make the natural world a place of wonder in addition to being a place of beauty.

Most of all, I walk slowly, examine closely everything I see and invite those who join me to do the same. This comes naturally to the forager and, once the habit is learned, becomes second nature in one's interactions with the broader natural world, even if you never pick so much as a field mushroom or a blackberry. I know I have done my job when I hear someone say that a walk will never be the same again. This has happened many times, and I always experience a frisson of joy and a hopeful expectation that the 'never' sticks. I can certainly take no great credit for this, as all I do is slow people down and tell them stories.

My approach in this book is, effectively, to take you on eight walks and do almost precisely what I do on my forays – find a plant, fungus, insect, field system, hedge, woodland or anything else and talk about it. Those who know me or have joined me on a walk will know my sometimes lamentable habit of digressing, and I have not held back here in talking about my pet subjects. These will be such things as conservation, agricultural practice old and new, what lichens *are*, the minutiae of fungal reproduction and what the point of wasps might be. Names are integral to any story and, indeed, always have a story of their own to tell; I will be relating many of these on their owners' behalf.

The corollary to the discovery of the variety, complexity and beauty of what may be seen on a simple walk is, of course, that people often did not know there were any such considerations worth discovering. When walking with friends, I am often appalled at their lack of interest in what is around them, the trees, hedges and fields just a pretty backdrop to their day.

I would imagine that most of my readers are not so incurious, but even the dedicated amateur naturalist will often be focused only on birds, or plants, or weevils, missing everything else. Thus I invite you to engage with the world you walk through in a way that is both expansive and detailed. We are told that we have damaged the wildlife of our planet, and this cannot be denied, but such a view often dismisses that which still exists, thrives even. The close observation that I encourage here will reveal to you ten times what you might have expected. There is more out there than anyone can imagine.

Identifying plants, fungi, hoverflies and almost everything else you might find on your walks is no easy task, and no doubt most people feel the water lapping against their chin when first exploring their local park or hedgerow in any great depth (*sic*). Nevertheless, it is a happy situation in which to place yourself, both a challenge and a joy. I suggest that you embrace it, but do not be too hard on yourself. Most of all, do not do what I did on these walks by attempting to understand and identify everything you see. Just take a few samples or very good photographs of what you find – three or four species should be enough – identify and learn about these, then go back for more. When taking a private walk to collect fungi for identification, I may well only gather two or three species, knowing the hours of work that may be before me.

Seven of the walks were taken during the late spring and the summer of 2021, when the plants and their many associated organisms are at their most visible, and one was taken during October, when the main flush of mushrooms occurs, in the south of England at least. There is much to find outside these seasons, but it is the principle of stopping, looking closely and wondering that is pursued so relentlessly in this book that matters. The locations have been chosen for their variety of habitats and geographical position. The general habitats explored range from urban and modern agricultural, to the uplands of northern England, the mountains of Wales and two islands at opposite ends of the kingdom. Within each of these there are numerous separate environments, so bogs, heath, hedgerow, mountainside, meadow, chalk downland, arable field edge, pebble beaches, dune systems, woodlands and many more are considered.

These were *my* walks, but it is *your* walks that matter. Yes, it is perfectly possible for you to tread in my footsteps, but where you walk may be quite different in ecology and season. It is the principle of walking with an open eye and its practicalities that I promote here, so do apply them to wherever you go.

This book has a strong personal thread running through it, though I have attempted not to swim too deep in the syrupy waters of self-indulgence. You will meet D, my wife of over forty years, who accompanied me on most of the walks, her roles being spotter of things to look at, recorder of what they were, my companion, carer and, all too often, compass. Six of the walks were taken at places I know, four of them intimately so. The remaining two were adventures into terrains unknown.

So that you know yourself not to be in the hands of an insufferable know-it-all, I have taken the considerable risk in this book in being honest about my level of knowledge about what I describe. I am a reasonably competent field mycologist with the ability to name fifteen hundred or so species in the field, and capable of identifying most of the rest when back home with my books, gently steaming chemicals and microscopes. With flowering plants and invertebrates, it is a few hundred of each and with mosses, liverworts and lichens we are down to the tens. In writing and researching this book I have learned much because I simply had to. Lack of knowledge is no sin, but not wishing to learn, I think, is. Casting myself, as I do, as the wannabe botanist, lichenologist, bryologist and, say, specialist in the Diptera,* I put myself in the shoes of most people, as no one can be all of these things, (though you will meet an exception later). I am also honest about my mistakes. There is an outstandingly egregious example of this recklessly placed in the first chapter, where I spent a couple of days researching and writing the story of a species that was not what I thought it was, and then needed to spend another two days writing about the species it actually was. I relate this humiliating story to show the perils of jumping to conclusions, that peril being infinitely greater if it is your dinner that is in question. Rest assured, this was my worst mistake. I hope.

While this book is certainly not a field guide, I have been liberal with my advice on how to identify individual species, with several practical processes that should prove useful. Some of them are neat short cuts (cheats), though these do not quite compare with the standard method, which involves careful

---

* Two wings = flies!

examination and a large pile of books! I do not dismiss the skill of proper identification, as it is the key by which the door to understanding is unlocked.

As the author of *The Forager's Calendar*, I could not neglect wild food. Every plant, fungus, seaweed, lichen and invertebrate with comestible potential that we found is noted and described. I also describe anything we found that is poisonous – everyone loves a bad boy.

Both common and Latin names are used throughout the book and, as a great fan, I make no apology for the latter. After the first mention, I use only the common name, if it has one. All common names will be capitalised where they refer to a species, rather than a group. Sometimes there will only be a Latin name, as the organism to which it applies does not have one that is common. The first mention of a name is rendered in bold. For the Families, Orders, Classes and Divisions into which we classify the natural world I have broken convention by capitalising them to avoid confusion with the everyday sense of these words.

The chapters are in no particular order, so you will lose little by dipping in and out – though the National Vegetation Classification system is mentioned throughout the book and explained in the first chapter. We did not discover everything there was to see on our walks or record everything we did see, and not everything we recorded found room in this book.

I have placed the references, plus other supporting material such as additional photographs and full lists of species found online at: www.foragerscalendar.net/the-observant-walker

Walk slowly. Look closely. Look up everything you can. Have fun.

Hayling Island, Hampshire

PEBBLE BEACHES, SANDY SHORES AND
DUNES, ACID GRASSLAND AND ESTUARY

FIVE MILES

7 AND 8 JULY 2021

DAY ONE

Hayling Island

I first visited Hayling Island in the late 1950s, or at least I presume I did. My family moved from Hook, in Hampshire, in 1957 to a conspicuously post-war Portsmouth: conspicuous because of the numerous bomb sites that were adventure playgrounds to us children. My father had always run a car and would take our still small family on trips at weekends, when a day out on Hayling Island was irresistible. From my first visit to my last, I have always thought it a place of wonders and mystery: another adventure playground, and one not *entirely* unlike those bomb sites in its appeal. Hayling Island is a glorious and endlessly interesting mess, and I love it. I took my daughters there when they were about nine or ten years old, and they, by contrast, thought it ghastly. The seafront was, they thought, tacky, dilapidated and of no interest, or, in their terms, 'a bit of a dump'.

An early nineteenth-century lawyer-made-good called William Padwick, who was just as fond of Hayling Island as your author, joined forces with others to replace or supplement the existing causeway (worryingly known as the Wade-way) with a bridge to the mainland. His associates in this successful venture were the Duke of Norfolk and Sir George Staunton of Leigh

Park. (Speaking as a Pompey lad, I should tell you that a Leigh Park address is no longer chic.)

In 1825 Padwick bought the manor, rectory and estates from the duke, acquiring manorial rights along the way. These rights included tithes, the rights over ferry operations and, mysteriously, 'mud rights', which are likely to have been for the oyster beds in Langstone Harbour to the west.

With the bridge in place, he turned his attention to transforming Hayling Island into a Brighton, a town whose bright lights glitter twenty-seven miles to the east. This involved the building of impressive villas and 'ornamental' cottages to encourage in-comers and hotels to accommodate holidaymakers. There were ornamental gardens and a hothouse for exotica. It does not seem that Padwick's dreams were ever completely realised, even with the arrival of the railway in 1867, gloriously named the Hayling Billy and much missed by all who remember it. (It stopped running in 1963.) Visually, Hayling seafront is nothing like that of Brighton in appearance, even with its scattering of attractive late Georgian architecture. Nevertheless, the population is now so large that most of the southern half of the island is built upon, and people holiday on Hayling still. Apart from the Misses Wright, they are not disappointed.

I had always intended to include a walk along the seashore, and Hayling Island is a place I know very well. It is blessed with at least three of the major coastal habitat types: sandy beach and dunes, pebble beach and estuary. Only cliff and rocky shore are absent. I rather missed the rocky shores, as it is there that one finds most of the seaweeds.

On a cool but dry and brightly overcast day, D and I set out early from Dorset, stopping to pick up my sister Carol, who still lives in Portsmouth and was keen to join us. We parked in the almost mile-long car park set above the pebble beach. I was on home territory as I know the pebble beach at Hayling well and am even more familiar with its more magnificent sister in Dorset, Chesil Beach. I did not expect to find too many plants that would involve head-scratching. I was wrong.

Hayling Island, like its neighbouring island of Portsea (Portsmouth), is roughly and appropriately in the shape of an anchor, with both islands bordered either side by large harbours with hooked spits projecting from both east and west. The five miles of the southern shore of Hayling stretches from a long, eastern spit to its mirror image in the west. The beach itself is pebble, giving way to gravel and sand, and just sand at the spits. Characterising the beach in this way does not allow for the vagaries of so dynamic a terrain, as a shoreline can easily be pebbles one day and sand the next, something I have seen on several occasions in Dorset.

It is the common experience of peripatetic teachers of botany that one sees three-quarters of all the plants there are to be seen in the first forty-five minutes of any walk. This was certainly not the case with our walk around Hayling Island: the great variety of habitats ensured that the plant species just kept coming.

Over half of the two-day walk was through or alongside a Site of Special Scientific Interest (SSSI) called Sinah Common. The SSSI narrowly encompasses the western half of the southern beach, widening to include most of the western peninsula. There are two unusual features of this protected area: first, a substantial proportion of it is a golf course, and second, its land area is accompanied by a massive tidal sandbar that runs south-east from the peninsula's tip. The latter feature is the mile-long East Winner and is exposed at low tide. Yes, there is a West Winner, a smaller sandbar that stretches south from the Eastney spit at Portsmouth. Both are created by the tidal dumping of sand from Langstone Harbour.

The most treasured plants to be found within the SSSI are the Childing Pink, *Petrorhagia nanteuilii*, with Sinah Common being one of only two British sites where it is found, and the Suffocated Clover, *Trifolium suffocatum*, also a rarity. The latter is striking in that its flowers are almost invisible and densely situated at the base of the plant, hence 'suffocated'. I found neither plant, not that it mattered – rarity is not a quality of notable interest, it is merely a state.

Sinah Common SSSI is an extremely complex and varied habitat, with pebble and shingle giving way to sand, sand dunes, dune heath and acid grasslands. These are complemented by a small area of pure heath, a lake, several ponds, scrub and woodland. Such plenitude is common in most seashore habitats, so your favourite seashore will not be found wanting, provided the hand of man has not been laid too heavily upon it. Vegetated pebble beaches, the main focus of our walk on the first day, are found all around the coast, though scarce on the east coast between Lowestoft and Dunbar. In Scotland they are most common on the south-west coast. Sandy beaches and dunes are similarly common, with only the south-eastern corner of England being largely devoid of them.

The Car Park

For much of the island's southern shore there is a broad band of gravelly grassland above the beach, with which it melds. The plan that day was to follow the beach west and then northwards for a total of one and a quarter miles to reach the Portsmouth ferry before turning back. We had six hours in which to accomplish this simple task but failed, only managing a single mile and abandoning the final quarter until the following day. This is a reflection in part of how very much there was to see, but *mostly* of how long it takes to set up a tripod.

It may also have been an indication of how much time we spent in the car park. I am a huge fan of car parks, and getting me out of one, even during a shopping trip, has sometimes found D losing patience. They attract pioneering plant species, and any associated, woodchip-covered flower bed will, at one time or another, contain unusual fungi. Car parks are also places where introduced plants, unable to make a living in well-established plant communities, do so on the disturbed periphery.

It is always a pleasure to find something unusual, something rare — such as the two above-mentioned celebrity plants — but we often ignore that which is common. So it is with the commonest of our lichens, **Xanthoria parietina**, which we found growing directly on several of the posts in the car park. It is a bright yellow/orange and can be found in almost every corner of the British Isles. I invariably hand people a loupe to examine any lichens we find, and the delayed 'Ooh' of surprise and delight always tells me when they have it in focus! Loupes can cost upwards of £300, but one that is perfectly serviceable can be had for about a tenner. Do avail yourself, as they are helpful in the identification of many organisms, notably lichens, for which they are essential.

Foraging and plant-spotting in car parks is often rewarding and most of the car park posts were garlanded with wild plants. One was engulfed in **Spear-Leaved Orache**, *Atriplex prostrata*, and the furry leaves and pink flowers of the statuesque **Tree Mallow**. The latter's Latin name, *Malva arborea*, is no great puzzle. It is not native to Britain, but has spread widely and sometimes too well, becoming an annoyance in some locations. It is edible inasmuch as it is not poisonous, and passable if you like your food hairy. In contrast, Spear-Leaved Orache is one of the many excellent edible plants found on seashores, though it does

23

not confine itself to a salty habitat. It is in the Goosefoot Family and related to spinach, for which it makes an excellent and free substitute. Other wooden posts were surrounded by **Sea Beet**, *Beta vulgaris* subsp. *maritima*, also a Goosefoot, their leaves hidden beneath a tangle of flower spikes. When out of flower, Sea Beet leaves are the best of the wild greens for the table. It also is related to and similar to spinach, but with a sweeter flavour and more succulent bite. These three plants are common, and we saw dozens of each. I had decided to restrain my collecting instincts on these walks, the cotton bags habitually kept in my pocket left behind. Still, it was hard to leave either of the two Goosefoots behind.

Yet another post yielded a plantain. Plantains (not to be confused with the banana-like fruit!) are disregarded plants, mere weeds wherever they grow, but sometimes they excel themselves, like the exceptionally well-turned-out specimen of **Ribwort Plantain**, *Plantago lanceolata*, we saw that day. Its seed heads hung from their ribbed stems with an artistic droop that would grace a watercolour. This post harboured a third edible Goosefoot Family member, **Babington's Orache**, *Atriplex glabriuscula*. While it was in its only habitat – the seashore – this particular plant was not in its customarily precise location – the strandline. I have seen this plant all around the British coast, clinging tenaciously to its unreliable linear niche.

The Pebble Beach

Finally, much to D's and Carol's relief, we left the car park to venture on to the beach itself and begin our walk proper. The beach was one of pebbles interspersed with plants – a vegetated pebble beach, one of the most exciting of all the British landscapes. Such a beach occurs on the upper shore, the pebbles nearer the sea being too mobile from wave action, to support any plant. We immediately found one of its typical inhabitants, **Curled Dock**, *Rumex crispus* subsp. *littoreus*. We dismiss all dock species, like the plantains, as weeds, their presence among more attractive plants a tiresome intrusion of a lower-class plant into an upper-middle-class neighbourhood. Such views are absurd, of course, and this species is more important than its common appearance may suggest. It, and the Yellow-Horned Poppy (of which more later), are integral to and thus indicative of one particular *plant community*, as defined under the National Vegetation Classification (NVC) scheme, one of a handful of classification systems that help ecologists define and understand the very many plant communities.

The NVC scheme set out thirty years ago to classify all of the natural and semi-natural British plant community types, such as blanket mire, chalk downland, heathland and pebble beach, splitting them further into sub-communities. Each community or sub-community is listed, discussed and described in a remarkable series of heavyweight and notoriously impenetrable books. The volume dealing with coastal plants is *British Plant Communities,* vol. 5, *Maritime Communities and Vegetation of Open Habitats.* What these volumes lack in native charm (and they lack it in spades), they more than make up for in being so very useful to ecologists and anyone interested in knowing precisely what is going on in any one place. Each community is named with a reference code, the hyphenated names of (usually) two of the species that are characteristic, followed by a brief and friendly description in plain English (such as 'dune grassland' or 'salt marsh'). To understand, manage and protect ecosystems, it is essential that they can be classified, rather than relying on vague descriptions that could apply to several types of community, only some of which are exceptionally worthy of protection. It is this classifying role that the NVC scheme fulfils. The presence of the two above-mentioned species *suggests* that the community here is 'SD1 *Rumex crispus* – *Glaucium flavum* shingle community', 'SD' meaning (unhelpfully) 'sand dune'. There are a worrying sixteen sand dune (SD) communities to choose from, each with numerous sub-communities, hence the tentative nature of my suggestion. Despite my reverence for them and their usefulness to any budding naturalist, I will not, you will doubtless be pleased to hear, relate the NVC status of every habitat we encountered on our walks, just a few to keep you on your toes.

Next to this, and dominating the beach as no other plant can, was my favourite of all the herbaceous plants, **Sea Kale**, *Crambe maritima*, another near-constant of the SD1 community. The mature plants were enormous at a metre or more wide and high, a typical size for Sea Kale. Their pale, frosted-green leaves are the size of dinner plates and the texture of slightly damp cardboard. This was a large and very welcome population and one that would stretch for most of our walk that day, but nowhere near as impressive as that on Chesil Beach in West Dorset, where thousands of these huge plants continue beyond sight.

Sea Kale overwinters as nothing but a root, producing a dense cluster of leaves from late March onwards. Most parts of the plant are edible: the leaf shoots and *young* leaves, the 'broccoli' of the immature flower heads, the flowers and the immature seed pods. It has long been gathered for the table or market, but its restricted habitat – the landward side of pebbly and gravelly beaches – indicates that collecting should be done with great care and only occasionally. One of the issues is that rare lichens that frequently share the shingle with Sea Kale could conceivably suffer from the habitat disturbance caused through commercial foraging activities. A report by an academic who had carefully examined a site on which commercial foraging was taking place, argued that the 'perceived threats to Sea Kale … have been greatly exaggerated', though I am unsure whether or not the threat to the associated lichens is exaggerated.

Still, I am always very careful as it is too beautiful a plant to risk its loss. A more serious threat than foraging to Sea Kale and the community to which it belongs is trampling. Light use by the general public and by the ever-cautious forager does insignificant damage. However, some of the long gaps in vegetation along Chesil Beach centre around the few seashore car parks that invite holiday makers, dog walkers and shoreline anglers. This heavy footfall has damaged not so much the mature plants as the frequent and delicate seedlings, ultimately leaving the beach barren. Fortunately, a substantial boardwalk has been constructed across Chesil Beach near the most used of these car parks, enabling the casual visitor to stroll comfortably from car park to sea and back again without harming the fledgling Sea Kale.

Clinging to the fence that surrounds the golf course and sitting in an area of grass, pebble and gravel was a cruelly trapped beauty, the aforementioned **Yellow-Horned Poppy**, *Glaucium flavum*. It is, as mentioned, one of the two plants included in the SD1 NVC designation and a few yards from its classic habitat. It is a familiar plant of pebble and gravel beaches, its brilliant yellow flowers and grey-green succulent leaves a joy to see throughout much of the summer. All poppies are poisonous, but the Yellow-Horned Poppy pulls no punches, containing a cocktail of alkaloids that could conceivably prove fatal in someone medically compromised. Even its seeds are poisonous. The most dangerous of its alkaloids is glaucine, one found in several poppy species. It has some underwhelming use as a cough remedy and a handful of other dubious medical purposes;

however, it is glaucine's ability to cause euphoria and visual anomalies (including bright colours) that has gained attention. A feeling of entering another world is one of its more appealing effects. I mentioned this to D, who said that I had been in another world for years, so why would I bother? Since all of the plant's alkaloids are classed as toxic, just remember that, should you tread this dangerous path, the other world you may enter may well be the next one. To distract you from such considerations, I give you the astonishing full chemical name (though in truth it is a coded description) for glaucine. It is the longest I have encountered and takes thirty seconds to read aloud: (S)-5,6,6a,7-tetrahydro-1,2,9,10-tetramethoxy-6-methyl-4H-dibenzo [de,g] quinoline.

The Golf Course

For good or ill, golf courses are familiar sights near the sea: one such, for example, can be found on the stretch of land between Deal and Ebbsfleet on the Kent coast, the entirety of Sandwich Bay. Perhaps it is the ready access to sand for the bunkers that swings it. The golf course that forms part of the Sinah SSSI abuts the car park to the east and to our right as we walked west. It is surrounded by the previously mentioned and serious fence, which gives every appearance of being there to keep the golfers in rather than the public out. But no doubt its main purpose is to prevent the frequent deaths that would result from high-velocity golf balls, to which the large number that had accumulated at the base of the fence bore sorry witness. I felt a strong urge to tackle the fence to retrieve these lost balls and sell them back to their owners. This inclination was an echo of a gratifyingly successful business I ran from 1960 to 1962, when I would crawl on my stomach through the dense low shrubs next to the school playground to retrieve lost balls which I would sell to other children.

Golf balls were not the only treasures on the other side of the fence; there were also several interesting plants. We often think of golf courses as barren wastes of overweening tidiness, and all too often they are. However, where a course is constructed on an area of dull arable land, the inclusion of rough areas and even the neat lawns can only be an improvement. Sinah Warren golf course is quite different. It was established about a hundred years before it became an SSSI and has managed to live fairly comfortably with its second role as a nature reserve. Indeed, the fact that it was declared as an SSSI while it was already a golf course indicates that there was much there worth protecting.

About twenty yards in I noticed something lying on the ground that looked like nothing alive and was in the shape of a cowpat. Using a telephoto lens, I managed to obtain a photograph good enough for an ID. It was ***Cladonia rangiformis***. This lichen is a relative of one I used to buy as a child to make trees and bushes for tiny plastic soldiers to hide behind on my papier mâché battlefields. *Cladonia* species are still collected for this purpose from heathland (their typical habitat) and have thus suffered from over-picking.

As well as the sunny heads of poppies, the irregular browns and greens of the golf course were lit up by countless spots of colour: the bright yellow flowers of **Lady's Bedstraw**, *Galium verum*, and the small blue scabious-like heads of **Sheep's Bit**, *Jasione montana*. This was once known as the Sheep's Bit Scabious because it looks exactly like a scabious. It is, in fact, in the Bellflower Family, not the Teasel Family (in which the scabious species reside). Such lookalikes are the bane of the amateur naturalist and must be tolerated with fortitude.

Not noticed on the day (it is so easy to miss things) but clearly visible in the same photograph is a newly minted **Marbled White**, *Melanargia galathea*. Whoever was in charge of making butterflies must have put their top designer on this true beauty, whose exquisite black-and-white patterning is complemented by a shock of grey fur running down the body and on to the wings. It is a butterfly that is doing extremely well in Britain at the moment, though triumph follows disaster and disaster follows triumph in the world of the butterfly. For them, the weather is (nearly) everything, with a bad season causing population numbers to drop like a stone.

Butterflies fall vaguely into 'specialist' and 'generalist' species, depending on whether or not they are fussy eaters. An iconic example of a fussy eater is the **Marsh Fritillary**, *Euphydryas aurinia*, whose larval food plant is the uncommon Devil's Bit Scabious. The larval food plant of the Marble White is, more sensibly, grasses, particularly **Red Fescue**, *Festuca rubra*, though it does require *long* grass. This is a ubiquitous plant, found everywhere from beaches to hilltops, and an excellent choice for a butterfly wishing to get on in the world, slotting the Marbled White firmly into the 'generalist' category.

The Shingle and Its Grassland

Back on the beach side of the fence we found a host of plants that can be classed as generalists or weeds, so I will pass them by largely unnamed. Among them, however, was a common plant that had worried me vaguely for years because, although I had seen it everywhere, it was never in a condition good enough to identify. In the high summer there is little to see but a large, wiry bush of tough, straight stems arranged at approximate right-angles to one another, the long seed pods pressed closely to them. The next year I found some in flower and leaf and discovered it to be **Hedge Mustard**, *Sisymbrium officinale*. It has four yellow petals on each flower and a leaf like that of Rocket, with a similar flavour, clearly placing it in the Cabbage Family, the Brassicaceae.

A plant that was to be with us for most of this walk was **Sea Radish**, *Raphanus raphanistrum maritimus*. It is extremely common beside the seaside, and a favourite of mine at this time of year for the immature seedpods. These taste like, well, radish, but with a better texture. The entire plant is untidy, large and nothing like the domesticated radishes that are uprooted long before their time.

Sea Mayweed, *Tripleurospermum maritimum*, a relative of Chamomile, was, as expected, present; I was to see a more unusual one later. **Restharrow**, *Ononis repens*, with its bright pink and white pea flowers in splendid display, was vastly easier to identify and tangled among the feathery leaves of **Yarrow**, *Achillea millefolium*. This last plant was once used as a bittering component in ale before hops were invented, and it still makes an indifferent tea. It has long been used to staunch blood and is named after Achilles, who presumably had it pressed to his wounded heel, albeit to no avail. A poor choice of name in my opinion.

Three hours had passed, and the grassy, herb-rich area behind the shingle, pebbles and sand had widened considerably as the golf course fence receded. In some places the soil there was almost black with dead organic matter. Sandy, nutrient-poor and acidic, it was lowland acid grassland. It is worth noting that, when talking about 'acid' soils, these are not steaming no-go areas infused with sulphuric acid, but nutrient-poor soils (generally a 'good thing' when it comes to wild plants) with a pH a little south of 7 (neutral). In other areas of grassland memories of the beach were clearly to be seen in the many patches of bare pebbles. Visually, these lands beyond the beach were still a sea of Lady's Bedstraw and Sheep's Bit. Among these plants were the extremely hairy-leaved **Mouse-Ear Hawkweed**, *Hieracium pilosella*, the pink pompoms of **Hare's-Foot Clover**, *Trifolium arvense*, and **Rough Clover**, *Trifolium scabrum*.

In one of the more shingly parts we found **Cat's-Ear**, *Hypochaeris radicata*, one of the endless dandelion-like plants sent to annoy amateur botanists. When studying these hawkweeds, hawksbeards, hawkbits and closely related others, including, of course, Cat's-Ear and indeed others lacking 'hawk' in their name, one must, as ever, look at the details rather than garner vague impressions. They are known, charmingly, as the Hawkish Complex. With hawkish plants it is the following details that set individuals apart: degrees of hairiness, whether the flowers grow on a single stem or from branching stems, the shape of the leaves, details of the bracts, calyces, sepals and more. Bracts, calyces and sepals may require a bit of swotting. Briefly, bracts are modified leaves just below the flower, calyces (singular 'calyx') are the part of the flower that protects it as it develops, and sepals are the individual and ultimately branching parts of the calyx. Well, I did warn you that they were details.

The unregarded weed near by, Redshank, which lay trailing across the pebbles, was not, on closer inspection, this at all, but **Ray's Knotgrass**, *Polygonum raii*. I presume that it is John Ray, the celebrated seventeenth-century botanist, after whom this plant is named (twice, in fact, as *raii* = Ray). It was once known as the subspecies, *P. oxyspermum* subsp. *raii*, having previously been split away from plain old *P. oxyspermum* before being accepted as a separate species. Ray was a notorious 'splitter', meaning someone who sees seven species where most people see only one, so it

32

is fitting that he is commemorated in a species of which he would have approved. I did find several bona fide **Redshanks**, *Persicaria maculosa*, not long after. It is very nearly a weed species but one that is attractive once closely observed, with its discreet but pretty pink flowers and richly red stems.

A frequent problem with species is that, despite Latin names supposedly being 'for ever', they change all the time. It is generic names that change most frequently, owing to a single genus being split into two or more genera, resulting in scores of species suffering a name change. Redshank was once called *Polygonum persicaria*, but the *Polygonum* genus was split into several genera, with *Polygonum* retained for the various knot grasses, and new genera (including *Persicaria*) created for former members that were not knot-grassy enough. Redshank's specific epithet was deemed sufficiently venerable to be promoted to generic status: that is, *persicaria*, its specific epithet, became the name of an entire genus, *Persicaria* and the new specific epithet, *maculosa*, was duly coined.

Lunch on the Beach and an Unsolicited Lecture

We were barely half a mile from our starting point. Sister Carol had displayed the early signs of impatience about ten minutes after we started, so it was agreed that lunchtime had arrived. We sat down on a convenient grassy knoll among the pebbles to eat and, obviously, drink. I wandered off halfway through my second beer to see what could be found in and under some nearby Blackthorn and Bramble scrub. Among the tangle was a **Dog Rose**, *Rosa canina*. Two of the leaflets were folded together either side of the central rib, in Cornish pasty fashion. On one of these the leaflet sported a bright, maroon-coloured blotch. The whole 'Cornish pasty' was a gall, created for the midge *Dasineura rosae*, whose tiny larvae will feed and develop within the safety of the envelope they have forced upon the leaflet.

On the grassy area around the scrub there were two species of fungi. One was a splendid find. It was *Agaricus bernardii*, a close relative to the Horse Mushroom, *A. arvensis*, a fact witnessed by its substantial size, its tendency to bruise slowly yellow and its almond scent. It is similarly edible, but not particularly common and found only near the sea. Best left in peace, I think.

I had set up my camera and tripod to photograph the other mushroom when a group of people who were passing asked what I had found. D, who was still near by, put her head in her hands. Having been asked a million questions over the last thirty years on my walks, I went into full professional mode and told them. After learning that I was photographing the mushroom *Psathyrella candolleana*, that it was one of the commonest and easiest to identify of a difficult genus, with its thin white cap, brown gills and slender white stem, and that you couldn't eat it, that the curled leaf near by was caused by a gall midge, and the names and interesting details of half a dozen nearby plants, they edged away and thanked me.

Mrs Paterson

I was pleased with having educated and entertained my unexpected students, and we continued our quest. The magnificent **Viper's Bugloss**, *Echium vulgare*, was everywhere; a 70-cm-high or more plant with numerous deep-blue flowers. These are formed one at a time – small, closed and pink, then open and blue – on many curved and bristly racemes (a raceme is a 'stem' on which a series of stemmed flowers form). Each flower forms a small trumpet, with five lobes ornamenting the edge. Viper's

Bugloss is largely a coastal plant, though frequently found inland. It does not take a botanical genius to notice that it is similar to Borage and Green Alkanet, the former familiar from the herb garden, the latter from waste ground. All three species are in the Boraginaceae Family and all are very attractive to bees. The puzzling name, 'Viper's Bugloss', appears to come from its presumed ability to cure snake bites; the ox's tongue bit is a reference to the bristly surface of the long, thin leaves.*

Later in our walk I would find a single specimen of **Purple Viper's Bugloss**, *Echium plantagineum*, a once rare species now seemingly recovered. It has an intriguing alternative common name, 'Paterson's Curse'. This derives from the belief that a Mrs Paterson took it with her from England to Australia in 1880. It seems to have preferred its new home and is now a widespread and pernicious weed in Australia. Unfortunately, it is toxic to stock, owing to the alkaloids it produces. These toxins also affect honey production as the honey too becomes poisonous, requiring it to be diluted with non-toxic honeys. Some genetic research has been undertaken to confirm or deny its origin. It seems that Mrs Paterson may indeed have taken it to Australia, but its curse cannot truly be laid at her feet as the plant had been there since around 1850, having come via a South African population, its seeds hitching a lift on the fleece of imported sheep. RIP at last, Mrs Paterson.

Viper's Bugloss has a personal resonance for me. Forty years ago, when I was beginning to fill the embarrassing chasm that was my inability to name anything much more than a dandelion and daisy, D and I would wander the fields, woods and coasts of Dorset looking for plants to identify. One day we were sitting on a low cliff, examining a plant we had not seen before. We

---

* *Bu* = cattle and *gloss* = tongue.

had just begun contentedly flicking through our *Wild Flowers of Britain and Northern Europe* when a passing, pompous know-it-all shouted 'Viper's Bugloss!' and went on his way. I quite like looking things up, so was a little annoyed that he should have spoiled my pleasure. Some people just don't know when to keep quiet.

Eggs, Sand and Sand Dunes

We were now nearly a mile from the car park, our path following the beach, which turns north, with the narrow channel between Hayling Island and Portsmouth to our left. Scrubby areas were easy to ignore among the plethora of specialist seashore plants, but two caught my eye. They were a **Blackthorn**, *Prunus spinosa,* and an apple tree. Both demonstrated the effects of the harsh environment in which they had found themselves by being 4 m in diameter and barely 1 m high!

I was pleased to see an area of the beach fenced off to provide a nesting site for Ringed Plovers, *Charadrius hiaticula.* This species nests on open beaches and has a difficult time raising a family with people and their dogs trampling over the nursery. Despite my lack of any profound interest in birds that do not come in a pie, I have had a fondness for the various plovers ever since I was asked to write about the historic collection of their eggs for food. Fascinating stuff, not least because plover eggs are really Lapwing eggs. Lapwings and plovers are close cousins in the Charadriidae Family, and the Lapwing was once considered to be a plover, the 'Sociable Plover'. Any wild bird's egg is now legally off the menu in Britain, but I do not think we are missing much. A bizarre experiment, a survey really, was conducted in 1953 on the palatability of the eggs from about one hundred species of bird.

They were marked on a scale from one to ten. Disappointingly, the ordinary hen's egg came top (8.7), followed by that of the Emu (8.4) and the Coot (8.3). The Lapwing's egg scored a relatively poor 7.5, but at least it was better than the Southern Black Tit, which managed a truly appalling 2.4.

Scattered here and there in the sand near the Ringed Plover nursery were tiny plantains, quite unlike their larger cousins in that their leaves were very narrow and branching at the tips. They were **Buck's-Horn Plantain**, *Plantago coronopus*. This is found throughout most of lowland England and coastal everywhere else in Britain. Right on the sandy strandline I found another of my favourites, **Sea Sandwort**, *Honckenya peploides*. Like many overtly seashore plants, such as Sea Beet, Sea Rocket, Sea Purslane and Annual Sea Blite, its leaves are succulent. The shore is effectively a desert, a place also known for its succulent plants. With little accessible water that is not extremely salty, any water they manage to acquire must be conserved. Sea Sandwort is very distinctive, with leaves that are pointed-oval in opposite pairs, closely stacked up their supporting stem and providing the whole with a geometrical appeal. Large seedpods succeed the small, five-petalled flowers, both emerging from the joint between stem and leaf. Sea Sandwort is headlined in the NVC title of the habitat in which it is found, the other being Sea Rocket: SD2 Honckenya peploides-Cakile maritima strandline community. Another constant of this community is the Babington's Orache I mentioned earlier.

I was disappointed not to find Sea Rocket, *Cakile maritima*, that day but presume that it does exist there and was just having the challenging time it often seems to suffer on well-trodden beaches. However, it is not unknown for a community type to be recognised for what it is even though one of its star species is sometimes missing. This is presumably on the principle that

Buckingham Palace is still a type of royal palace even if the king is not in residence. Sea Rocket is edible and quite good if you like flavours that cause you to gasp, choke and cry.

Sitting among the many shorter plants in the sand of the level upper shore next to the dunes was the good-looking **Hare's-Tail Grass**, *Lagurus ovatus*. The generic name literally means 'hare's tail' and the specific epithet 'egg-shaped' a reference to the shape of the seed heads. This is one of the plants that began life in domestic gardens and has taken its place with native plants without being too troublesome – a remarkable trick when so many other plants seem determined to make a thorough nuisance of themselves.

As the landscape became dominated by sand and dunes, one of the botanical gems of the British coast began to appear: **Sea Holly**, *Eryngium maritimum*. A *strictly* coastal plant, it is found in sand dunes and sand-rich upper beaches around most of Britain. It is largely absent from the east coast north of Hull and all around Scotland to Galloway, but with scattered populations in the Western Isles. It has the accolade of being the prickliest of all British plants (with Juniper being an arguably close second), making it a treacherous plant for holidaymakers wandering barefoot (or bare anything) through the dunes. The multiple drinking-straw-diameter roots that can sometimes be seen hanging out of eroded sand dunes were once candied to make a sweetmeat that was reputed to be an aphrodisiac. It isn't, I've tried. The most surprising thing about this attractive plant is that it is in the Carrot Family, the Apiaceae. *Nothing* about it – not the holly-like leaves or the pompom of brilliant blue flowers – looks remotely like anything possessed by other members of this Family, but relatedness does not necessarily imply similarity. Sea Holly is protected in many parts of Europe, though, as is often the case, it is its habitat that really needs protection.

We were now firmly in sand dune country, another exciting habitat, and one I wanted to examine further before the day had ended. But for domestic reasons (sister Carol's) we had to beat a retreat.

DAY TWO

The Ferry and an Unfortunate Butterfly

Carol felt that we had entertained her sufficiently and did not come with us on the second day. We parked near the ferry, half a mile north of where our adventure of the previous day had ended. The bright blue sky and warm breeze that greeted us shamed the day before. I had allowed two days for the walk, but at five miles of fairly light walking, it could easily be completed in two hours by anyone not stopping to take a photograph every five minutes. The area in which the car park was situated was the part of Hayling Island I knew best. Our plan that day was to walk back to where we had finished our walk the day before, and to continue from there.

A day trip to Hayling Island from Portsmouth, and especially from Southsea, the southern part of the city and where I once lived, could easily avoid the bridge to the north of the island by taking the ferry. It runs between the two spits across a 320-m-wide channel and on occasions can be an exciting ride. The first thing one notices is that the ferry only points consistently towards its destination pontoon during slack water. At full ebb and full flow it will begin its progress by pointing almost at right angles to its destination and follow a parabolic route thereafter. Spring (high) tides make matters more exciting because of the stronger current, and inclement weather makes the ride positively exhilarating. The ferry service has been running off and on for a couple of centuries but is a difficult business to maintain, so do support it should you ever get the chance.

Few of my memories from primary school are particularly pleasant. All that comes readily to mind are Friday science classes, which I loved with a passion, the time when the dressing-gowned Joy Parsons flashed her knee for me (complete with a coy, knowing smile) in the backstage changing room during the Christmas concert and the two weeks when we were treated to a cheerful student teacher who was anxious to please. He took us on the ferry to the same beach D and I were on that day. We were required to throw quadrants over our shoulder and record the organisms we found within its bounds. I have no recollection of what plants and bugs I saw, but it felt like *real* science, and I was duly impressed. And, of course, it was a day of not being stuck behind a desk or, worse still, of sport.

Inspired by this and taking a later (and passing) interest in butterflies, your fourteen-year-old author took his eight-year-old sister (another one, Trish) to Hayling Island. We were armed with a ponding net, some small boxes, my *Observer Book of Butterflies* and a notebook. We found only a single butterfly and duly caught the unfortunate creature. It was the most boring of them all, the Meadow Brown, *Maniola jurtina*. Still, I was pleased to have identified it. We took it home and I consulted my ever-handy Boy's Book of Unpleasant Things to Do. I 'put it to sleep' in a jam jar containing a small amount of dry-cleaning fluid stolen from the kitchen, then 'set' it with strips of paper pinned over its outstretched wings. Happy days.

Subspecies

After walking back to the sand dunes of the previous day, we continued our mission just above the tidal zone. I have not recorded many subspecies in this book because it takes a brave amateur botanist to claim a correct identification. Nevertheless, I found a chamomile-type plant, a mayweed, that looked quite different from the Sea Mayweed we had seen everywhere the day before. Sometimes a 'sub' will be distinguished by its habitat or perhaps by being a different colour (as in this case), but in the absence of so clear a clue one is looking at fine details. Fortunately, this plant presented me with an obvious clue.

One of the peculiarities of the rules that govern taxonomy is that, if no subspecies is associated with a species, then its original binomial (genus name plus specific epithet) is all you need. However, if someone declares a subspecies, then the original species automatically becomes a subspecies too. In formal writing, all subspecies must be referred to by a *trinomial*. The third name is up to the author of the new subspecies, but the original species must repeat its existing specific epithet. Human beings, for example, are a subspecies, as there was at least one other, the long extinct *Homo sapiens* subsp. *idaltu*. Hence, our full title is *Homo sapiens* subsp. *sapiens* L., the 'L' being for Carl Linnaeus, who gave us our name. This has confused people over the years, the misconception being that we are so clever we were called 'clever' twice. Incidentally, every species that receives a scientific (Latin) name should have a specimen saved for posterity as the 'type' specimen. Ideally it will be the one most closely studied by the naming taxonomist. These are kept in universities, museums and botanic gardens, though many are in private collections, such as the chalet bungalow in Dorset that hosts the famous (among lepidopterists) Sterling Collection of micro-moths. Types were retained only inadvertently in the time of Linnaeus, so he did not keep a specimen of human being tucked away in a drawer for later study by zoologists. We do, however, now have one since it was declared in *Nature* in 1959 by the distinguished taxonomist Willian Stearn, who pointed out that the specimen most studied by Linnaeus was Linnaeus himself and declared him to be our type specimen. Since this declaration was announced publicly and in print, it automatically became fact.

The species, *sub*species, I *might* have found that day was growing in the sand next to a Sea Kale. It was a chamomile-like plant – sprawling habit, feathery leaves – called *Tripleurospermum maritimum* subsp. *vinicaule*. The subspecific epithet means 'wine-coloured tail', a reference to the dark purple colour of its stem. It is a subspecies of Sea Mayweed. There are barely thirty records of it in Britain, but one is for Hayling Island. Everything fits nicely, and I am fairly confident in my identification – but I fully expect some smart Alec or Alice botanist to sidle up and say, 'Nah, mate, not with them anastomosing epicalices.'

I have said nothing about marine organisms so far, unsheltered sandy beaches often being devoid of seaweeds and shellfish. I did, however, find at this point some seaweed clinging to a piece of wood, together with some barnacles. The seaweed was one of the familiar filamentous green species in the genus *Ulva*, though which one must remain a mystery. These are generally edible when deep-fried and reminiscent of chewing a ball of green cotton thread when raw. The barnacles will also remain unnamed, so you will have to be content with my favourite barnacle fact – that the males possess the largest penis-to-body ratio of any animal, the necessary appendage being five times as long as the shell is wide. If you are stuck to a rock and likewise your amour, there is nothing else to be done.

Back to the Sand Dunes

In the sand below the dunes I found my third stonecrop species of the walk, **White Stonecrop**, *Sedum album*. Those I forbore to mention from the previous day were **Biting Stonecrop**, *S. acre*, and **English Stonecrop**, *S. anglicum*. Both of these have flowers that are spectacular in colour: respectively yellow and pink with red. You can guess what colour White Stonecrop is. All are succulents that could, and do, grace the domestic garden. Also here was my first ever 'spurrey', **Lesser Sea Spurrey**, *Spergularia marina*. It is an extremely hairy plant, to the point of being sticky, and its flowers have five pale pink petals.

Above the sand of the upper shore were the dunes proper. They were, of course, dominated by **Marram Grass**, *Ammophila arenaria*. In one of the delightfully absurd constructions that brighten the world of taxonomy and biological nomenclature, the Latin name of this grass translates roughly as 'the sand-loving sandy thing'. It is beyond my powers and your patience for me to go far into the subject of sand dunes, as they deserve (and have) a book of their own.* With the sixteen aforementioned NVC classifications plus sub-communities with the word 'dune' in them, and my failure to take sufficient notice at the time, I can only presume that the dunes I was standing in were the familiar Marram Grass dunes, classified as the 'SD6 mobile dune community'.

Other, more seaward and less impressively clean and tall dunes will contain other grasses. These are usually dominated by either *Elymus farctus* or *Leymus arenarius* (respectively Sand Couch-Grass and Lyme Grass). Well, I found one of these species on the seaward side of the Marram Grass dunes, but they are not

* M. Anwar Maun, *The Biology of Coastal Sand Dunes* (Oxford, 2022).

easy to differentiate, so I am unable to say which it was. Mostly, it is enough just to notice that there is grass on a sand dune – and to know that it is, frequently, a mix of different species. Incidentally, the two generic names of these two grasses are simple anagrams of each other. *Elymus* is an old name, applied by Linnaeus, but *Leymus* is later, and the obvious suspicion is that it was divided from *Elymus,* and the new genus created by moving the 'L' one place to the left. Such playfulness (or laziness) is common, and often an informal indication that the two genera concerned are likely to tax the patience of anyone wishing to identify them.

Marram Grass dominates its dunes because it is the only grass that can easily withstand the inundations of wind-blown sand that characterises its habitat. More than this, Marram Grass helps create dunes by binding the sand with their substantial roots. Other plants may also be able to tolerate these inundations, if not so well, but the Marram Grass will get there first. Marram Grass is also found in the safer environment of more inland dunes, but here it is accompanied by other plants that are now, away from the sandy and salty winds, able to establish themselves. Incidentally, such plant-rich dunes are known as 'grey dunes'.

I looked around for dune fungi but found none. It was too early in the year, no doubt. That dunes have their own mycota (population of fungi) may come as a surprise, but there are hundreds of species that can be found in dunes, a small but significant proportion of which are *only* found in dunes, mostly among the Marram Grass. Several of these have 'sandy' names: *Inocybe arenicola, Coprinopsis ammophilae, Peziza ammophila, Psathyrella ammophila* and more. I have a loathing of the recently invented names for fungi, but am nevertheless prepared to relate that the first three are respectively called the Sand Fibrecap, the Dune Inkcap and the Dune Cup, with the last species spared such ignominy. The *Peziza* species is a brown cup just poking out of the sand and fairly common. *Psathyrella ammophila* is also relatively common. I always look at sand dunes closely just to see if there are any fungi there. This sort of dedication can be excessive, and I'm afraid it extends even to fictional representations: I recall watching a film where a couple of bikini-clad young women were lying among sand dunes and found myself not paying attention to them or their dialogue but instead scanning the sand for fungi. All rather sad, and doubly so as there were none to report.

Bees in the Dunes

The dunes that day had little in the way of other plants, but they did have bees, scores of bees. There is a common misconception that there are honeybees and bumblebees and nothing else. But in Britain alone there are 275 bee species, a couple of dozen of them bumblebees (*Bombus* spp.) and the European Honeybee, *Apis mellifera*.* The rest are 'solitary bees', that is, bees that do not form social colonies. In the open sand between dense stands of Marram Grass there were many tiny holes into and out of which flew the solitary bees that nested there. I had determined not to collect any, or at least many, samples, but thought it worth the guilt to bring home a bee which I could later study under my microscope. In my defence, anyone who walks anywhere will kill innumerable invertebrates with every step, leaving a mini-massacre in their wake.

After much scratching of the head, thumbing through my book on solitary bees, following its key ('keys' are explained in the chapter on The Drift), not getting anywhere, I resorted to my

* 'the bee that bears honey'.

melittological friend, who told me that it was the **Silvery Leaf-cutter Bee**, *Megachile leachella*. The females of several members of the Megachilini carry a handy 'razor blade' between their mandibular teeth to cut very neat circular or semicircular leaf sections from plants with fairly tough leaves. They take these to their nests to build partitions to separate and line the brood cells. This may well explain the extremely neat semicircles cut from the leaves of one of my garden roses – they are so precise that their use as mere food seemed unlikely.

Langstone Harbour

We walked north and rounded the spit eastward. For the first time we could see the full extent of Langstone Harbour. It is a place where I used to go cockling with my mother, father and sister Trish, back in the 1960s, and the place where I sat for three hours with two friends failing to catch flatfish in the rain from a rowing boat. It is also where I have led a couple of organised walks and carried out research for two previous books. My maternal grandparents lived in Portsmouth, about 150 yards from the western coast of Langstone Harbour. The part of the harbour near to them was closed off with a causeway in the '60s in an attempt to reclaim the land, though 'claim' seems a more accurate word. Drained, it became a vast area of cracked mud that became a test range for some of my more successful home-made rockets and then a municipal rubbish dump. It is now an excellent nature reserve, though I presume that the original planners had more lucrative ambitions for the land.

With no rockets on me to test, our walk that day was to be more peaceful, just a gentle stroll from the ferry, east along the straight country road sandwiched between Sinah Common to the south and Sinah Warren to the north, followed by a northward return to the west-facing shore of Langstone Harbour via the track that occupies the length of the old railway line.

The Kench and Samphires

But first, a sheltered area of mudflat and salt marsh demanded our attention. The Kench, as it is called, is effectively a harbour, if only for small boats. It is bounded by a long stretch of Ferry Road to the south and the complex double spit that arches around to the west and north. To the east there is an area of scrubland.

Apart from the wildlife and occasional small boat, the main inhabitants of the shoreline of The Kench are chalets and houseboats. I think I may have spent an evening in one of the chalets in 1969, when I and my friends (one of them having evidently obtained the key from his parents) went there with a teenage determination to have a good time. The Swinging Sixties, however, never made it to Langstone Harbour, so we didn't.

We continued along Ferry Road with the mudflats to our left exposed by the low tide. The mud has been washed from the land over countless years and deposited in the sheltered waters of the harbour. Plants invariably establish themselves just above the high tide in the mud and gravel, or in the intertidal zone where it may be just mud. Here the narrow beach below the sea wall consisted of a mix of plants already seen and plants that were happier in the more sedate environment of the harbour. The beach was, unfortunately, inaccessible owing to a wire fence which I would normally have climbed over, but there were some intimidating 'Private Beach' signs which seemed to come with an implicit threat of bloody vengeance, so my observations were from the high pavement. Above the high-tide mark there were those plants already recorded: Sea Spurrey and Buckshorn Plantain, for example, but there were a few true salt marsh and mudflat plants too. Sea Purslane was one and Marsh Samphire another.

Marsh Samphire encompasses several species. The Common Glasswort, *Salicornia europaea*, is probably the correct name for what I saw, but the ten species that it could have been are almost indistinguishable from one another – except by a handful of botanists who do not necessarily agree with each other. I have met many people who, perhaps understandably, think that Marsh Samphire is a seaweed, but it is not, being instead one of the more surprising plants in the Goosefoot Family. Despite appearances, it has flowers that grow from the joints of its stem/leaf: they are minuscule. Marsh Samphire is edible but must be cut with scissors, as just pulling it out of the ground uproots the entire plant. This contravenes the law that requires permission to be obtained from the owner of the land from which a plant might be uprooted. The primary purpose of Marsh Samphire roots is to prevent it floating away, not to provide nutrients, since it is already immersed in nutrient-rich water for much of the day. If the plant is cut just above the roots, that would be legal but pointless, as it is like cutting your annual bedding plants at ground level with a scythe and expecting them to survive. Cutting higher up might help, but I should not worry about this too much – just don't tread on any. Here the Samphire was in small clumps among the mud and stones, but it often grows in pure intertidal mud to form what looks very much like a neat lawn.

The most exciting, indeed magnificent, plant along that stretch was **Golden Samphire**, *Limbarda crithmoides*. It is a strictly coastal plant, found in scattered populations around southern Britain. It is considered to be 'threatened', in that its habitats are threatened, but the populations appear to be stable. Golden Samphire is edible, just about, not that you would consider eating a threatened plant. It was once collected in Britain as a poor substitute for Rock Samphire in the pickle. Frankly, it could not be worse than pickled Rock Samphire, so you would be luckier if you bought the dud.

We would later find **Rock Samphire**, *Crithmum maritimum*, a mile north among the low rocks above the shore. The succulent, branching leaves were once – and, to a *very* limited extent, are now – collected for pickling. The flavour of the fresh plant is plain horrible, consisting of carrots and kerosene. The flavours are due to Rock Samphire being in the Carrot Family and to the plant actually containing kerosene (paraffin), otherwise known as alpha-pinene. Once it is pickled, these flavours are unmoderated and made worse with the added burden of acetic acid. I have never understood why anyone would think (as seems to be the case with many pickle ingredients) that steeping something unpleasant in vinegar will miraculously improve matters. One more characteristic of Rock Samphire that I should warn you about is its tenuous nature. Eat one sprig and you will be tasting it for six hours. My work here is done.

All samphires are succulent coastal plants, and all are edible. The word derives from *herb de Saint Pierre* which was shortened to *sampere* or *samphire*. Christ called St Peter his 'rock' (the name Peter is from the Greek for 'rock', *petros*, and it is Jesus' only recorded joke), so it seems likely that it was originally applied to Rock Samphire, which is famous for growing on cliffs and rocky shores. These three species belong to wildly different Families of plant: Golden Samphire is in the Daisy Family, Rock Samphire in the Carrot Family and Marsh Samphire in the Goosefoot Family.

We found yet another maritime Goosefoot later in the day, well above the high-tide mark. It was **Annual Seablite**, *Suaeda* *maritima.* It formed neat, six-inch tufts of succulent leaves among the dried seaweeds and pebbles. It is an edible, if largely tasteless, species, but with a pleasant degree of crunch, very much the sort of thing you might consider collecting to sell to posh restaurants for an absurd sum.

To our right (south), as we walked westwards along Ferry Road, was the northern side of the Sinah Common golf course, with glimpses of a fine and mature heathland, purple with **Bell Heather,** *Erica cinerea,* which contrasted nicely with the yellow of a species from the 'hawkish complex'. Sorry, best I could do at the time. The heathland represents a late stage in the development of the dune system. A little to the west it was developed further with dense gorse cover and then the final stage, a climax woodland, providing a neat display of successional development of an ecosystem within a mere 10 hectares.

The Hayling Local Nature Reserve and a Birder

At the south-eastern extremity of The Kench is an entrance that leads to an LNR, or Local Nature Reserve. Just to the left of this entrance there was a Dog Rose. These always draw my attention, either for their lovely flowers, to pick their rosehips or to look out for the prettiest of all the galls. My attention was rewarded with a neat specimen of Robin's Pincushion. This flamboyant composition of wiry, bright red threads is unmistakable. Galls are created for a parasite (which may be an insect, a mite, a fungus, a nematode worm or a bacterium) by the plant, under instructions from the parasite. The parasite in this instance was the gall wasp, **Diplolepsis rosae.** The mother wasp will lay multiple eggs on multiple leaf buds, each egg and, subsequently, larva forming a chamber in which it will feed and enjoy protection. If you cut an empty Robin's Pincushion in half, you can see those several chambers.

Behind what I assumed to be a Second World War lookout post we noticed a man and woman sitting on a bench, the man wielding binoculars with intent. They glanced in our direction, so I took the opportunity to introduce the pair of us and explain our mission. I politely asked about their own, obvious though it was. There is a single-mindedness about 'birders' (a term used to distinguish them from the more casual 'birdwatcher') that is difficult for most other naturalists to understand. My speciality is mycology, but even on a fungus foray I would not walk past, say, a broomrape in full flower without stopping, photographing it, putting it on social media and telling everyone for the next month about what I had found. Birders, however, only see birds, and any expressed interest in plants only reaches as far as how they might affect their objects of devotion: a foodplant or habitat, for example. Fungi do not exist as far as they are concerned, and with other animals it is whether or not they might steal bird's eggs or eat the mother. They tend not to like cats.

I am being playful here, but there is a degree of truth in what I say. I do not think that Mike was quite so extreme, and I found him very likeable and helpful. He told me about the various birds he had seen that day: a Kestrel, a Curlew, some gull or other and … I can't remember the rest. And he very kindly offered me a photograph of a Curlew he had seen a little further to the north and gave me permission to use it. It is the only photograph of a bird in the whole book, so do enjoy it.

Sinah Warren

Eastwards, beyond the LNR, we followed Ferry Road, alongside Sinah Warren to the north. A possible origin of the name Sinah is indicated here. A warren is where rabbits were kept in the Middle Ages, after their introduction from Spain. Used to the warm Iberian climate as they were, they found it difficult to survive in Britain and needed wardens (hence 'warren') to look after them, complete with ready-made burrows known now as pillow mounds. Sinah, it is thought, may have been the name of a long-tailed rabbit variety that was kept there. The wardens in this instance were monks, who operated an early incarnation of a health farm, though I doubt it was much fun.

For a short period during the Second World War, Sinah Warren's then owner, the wealthy Andrew Arbuthnot, created what is believed to have been the first factory farm for chickens. This was an arguably noble attempt to both alleviate wartime food shortage and infuriate the neighbours with the intolerable smell from the mountains of chicken manure that piled up. Arbuthnot also planted hundreds of trees from all over the world.

We did not walk around Sinah Warren that day, but I have since taken a virtual stroll. It is now a restful-looking hotel/ holiday park. I thought I might stay there for a few days to undertake a more comprehensive survey of The Kench, but apparently they have 'entertainments' and you can never be sure whether or not they are compulsory. Still, it might be worth the risk as the trees are mature and some of my best fungal finds have been in the grounds of country hotels.

The Hayling Billy

After a long walk east along Ferry Road and wiggling our way through a complex of houses, we reached the southern entrance to the Hayling Billy Coastal Path. The much-lamented Hayling Billy railway service between Hayling and Havant was opened in 1867 and closed in 1963 by the notorious and spectacularly ill-conceived Beeching cuts. This was the abandonment of around half of Britain's railway capacity owing to the competition they had suffered from increased use of motor vehicles. It was both unpopular and understandable at the time, with only hindsight bringing its extreme folly into sharp focus. There are many aspects of the policy that are open to criticism, but the most damning one, I think, is that many of these lines of communication were casually disposed of by British Rail and became useless for the many subsequent purposes to which they may have been applied – power lines, broadband lines, cycle paths, footpaths, new roads, *railway lines* and so on. If one person holds a tenacious claim to a metre of the land along a discontinued railway line, then any such scheme must be abandoned unless expensive and unreliable legal action is taken.

One wonders if the Hayling Billy would survive commercially or provide a public good in the twenty-first century, but its loss is, at least, compensated for by this fascinating footpath. It stretches from Sinah Lane to just short of the Hayling Bridge in the north, a distance of nearly five miles.

We stayed on the path for about half a mile, with a long spinney to our left, a hedge to our right and arable land beyond. This was a linear haven for wildlife. There were some of the plants typical of hedgerow and wood-edge along this stretch: an unspecified St John's Wort, **Hedge Woundwort**, *Stachys sylvatica*, **Greater Mullein**, *Verbascum thapsus*, **Dogwood**, *Cornus san-*

guinea, **Garlic Mustard**, *Alliaria petiolata*, **Common Figwort**, *Scrophularia nodosa*, and a patch of **Hemlock Water-Dropwort**, *Oenanthe crocata*, in a damp area towards the end. The last of these plants is deadly poisonous, causing fast and furious liver failure accompanied by a horror movie of symptoms. Nevertheless, I have known people who have eaten the leaves (almost identical to flat-leaved parsley) and survived. The leaves are less poisonous, they ate only a tiny amount and they were cooked. The roots, however, are utterly deadly, but strangely appealing once dug out of the mud and given a wash. They look just like a bunch of carrots, except that they are white.

Just as we entered, I saw a plant that was new to me (always a thrilling moment), though its name was not. It was **Field Madder**, *Sherardia arvensis*, a plant with four tiny pink petals. It is a relatively common plant, especially in arable fields on chalk, so no doubt it is one of my many failures of observation. The roots of Common Madder are used to make a dye (whose effects range from reds to oranges), but those of Field Madder produce merely a fugitive pink. We also saw our third gall of the trip in the form of multiple and impressive raised bumps on the leaves of a **Holm Oak**, *Quercus ilex*, caused by the mite *Aceria ilicis*.

The best of this linear show, however, was attached to a seriously denuded Hawthorn branch. This branch was covered in a loose, stocking-like web. Inside the web were about forty orange/brown larvae, plus hundreds of 1.5-mm-diameter black and vaguely spherical particles, which I presume were their droppings. I had never seen this species before, and did not know what they were, moth larvae being my first guess. A little research quickly found them to be the larvae of the **Social Pear Sawfly**, *Neurotoma saltuum*. Presumably, pear trees are its favoured larval food, but it is known from plum, cherry and cotoneaster. It is locally common in Britain, with a vaguely south-western distribution. We will learn more about sawflies in the chapter on The Drift, the main thing to note being that they are not flies (Diptera) but instead accompany wasps and bees in the Hymenoptera.

I saw one other oddity along this path, one that has puzzled me for years. It was a thin elm branch with distinct, corky ribs running along the stems. Corky ribs (or wings, as they are more commonly known) are not seen on all elms and may occur on only some of the branches of a single tree. There is something called 'elm-wing virus', but no amount of research has uncovered any details.

It had been a while since we had seen the sea, the present path being one field away from the beach. We took the opportunity to remedy this by following a westerly path seawards alongside an area of neglected rush pasture. Just before we arrived at a bank that had clearly been constructed above the beach as a sea defence, we saw a sprawling mass of brilliant yellow flowers. It was **Dyer's Greenweed**, *Genista tinctoria*. There is a subspecies, *G. tinctoria* subsp. *littoralis*, which, with 'littoral' meaning 'beside the seaside', seems a likely candidate as it was very close to the sea. While nearly all the records for this species are further west, an ecologist friend told me that it was possible, likely even, that the one I found that day was indeed the subspecies. Dyer's Greenweed is in the same botanical tribe as gorse and broom, and indeed 'Dyer's Broom' is another name for it. The dye produces a yellow colour (as do gorse and broom), something that is surprisingly rare among plant and fungal dyes as it is more common for them to produce a colour dramatically at odds with the source material.

I cannot leave this plant without mentioning its generic name, *Genista*, which is the origin of the name of the Royal House of Plantagenets. It was adopted, probably via the old Latin name for the (related) broom, *Plantagenest*, because its flowers' intense yellow represents gold and thus wealth.

Cord Grass and a Terrible Confession

Beyond the sea bank we are at last back on the beach. Here the environment is one of a clay bank two metres high, then ten to fifty metres of pebble, gravel, sand and mud, then just mud or muddy sand. It is a landscape I know well, having spent many days here collecting cockles and clams.

Whatever small confidence you may have in me by now will now be shattered by what happened with my next find. I had intended to keep quiet about it, either passing it by altogether or making it less embarrassing than it really was. But honesty has won the day and, anyway, nobody likes an infallible smart arse.

About thirty metres below the high-tide mark, nestling in the mud, sand and pebbles, were several incongruous near-circular patches of upright green leaves. 'It's seagrass!' I exclaimed excitedly to D, digging the hole deeper by adding that it was a species of *Zostera* and that Eelgrass is another of its common names. I had done some minimal research prior to our mini-expedition and knew that Langstone Harbour was noted, famous even, for its seagrass. I had never knowingly seen seagrass before, and given that it was a grassy-looking plant, growing in the intertidal zone and in an area renowned for its presence, what else was it going to be? I am sure that a few of you can cheerfully answer that question.

I spent a day or so writing it up for this book, checking with photographs online, research papers, distribution maps and reports, and was quite pleased with what I had written. Except that nothing quite fitted. *Zostera* species are not grass, just 'grass-like', and my find was very obviously a grass, even to me. I was just in denial and so battled on. Some *Zostera* species, I was reassured, take different forms, depending on whether they grow permanently under water or are revealed by the tide on occasions. The latter forms are more robust, perhaps explaining why the 'seagrass' I had found did not look much (OK, *remotely*) like the photographs I had taken. I delved deeper. Re-reading these papers with the care they deserved the first time, I found I had got things the wrong way round, and that those I had seen should have been *less* robust.

In gentle despair I checked my suspicions with my dear friend Bryan (the fellow who knows everything that I mentioned in the Introduction). He flatly said it was Cord Grass, not a seagrass. He did not add that I was an idiot as it really didn't need saying and, anyway, D said so when I told her. I knew about Cord Grass, but did not notice it if I have ever seen it. I knew it was a plant of salt marshes, but what I did not realise was that it was content to take a *complete* saltwater bath twice a day; indeed, and in fairness, it *is* unusual. Still, my failure of observation was utterly shameful.

I have pleaded with people for the last thirty years that if the mushroom they have in their hand does not completely match the description in the book of what they *think* it is, then it isn't. Sound advice of the highest quality, and something I should consider taking myself. Now, where were we, or rather, where should we be? Ah, yes!

About thirty metres beyond the high-tide mark, nestling in the mud, sand and pebbles, were several incongruous near-circular patches of what I immediately recognised to be **Cord Grass**. There are five species and one hybrid in Britain; this one was *Spartina anglica*. There is an extraordinary story about this species, the most fascinating part of which is that we know almost to the year how old it is: circa 1888. By this I do not mean the year in which it was named (we know that for almost every named species), but quite literally how long it has been in existence. This may come as a surprise to anyone who is a little vague about evolutionary processes. Surely, they might say, species change very slowly from generation to generation, until sufficiently different from their distant ancestor to count as a new species. In this case, however, a major genetic change happened suddenly (twice, in fact), and a new species branched off from an existing one.

When a species of Cord Grass, *S. alterniflora*, was introduced to the Solent in the middle of the nineteenth century, it hybridised with the native species *S. maritima*. This hybrid was sterile, reproducing only vegetatively, like strawberry runners or plant cuttings. It is called *S. × townsendii*, and still thrives locally. (The '×' here is used to indicate that it is a hybrid species.) Cord grasses are known for their excessive polyploidy, where many more than the customary two sets of chromosomes exist within their cell nuclei. Without going into impenetrable details, *S. × townsendii* subsequently underwent polyploidy, which, it so happened, made it fertile. It was described and named in 1888, so we know more or less when it came into being.

S. anglica is considerably more vigorous than its close cousins (as often happens in polyploidal species) and, fortuitously, with an exceptional talent for stabilising the seabed with its substantial roots. It has been exported to temperate zones (its preferred climate type) all over the world for its stabilising talents. As hinted earlier, it is more usual to find this grass on the raised, muddy edge of salt marshes, often defined on the seaward side with mini, muddy cliffs. In this more common mode, it is reported to be capable of raising a salt marsh by up to two metres!

S. anglica is not without its problems as it can be invasive, taking over oyster beds and displacing less vigorous plants. It once covered huge areas within the broader Solent area, including Hayling Island, but has died back dramatically and quickly. Various explanations for the retreat were considered – bacteria, fungi, pollution – but it transpires that the plant was, effectively, poisoning its own habitat. In estuarine habitats, where sand forms a reasonably high percentage of the sediment, it continues to grow well, but with the fine mud that characterises much of its home patch its roots found themselves attempting to grow in the anaerobic conditions typical of mud – it effectively chokes itself.

Since Langstone Harbour is, as I say, noted for its *seagrasses*, it is worth relating their story briefly, even though we did not see it. As already noted, seagrasses simply aren't grasses but are grass-like plants, much as reeds, rushes and sedges are grass-like. Individually they are referred to as 'eelgrasses', as in Common Eelgrass, *Zostera marina*, Narrow-Leaved Eelgrass, *Z. angustifolia*, and Dwarf Eelgrass, *Z. noltii*. The first and the last of these are found in Langstone Harbour. 'Seagrasses' suffer from too many names, with Zos, Zos-Grass and Wigeon Grass being three more.

Both male and female flowers are formed on a single 'stem', and the pollen is dispersed not by wind but by water. This happens either by submarine transport, where the pollen arranges itself into tiny, brush-like structures to be carried along by currents, or by surface transport in which they arrange themselves into small, snowflake-shaped rafts that float around, trusting that they might bump into a female flower.

Zostera spp. are important not only in themselves but also for the creatures they support, seahorses and pipefish being particular seagrass specialists. The eggs of herrings can be highly concentrated in seagrass and likewise various shellfish such as Cockles and Brown Crabs. It also feeds several bird species, such as Brent Geese, Swans and, of course, Wigeon.

Cockles and Winkles

Moving on, or rather, walking with great care across the mud, I found a few live **Cockles**, *Cerastoderma edule*. Some were lying on their sides, but more were in their preferred arrangement of being mostly buried with their hinge vertical. This keeps the two siphons free of the mud so that they can feed. There were a few empty **Palourdes**, *Ruditapes decussatus*, and oyster shells, and very many **Winkles**, *Littorina littorea*. Palourdes are similar to cockles, but larger, more stylish and with a better flavour and texture. Sadly, not many people eat Winkles in modern Britain, which is a pity as they are high in protein and taste nice provided you don't look at them first. They were once a staple of the poor and sold by street vendors in London in the nineteenth century, and more recently on whelk stores at seaside towns. They were a traditional treat in our family via my father, who was the son of a Lowestoft herring skipper, for whom it was also a tradition. Anyway, we liked them, they were free and they were fun to collect. If you are tempted to gather these for yourself, then go on an ebbing spring tide and leave before the flood. Steep them overnight in a wide, shallow tray of salt water (3.5 per cent) to purify them and use a safety pin to extricate them from their shells once cooked.

A Hoverfly and Two Exciting Plants

Our walk was nearly over, but the plants kept coming, and above the beach I managed to take a reasonable photograph of the **Marmalade Hoverfly**, *Episyrphus balteatus*, conspicuous with its three broad, black bands, separated by two, thin, black 'moustaches'. I had taken guided walks in this area fairly recently and knew what plants to expect. One of these was **Sea Lavender**, an attractive plant of the upper reaches of salt marsh. It has broad, succulent leaves and strings of pretty lilac flowers. Years ago, attracted by the succulence and knowing that Sea Lavender was, at least, not poisonous, I ate some. It was truly vile. I have not provided a Latin name as I simply do not know which sea lavender it might be, because there are dozens of them and no strong agreement between taxonomists who ponder such things. Most people go with *Limonium vulgare* and leave it at that.

We then found one of the great treasures of salt marshes, **Sea Wormwood**, *Artemisia maritima*. I am familiar with this delicately beautiful plant from my many visits to the coast of East Lothian, where it grows in great profusion. It is found on the edges of salt marshes all around Britain. Despite its wide occurrence, it is less frequent than in the past, owing to habitat loss. More robust in stature and less fussy about where it lives, is its relative, Wormwood, *A. absinthium*. I have used this in tiny quantities to make bitters for cocktails, though even for a bitter it is *extremely* bitter. This is unfortunate, since the aromatics it contains are very pleasant. Sea Wormwood, however, is much milder and potentially more useful to the cocktail maker. Or possibly the gin maker. I have done a little work for gin producers who were looking for wild aromatic plants to include in the formulae. On all of the three occasions it has been by the sea and the subject of Sea Wormwood has come up. I have recommended it highly, but pointed out that it will nearly always grow in protected areas and that if they wished to use it they would need to source it from a grower.

The Taxi

Our day ended at 5.30 in the evening, and we were extremely tired, having walked five miles plus diversions that day. We staggered the short distance to the bus stop, waited and watched a couple of buses zoom past before realising that buses are not what they once were, and we would need to book. An app was duly downloaded but proved impossible to make sense of, so we tried to phone for a taxi. There were few companies to choose from, and those we found either did not answer or told us they could pick us up at 11 p.m. at the earliest, mate. One said he could take us to Gatwick in a limo, but that was all. Walking the five miles back to the car seemed the only option, so we set off. After an exhausting quarter of a mile we gave up and tried some taxi firms from further afield. One of these said it was too far to come but he knew a taxi firm on Hayling Island who, he told us, would not answer their advertised number (we knew, we had tried) but would probably pick us up if he put in a good word. They were there in fifteen minutes.

Fulham to Marble Arch

URBAN STREETS AND PARKS

FOUR MILES

20 MAY 2021

Hayling Island, Hampshire

The car park

Xanthoria parietina

Restharrow and Sea Kale

Viper's Bugloss

The fine detail of a hawkish seed head

Sea Holly

Sea Sandwort

Salt marsh east of The Kench

Curlew (courtesy of Michael Woffinden)

Sea Purslane and Marsh Samphire

Social Pear Sawfly

Cord Grass flowers

Langstone Harbour sea defences

Fulham to Marble Arch

The cemetery at St Thomas

Herb Robert up close

An urban plant community

Procumbent Pearlwort

Brompton Cemetery

Lecanora muralis

Cow Parsley and Green Alkanet

Wood Sorrel

A pollarded Lime Tree

A mushroom ring *sans* mushrooms

A managed mowing regime

Comfrey in a wild corner

A Grey Squirrel

Urban Bounty

Some of the most exciting plants and fungi I have found over the years I have discovered not in the wilds of Britain but in its towns. For example, a few weeks after this visit to the London area, I found a dozen fine specimens of Ivy Broomrape, *Orobanche hederae*, growing along a path west of Kingston upon Thames. I have found St George's Mushrooms in Farringdon, Sea Beet in Dagenham, Wild Rocket in Hackney and a splendid collection of Horse Mushrooms in Fulham.

Towns and cities are often dismissed as barren wastes for wildlife, but this is a gross misrepresentation. When a new town or development is proposed on a greenfield site, I will not be writing immediately to the council to complain, instead I will look at the proposed site first. If it involves the destruction of ancient woodland, hedgerows that buzz with life, herb-rich pasture or the draining of a bit of wetland, then I will draft my objection. But if it is to be built on *intensive* arable land, then I hold my peace. While we certainly need high-output arable land, its loss is, for the most part, directly ours, not that of the organisms that live there – indeed, there will be few to lose. Once all the building is complete, semi-wild areas are established, trees and gardens planted up and it will boast a thousand times the biodiversity of what was there before.

Towns are where most people live, take their constitutional walk or walk to the pound shop, hairdresser's or doctor's. They also visit parks, and this particular walk included three, two of them Royal. As we wander from place to place, be it town or in country, it is always worth looking around you; there will be more to see than you might imagine.

But why, you might ask, choose Fulham to Marble Arch? Well, it had to be somewhere, so I made it personal by honouring my maternal grandparents. It is simply that my grandfather was born in Fulham and met my grandmother at Marble Arch. He was of that most honourable breed, a pre-war soldier, a Coldstream Guard, in which he had the added honour of being the shortest soldier in the regiment at 5 foot 8 inches. It was while in his uniform at Marble Arch that my grandmother spotted him and, I have always fancied, jumped on him. He was shy and she a passionate redhead from rural Wiltshire. My noble and well-read grandfather and I were very close, and I would tell you more about him but will settle for his most striking peculiarity: he didn't believe in static electricity. We all don't believe in something, but why pick on static electricity? He never said. I suppose it is better than my late mother-in-law's disbelief in Elvis Presley. Not 'didn't like' but 'didn't believe in'. No explanation for this mad assertion was ever forthcoming either.

Wild Surbiton

D and I stayed with our daughter the night before our venture. Her flat was in Surbiton. Surbiton (= 'the place where barley is grown') is famously a leafy suburb, as was clear from the view of the small garden from her top-floor window. Bright green **Rose-Ringed Parakeets**, *Psittacula krameri*, were everywhere, with three or more visible at any one time. This bird is obviously not native, having established substantial populations descended from several and frequent escapees from domestic incarceration. Legendary explanations involving Jimi Hendrix or Humphrey Bogart have been dismissed as, well, legendary. It can be found almost anywhere in Britain, chiefly in urban areas, with London being Parakeet Central. Across Britain their numbers are in the tens of thousands. Something usually has to give way with the introduction of so enthusiastic a species, and in this case it is presumed to be native birds, with Starlings, Nuthatches and Woodpeckers out-competed for nest-holes. Bats, too, are thought to be threatened by this colourful pest. Culls have been considered, and over a hundred were shot in Richmond Park between 2017 and 2019. There is also the Monk Parakeet, *Myiopsitta monachus* (just as bright green as its cousin, but with a white belly), but its numbers appear to be small – for the moment.

Decidedly native, but seemingly on its way to forming an urban subspecies, is the **Red Fox**, *Vulpes vulpes*. These too could be seen in that suburban garden as they never could be in the countryside. We watched them lounge and play on the lawn, and my daughter told me she had seen the vixen teach her cubs the elements of hunting, ticking them off when they brought her empty yoghurt cartons. Despite having heard of a population of Soprano Bats in the area, we decided not to brave an after dark walk around what passes for the great outdoors in Surbiton and retired for the night.

Church of St Thomas of Canterbury and the Classification of Urban Communities

According to the 1911 census, my grandfather grew up in his father's greengrocer's on 14 Campbell Street, Fulham. But as far as I could see, no such street exists in today's Fulham. Still, I needed a suitable place to start our walk, so I chose the Catholic church of St Thomas of Canterbury. Of Irish descent, my grandfather was a Catholic all his life but, having married a Protestant, seldom went to church. I do not know if he went to St Thomas's, but it did once have a school attached, so it would have been a suitable choice.

I spend a fair amount of time wandering around cemeteries, as their permanence often leads to some unusual plants, fungi and lichens. While we were attending the funeral of a friend, D was moved to have a serious word or two with me (in fact it was two: 'not' and 'now'), after I was distracted by a particularly magnificent group of mushrooms called *Agaricus bresadolanus* in the grass among the graves. *A. bresadolanus* has unusual rhizomorphs, don't you know?

Nothing so fascinating met our eyes in that cemetery, with lime trees and a palm tree and a rough understory of the usual weedy suspects. The palm tree seemed incongruous, but a moment's thought back to Sunday school made me realise my error. The 'weeds' were predominantly **Green Alkanet**, *Pentaglottis sempervirens*, the ubiquitous **Herb Robert**, *Geranium robertianum*, **Ivy-Leaved Toadflax**, *Cymbalaria muralis*, some wan-looking **Bluebells**, *Hyacinthoides non-scripta*, **Wood Avens**, *Geum urbanum*, **Prickly Sow Thistle**, *Sonchus asper*, **Cleavers**, *Galium aparine*, **Daisies**, *Bellis perennis* ('perennial beauty'!) and the very common **Annual Meadow Grass**, *Poa annua*. The leaves of several of the Sow Thistles were decorated with the whitish channels of the **Sow Thistle Miner**, *Chromatomyia atricornis*, a small fly. These are all very familiar and often untidy species, but beautiful nevertheless in their close details. This beauty is quite literally magnified once that closer look is taken, as can be seen in the close-up of Herb Robert shown here.

Such sights were to attend much of our walk that day. Plants that grow at the join between wall and pavement, between pavement slabs and underneath street trees, are the common, uninvited companions of our urban lives. They have long been disregarded by the urban dweller, but a popular movement was instigated in 2020, where they became a saviour of sanity for many. During the various lockdowns that accompanied the Covid-19 pandemic, people began to take more notice of their environment during the short daily walks that were permitted under the sometimes damn fool lockdown regulations. This took visible form when people began to write the names of plants in chalk on the pavements. Some attempted to find a new species every day and would proudly post their finds on social media. That they sometimes got things wrong is of little importance; it was the fact that they became interested in a previously invisible aspect of their environment that mattered.

One would think that the professional or serious amateur naturalist would dismiss the plants that make a living in the urban setting, but it is not so. Science is, or should be, the description of what is, not what we would like it to be. Urban ecosystems, therefore, are described and recorded in the same way (if not to the same extent) as any pristine nature reserve would be. The National Vegetation Classification (NVC) scheme has categories into which the various urban plant communities fall. These can be found in volume 5 of *British Plant Communities*, as 'vegetation of open spaces'. Some of these will be wild or semi-wild, such as crevices in rocks, field edges, periodically flooded areas and so on, but many cover the nooks and crannies of the urban landscape. As usual, they come with the sorts of name not much welcomed by the average person (literally, in this case) in the street: OV25 *Urtica dioica-Cirsium arvense* community, for example. The authors of the five volumes of *British Plant Communities*, in which the NVC is described in minute and painful detail, freely admit that some communities are difficult to identify with great certainty and that sometimes the various populations can vary so much within a few square metres that no sensible class can be ascribed to the collection of plants that find themselves there. I certainly had trouble with the mixed habitats I could see through the cemetery gate, but I was to be luckier later in the day.

Just as we left the church, a small cluster of the very common **Glistening Inkcap**, *Coprinopsis micaceous*, came into view, but forming a soggy mess rather than a neat collection. Healthier were sprawling masses of **Chickweed**, *Stellaria media*. This is an edible plant, and first class in a stir-fry or bhaji. However, at the base of a tree along any street in the world is not a good place to collect your dinner.

A Maze of Roads and Their Plants, and the Complexity of Dandelions

Apart from start and end points, there was no plan for the day. Unlike in the countryside, where fields and private land restrict the walker to footpaths, in a city we are free to wander down pretty much any road we want. I wanted it to be a 'natural' walk, not one that had been selected for its green credentials, so we consulted our online map and followed the shortest route. We crossed the road to go east-north-east along St Thomas's Way.

The danger in our method was that some roads might not have anything of interest. This was the case with St Thomas's, which was attractive enough, but a near-desert apart from the young Plane trees scattered along it.

But we had better luck on Haldane Road, where front gardens line both sides for most of its length. A three-metre-long paved path between two houses displayed flora not so different from that of the little of the cemetery that we had seen earlier, except that several **Dandelions** were also there. Finding both Dandelions and Annual Meadow Grass enabled me to tentatively give this tiny patch of land an official classification: OV22 *Poa annua-Taraxacum officinale* community.

The taxonomic standing of the otherwise humble Dandelion is hideously complicated. It is generally called *Taraxacum officinale* agg. or just *Taraxacum* agg. in polite company, indicating that the writer knows it is a Dandelion but is not prepared to hazard a guess as to which one. *Taraxacum* is an odd genus in that it is separated not so much into what some might call 'true' species as into micro-species. These are almost invariably clones (also known as 'apomicts' from 'apomixis', meaning 'without mixing'), with seeds that produce offspring genetically identical to the parent plant. There are a few sexually reproducing Dandelions, complete with the customary two sets of chromosomes, while the clonal (apomictic) lineages have more: that is, they are polyploid. Micro-species can, however, *sometimes* give up their vows and reproduce sexually. *T. officinale* (an apomict) is the Common Dandelion, but there are over two hundred more recorded and named in Britain alone. A (very) few people are able to identify them, but I have always suspected that if you gave the same specimen to five taraxacologists (for so they are called) you would receive five different names. Some authorities dismiss much of this, just lumping all Dandelions into a handful of groups. Frankly, it is a nightmare beyond the understanding of people with better things to do with their time – a Dandelion is a Dandelion.

We continued our zigzag path along the broad Racton Road. Cars were parked both sides, which gave me a reasonably safe chance to get close to the plants of pavement, kerb and gutter. I laid down in the gutter and duly examined a few plants through my loupe and took several photographs. Inevitably, a woman walking by expressed her concern. 'Is he OK?' she asked. D was watching with interest, so her usual claim – that she had never seen me before in her life and that, whoever I was, I looked OK to her, just drunk – was too implausible. And the photos I took? They were of **Germander Speedwell**, *Veronica chamaedrys*, and **Rue-Leaved Saxifrage**, *Saxifraga tridactylites*, the latter plant conspicuous with its red leaves and brilliant red stem. One wonders about how some of these plants earn their common names; sometimes no one knows, but these two have a known etymology. 'Germander' can be traced back to the Hellenistic Greek as χαμαίδρυς, meaning 'ground oak', presumably because it is a fairly low plant and the leaves look vaguely like those of oaks, and the Greek was later rendered in post-classical Latin as *germandra*. 'Speedwell' employs an old meaning of 'speed' – that is, 'to prosper' – while the 'well' is used in the almost lost sense of 'morally good'. So, while most people will just settle on the plant being a lucky charm for travellers, my interpretation is that it is an encouragement to behave well. Leaving the meaning of 'rue' to one side, 'saxifrage' means 'breaker of rocks', owing to such plants often being found in rocky crevices, as one was here, albeit between paving slabs.

I also found more Dandelions, Annual Meadowgrass and some **Hairy Bittercress**, *Cardamine hirsuta*, its tiny, four-petalled white flowers just opening. This is an edible plant with a mustard-and-cress flavour, but best picked far away from a gutter. Untidily entwined with these three plants were the bronze trefoil leaves of **Procumbent Yellow Sorrel**, *Oxalis corniculata*, though its yellow flowers were not in evidence. It is a relative newcomer to Britain, having been here only 500 years since it arrived from South-East Asia. It seems to have fitted in well enough, being common in Britain and with a southern and western distribution. All four of these species are standard pavement fare. Near by there was a fifth such plant, **Procumbent Pearlwort**, *Sagina procumbens*. It too has white petals, four of them, though they were still closed that day. It is an attractive plant in delicate miniature, with leaves that are dark green and slightly succulent, and one that you may have trodden on twenty times today as gaps in pavements seem to be its favoured habitat. It has potential use on patios, where it may be sown to fill in gaps that would otherwise be taken by more troublesome weeds. It has a companion species, Heath Pearlwort, *S. subulata*, also known as 'Irish Moss', which can also be used in the garden, this time as ground cover and even as a lawn. It is native to Britain but restricted to Scotland and south-west England.

Street Trees and Their Under-Stories

The dominant tree in London is, of course, the London Plane. Its Latin name is *Plantanus* x *hispanica*, the 'x' indicating that it is a hybrid. The parent species were *P. occidentalis* and *P. orientalis*, marking a providential meeting of west and east, with the two trees planted close to one another, it is presumed, in seventeenth-century Spain. It is larger than its parents and more robust, and 'heterosis', also known as 'hybrid vigour', would be a good explanation for this. Heterosis is when closely related species of plants (or, indeed, animals) that are nevertheless genetically some distance apart mate with one another, increasing genetic diversity. It does not always work out so well, but in the case of the London Plane it has done so admirably.

The London Plane has been in Britain for centuries, with one of the two earliest known being at Ely Cathedral and the other, fittingly, in London, at Barnes. They are over 300 years old. The London Plane was introduced into London as a street tree around 150 years ago, chosen for that vigour, for its beauty and for its ability to tolerate the trials of living in a polluted environment.

I consider it to be a beautiful tree, but it has one failing in my opinion. The English Oak can support perhaps 500 species, including insects, lichens and fungi. By contrast, the London Plane, neither of whose parents lived closer than southern Italy, supports three unassuming microfungi, no larger mycorrhizal fungi, no galls and nothing much of anything else apart from the Grey Squirrel. Not even lichens can readily grow on it, because the bark continually peels away. London would have been vastly more lively had Oaks been planted instead, but perhaps they would not have survived as well as the ubiquitous London Plane. Not everyone appreciates bugs and fungi in their trees, so one must wonder if their lack of such 'pests' was among the reasons it was chosen. Another option might have been the species-rich limes, which tolerate city life well and might have been a better choice – except for all the honeydew they produce with sticky regularity.

Although Plane trees may be the favoured tree of London's urban planners, they are not necessarily what most residents and indeed planners choose for smaller streets, and few residents will choose the enormous London Plane for their own gardens. Paul Wood (nominative determinism), in his excellent *London's*

Street Trees, tells us that there are 400 species of tree found along London streets, from the Almonds to Maples and from the Nettle Tree to Whitebeams. There is much to occupy and entertain the amateur dendrophile in London.

Down a residential street near by I noticed some cherry trees. Many of these are likely to be ornamental, while some will produce edible cherries. Few people trust their plant ID skills enough to pick berries from any street tree, their mothers' warnings still fresh in their minds, but cherries and the Cherry Plum (not seen that day) are safe and easy enough to identify. Fruity treats aside, I look at street trees with the eyes of both forager and (former) furniture-maker. One cherry tree caught the latter eye. It had either suffered a serious misfortune or been recklessly pollarded, as its broad trunk stopped at two metres up, then started again with half the diameter. Planked-up, the clean, straight primary trunk would have made a splendid fruitwood desk.

Speaking of pollarding, two hundred metres or so south of the Hotel Lily there was a large Lime tree in full leaf, if not in full branch. It was one of the thousands of London trees that had been pollarded. In the confined spaces provided by an urban street, control must be exercised over any substantial tree determined to grow to its full potential. Lime trees can be enormous, with the Broad-Leaved Lime possibly forty metres high and thirty metres wide. The answer is pollarding, where the trunk is kept free of low branches and the higher, spreading branches cut back to acceptable lengths. Multiple young shoots will soon start to grow from wherever the tree has been cut, and after a few years (typically five) the new shoots are cut back to grow again.

Street Limes have long been kept under control in this way, their pollarded nature clear for all to see when the leaves have fallen. This particular example was clothed with leaves up most of its trunk from the cut-back side-shoots, as is typical with Limes. The leaves are a bright, almost translucent green at this time of the year, or any time they have produced new growth. They are edible, with a mild flavour and slimy (in a good way), succulent texture, just about acceptable as an on-the-go snack and marginally more so in a cheese sandwich. The sliminess is a reminder that Lime trees are in the Mallow Family, the Malvaceae.

The basal growth of Lime leaves had an 'understory' of the plants we had seen already that day: Annual Meadowgrass, Sow Thistle and a lush carpet of Chickweed, plus **Common Groundsel**, *Senecio vulgaris*. The Latin name of Groundsel means, literally, 'common old man', a reference to the grey hairs on the seeds, with the 'man' implicit. Slightly offensive, perhaps, but nowhere near as much as its cousin the Oxford Ragwort, *Senecio squalidus*, which means 'dirty old man'. Common Groundsel appears to be native to Europe and possibly North Africa but is one of the world's great successes, finding a home on all continents save Antarctica. A few inches away on the pavement was a reminder of why it would not have been sensible to pick any of the Chickweed, lush or not. Such unpleasantness soon forgotten, my mind turned to a mystery that has troubled me for years.

How Street Trees Obtain Their Water

How is it that trees growing in urban environments where the soil in which they grow is entirely covered in largely impervious paving, excepting perhaps a small area at the base of the tree, find sufficient water to thrive as they do? I had no answer then and have only a few observations on the matter to make now.

I thought someone would know the answer, but a trawl through my library and a search for papers and reports on the subject found very little. The only reasonably direct answer came in a thesis from an American PhD student, backed up by a brace of professors, the final and completely unedifying conclusion being that no one knew where the water came from! The other issue is 'compaction'. Trees, indeed most plants, do not thrive in soil that is compacted, since it creates resistance to root growth, poor flow of water and a lack of air pockets. But still the street trees grow. With the absence of both authority and investigation, only speculation remains.

The tiny area of exposed earth at the base of most, though certainly not all, street trees does not seem anywhere large enough to absorb sufficient rainfall, even with the occasional run-off from the adjacent pavement. This is certainly the case but may be ameliorated by the ability of some trees to 'funnel' the water down the trunk to settle in the earth below. Some water must percolate through the gaps in the pavements and between kerb and road, and in some places a tree will be sufficiently close to open ground (a garden, perhaps) to acquire water from there. Beyond that there is only groundwater, and this seems the most likely primary source.

In *London's Street Trees* Paul Wood attributes the survival of London's trees to the 'spongy clay soil', which is especially talented at holding groundwater. He also points out another potential source – the broken Victorian drainage pipes, which release 'water' into the subsoil. These are slowly being replaced, which, with their contribution to the life of the city's trees unmeasured, could be a disastrous move for the trees that depend on their inefficiencies. Much the same can be said of the notoriously leaky pipes used to supply water.

Sycamore and the Invasive Species Controversy

We turned right on to Lillie Road, past the Hotel Lily. Having suffered with everyone else during the lockdown trials of the previous fifteen months, the bare area in the hotel grounds next to the road looked a little neglected, with several weed species making a land-grab. One was Hedge Mustard (not to be confused with Hedge Garlic). It was joined by **Petty Spurge**, *Euphorbia peplus*, the commonest of our spurge species and often classed loosely as a weed. Most of the rest we had seen before, but two species had staked a more substantial claim: **Buddleia**, *Buddleja davidii*, and **Sycamore**, *Acer pseudoplatanus*. These are both weed species in this situation – unplanted and unwanted. Incidentally, I must point out that Hotel Lily has subsequently tidied up the area very nicely!

When we lived on top of a Dorset hill (see the chapter on The Drift), there was a Buddleia behind the barn that spent its summer as an unseasonal Christmas tree, decorated not with baubles but with long cones of lilac flowers adorned with butterflies. It was always a lovely sight, one unparalleled in any native plant that I have seen. Great for butterflies, yes, but it is counted as an invasive species found in large numbers throughout lowland Britain. They are, I think, acceptable in gardens, provided they are cut back immediately after flowering to prevent the highly mobile seeds from spreading, but not elsewhere. I always want to wield a chainsaw, then a pickaxe (to make sure), whenever I see them, with or without the owner's permission. The RSPB recommends a few alternative butterfly-friendly and less troublesome shrubs that might take its place, of which I would choose any of the three native genera or species: heathers, Dogwood and currants.

I have similar mixed feelings about the Sycamore. Again, it is not a native, having been introduced in the sixteenth century. However, my feelings for the Sycamore are much warmer as it gives back more than pretty flowers and a dinner for butterflies. It can live for about 500 years, and mature trees are beautiful. Mature trees also form an invaluable substratum for mosses, and the near-neutral pH of its bark provides a habitat for some uncommon lichens.

Sycamore is also attractive to its host-specific aphid, *Drepanosiphum platanoidis*, which exudes a clear sugar syrup called 'honeydew' from its rear end. This, in turn, forms a food supply for a variety of organisms. Honeydew is, of course, the material that will noticeably cover a carelessly parked car in a day or so, as I know to my cost. The sticky, sugary nature of honeydew will soon be colonised by dust particles and ruin the bright paintwork until you wash it, again. I am not one for washing cars and once, when challenged over my honeydewed, grey mess of paintwork, I told my importunate critic that it wasn't dirt, it was camouflage. I did, however, notice something remarkable in the sugary dirt. The entire top of my beloved pickup was covered in minutely zigzagged tracks from the radulae of foraging snails with sweet teeth.

Apart from snails on pickups, the honeydew from a Sycamore (or any other tree that hosts aphids) can support many other organisms and, in turn, the organisms that consume or parasitise them. These include the Diptera, Hymenoptera, Lepidoptera, Coleoptera and Neuroptera as beneficiaries. In plainer English and respectively, these might be: flies; wasps, bees, ants and sawflies; butterflies and moths; beetles; and lacewings. Sometimes honeydew is sourced from whatever surface it lands on – leaves for the most part – or directly from the rear end of the aphid that creates it as waste. The aphids themselves feed from the leaves, tapping into the pipework that transports dissolved sugar and amino acids from the leaves to other parts of the tree and known as the phloem vessels. The aphids require mostly the trace amino acids, excreting the surplus sugars. A single drop of honeydew is produced by the aphid every twenty minutes on average. I have tasted honeydew using the simple technique of licking my Ford pickup – it is pleasantly sweet, if a little gritty. A more hygienic way is to buy a jar of honeydew honey, made by bees that collect honeydew and convert it to an unusual type of honey – though to enjoy it you will need to forget its origin.

The timber from Sycamore has historically been used in making barrels for dry goods, kitchen utensils, butcher's blocks and musical instruments. It is usable in furniture-making when it is 'clean' – no knots or swirling grain – and especially so when it displays a 'ripple pattern'. I used it several times in my cabinetmaking days and found it a little difficult to work or obtain a high polish – 'woolly' and 'stringy' being the words that come to mind. It also suffers terribly from woodworm. Despite my underwhelming opinion of this tree, high-quality furniture can be made from it if the boards are chosen carefully.

My reservations on Sycamore as timber aside, the serious problem with this tree species is its invasive nature. Mature trees can be splendid affairs, but the Sycamore's ability to set seed almost anywhere can change the entire character of an existing woodland. The prime reason for this is that it is highly shade-tolerant and can grow even where there is a dense canopy, eventually supplanting the original tree species. I visit private woods every year to take fungus forays, and my heart sinks if I see Sycamore in it beyond a few standards. My dismay is partly because there are no mycorrhizal species associated with it that produce visible fruiting bodies (that is, mushrooms), but mostly because of its disruptive effect on the wood in general.

Evidently, the management at Hotel Lily was similarly wary of Sycamore, as the leaves I saw were attached to groups of cut stumps. But there is always something of interest wherever you look, and some of these leaves bore the handsome galls of the **Sycamore Gall Mite**, *Aceria macrorhyncha*.

It is likely that such views on alien species may seem difficult to some people, and I have often felt the need to justify my disdain for troublesome species that have found their way to Britain as being just that and no more – in other words, I am *not* talking about people. However, louder voices than mine have been raised explicitly equating how we view alien plant and animal species with how we view the migration of people. There are dozens of articles and academic papers, with titles such as 'Why We Should Rethink How We Talk About "Alien" Species', 'Biodiversity and the Use of Nativist Language' and 'People, Plants and Racism?' being more than enough to give you the idea.

The general points being made to varying degrees within such published work is that ecologists may be misdirected in their ecological endeavours by the racist tenor of the language and ideas, or that racist ideas may percolate into their own, previously innocent, value system or that the language and concepts they employ merely reflect a predisposition to racist attitudes.

It is all too easy to see the issue: the *polite* words used when discussing the two views are very often identical: alien, exotic, foreign, native, natural, invasive, competition, displacement, integration (or failure of integration), and even, *in extremis*, eradication. So an ecologist might say that a species that had somehow found its way to any particular new territory will disturb the local habitat, replace indigenous species, form troublesome hybrids and corrupt the purity of the ecosystem, and that they should be rigorously excluded or removed. Even expressing any advantages of alien species is difficult as it invites the judgements sometimes employed in discussions about immigration. On one of my seashore walks, for example, I might talk about the seaweed known as Wakame, *Undaria pinnatifida*, saying how good it is to eat and that (despite being an alien) it has behaved itself by integrating almost seamlessly with the indigenous biota and is nothing like that horrible Wireweed, *Sargassum muticum*, which has been a wretched nuisance since it arrived and is completely useless.

It does not help that both racism and concern over invasive species are emotive concepts, albeit racism clearly wins in any competition over which is the most emotive of the two issues. Nevertheless, Ash Dieback, for example, has been caused by the invasive species *Hymenoscyphus fraxineus*. The loss that this fungus has caused is vast, and everyone who loves the Ash tree is heartbroken. Similar emotions have been engendered over the Grey Squirrel for ousting *our* Red Squirrel, the Signal Crayfish that has displaced *our* crayfish and Himalayan Balsam that has clogged *our* rivers and usurped *our* native plants. Such 'our's may feel divisive, but I defend them because they express the intensity of possessive feeling that many cultures bear towards their own countryside and the organisms that share it.

While I understand the concern of those writers who find the language of invasive species problematic, I believe they are not, wilfully or innocently, giving people credit for understanding the context in which a word or idea is used. If there are species that make their way to a new territory and, perhaps, cause problems, we must talk about them, and, unless painful circumlocution is employed, the obvious words listed above are the ones to use. To say that they cannot be used because they cause offence is handing the bricks of our, or anyone else's, language to the bad guys. For my part, I will continue to feel slightly uncomfortable while talking about invasive non-native species and continue to point out that I am not, absolutely not, talking about *people.*

Leaving this knotty issue and the charming Hotel Lily behind us, we walked for two hundred metres along Lillie Road. Although this chapter champions the organisms that live with us in urban areas, some are almost devoid of uninvited life. Our short walk along Lillie Road was as barren of wildlife as any part of London I had seen, with the possible exceptions of the area around Borough Market, and Primrose Street in Shoreditch. I remember Primrose Street from when I used to go to Shoreditch to buy veneer for furniture-making projects. In those days its old, grubby, red-brick destitution had clearly not seen a primrose for a couple of hundred years, and now, all glass, stainless steel and expensive paving, the street is not likely to see one ever again. Perhaps the only bit of green, situated in and around a large courtyard on the northern side of the road, might accommodate a few in its raised beds; indeed, perhaps it already does.

Brompton Cemetery

Everything changed after we crossed the railway bridge to join the Old Brompton Road. To the south of the road a long arch-and-pillar brick wall came into view, every one of its many win-dowed arches guarded by cast-iron railings. Through these we could see some of the many marvels that it contained, not least the gravestones. It was, of course, Brompton Cemetery.

You can easily find the history of Brompton Cemetery, so my introduction to it will be brief. It was built as a grand, out-of-town 'overflow' cemetery to accommodate the demand from an increased population and urban expansion. Furthermore, the cemetery and burial business had fallen into corrupt and incompetent hands through a system of sinecures and absentee clergy. Brompton Cemetery is one of the so-called 'Magnificent Seven' garden cemeteries in London, Highgate being the most famous of them. They are all *secular* cemeteries, reflecting the Enlightenment sensibilities of the time. Brompton Cemetery was bought by the Crown in 1850 and is now managed by the Royal Parks, though it is not a Royal Park itself, any more than are the gardens of 10, 11 and 12 Downing Street, which are managed by that same august body.

Maps and drawings of the area in the early nineteenth century show that it was very much out of town. The construction site is shown as four fields (possibly enclosing a market garden) in Meale's 1830 map of London, and they are thought to have been used briefly for brick production immediately prior to their new career as a cemetery. The rectangular forty-acre site once lay alongside the Kensington Canal, formerly the path of a tributary of the Thames, Counter's Creek, and subsequently an overground part of the District Line. A remnant of the creek known as Chelsea Creek can be found where it meets the Thames.

The general design revisited the formal symmetries of the seventeenth century, eschewing the contemporary fashion for romanticism. This is clear from any aerial photograph, or from what looks remarkably like the first-ever drone shot but is actually a lithograph of 1840, drawn by an evidently talented fellow called G. Hawkins.

It was opened for business in 1840 as a near-barren site: 'Not a tree and scarcely a shrub adorn the place', as a contemporary report had it. This was presumably on the understanding that its clientele would be prepared to wait patiently for the provision of such mod cons. They were. Construction continued and was completed in 1844. Business was brisk (cholera epidemic), so the investors were paid off quickly and were receiving a return on their investment by 1850. It was then that it was bought by the Crown, and it is still the only public cemetery in its possession.

We walked through the subdued but welcoming entrance and found the place to be quiet. Well, I suppose it would be, but I mean there did not *seem* to be many people about. However, Brompton Cemetery receives an average of around two thousand people a day, and considering the size of the place, it was likely to have been an average day.

As always in cemeteries, our thoughts, everyone's thoughts, immediately turned to its permanent residents. In Brompton Cemetery there are in excess of two hundred thousand; the dead here outnumber the living by one hundred to one over a single day. The most expensive plots were along the eastern edge, with the relatively poor doomed to await the Day of Judgement in the west, presumably because you are judged sooner in the east with the rising of the sun. For myself, I would rather wait as long as possible. But contemplating the thousands of lives, loves and hopes of those that surrounded us was not the task of the day, so we began to look at the plants, lichens and anything else that might catch our eyes.

The Lichens of Brompton Cemetery and of London

All cemeteries are effectively parks. Parkland appeals to people, so the theory goes, because we evolved in a savannah region of Africa which looked very much like a park in that it consisted of well-separated trees with grass and other low vegetation between. We feel at home. In cemeteries this habitat is complemented by any amount of granite, limestone and marble, providing habitats for those most overlooked of God's readily visible creations, lichens.

Lichens, that extraordinary and sometimes colourful symbiosis of fungi and algae, have suffered the most extreme of bumpy rides in London, with central London down to a truly telling single species in the 1960s. Or maybe it was two: both *Lecanora dispersa* and *L. conizaeiodes* are mentioned in the literature, and both fit the bill as they are known to tolerate high sulphur dioxide levels. *L. dispersa* (also, and annoyingly, known as *Myriolecis dispersa* – species *should* have only one name) is a common native lichen, while *L. conizaeiodes* is believed to have originated from somewhere like Iceland, where it had adapted to the sulphurous fumes in volcanic areas. It was once very rare in Britain but came into its own in the toxic air that arrived with industrialisation. Its toleration of noxious air quality does not, however, mean that it *requires* it, so it has stayed and is moderately common everywhere in Britain even now that our air is (somewhat) cleaner than in the past.

That lichens are excellent 'at a glance' indicator species for air pollution is well known. They can also indicate what *type* of pollution is causing the local problem, as different species can tolerate differing levels of the various pollutants, most usually by tolerating only a narrow range of atmospheric or substratum pH values. Of the 1,700 or so lichens found in Britain about 130 were known from within a 16-km radius of Trafalgar Square prior to 1800. By the 1960s the polluting effects on London's lichens were being discussed in academic papers, with the blame put squarely and accurately on sulphur dioxide. Various clean-air acts followed, and the turnaround in the fortunes of lichens was dramatic. By 1981 the researchers D. L. Hawksworth and F. Rose were reporting two dozen or so recolonising species and, in 1989 they reported more.

There are, unfortunately, still problems. The substrata on which lichens live or lived have not necessarily recovered from the acidity they acquired years ago. While the stone surfaces of buildings and gravestones lost their toxicity quickly, tree bark has been slow to recover. With a few exceptions, lichens either grow on bark or they grow on stone, with some species not seeming to care what they grow on. This can be seen in the surveys which have been undertaken that show lichens on stone surfaces to have recovered well, while those on bark seem to be lagging behind by a large margin.

Sulphur dioxide levels are now relatively very low, with its sources from the burning of coal and vehicle emissions removed or better controlled. However, any amount of SO_2 is too much for the more sensitive species. Nitrogen oxides are also toxic for many lichens, and their levels have reduced by only 75 per cent, still too high for many species. On the other hand, there are many lichen species that are nitrophiles, able to withstand nitrogen pollution, or eutrophication, as it is often known. Nitrogen pollution in the form of ammonia can still be a problem in rural areas, in the form of decomposing animal waste.

In London, although the recovery was fast for some species, they did not re-establish as one might have expected – one by one in the reverse order to which they were lost, according to their tolerance of sulphur dioxide. Many did not return at all. This has been dubbed 'zone-skipping', where a 'zone' is those lichens that tolerate a defined narrow range of sulphur dioxide, with some failing to re-establish due to missing their window of pH tolerance. One paper I came across suggested that London's lichens were trapped in successional stasis, like that of a successional woodland that cannot develop beyond low shrubs.

The upshot of all this is that London's lichens are doing vastly better than they were, but not as well as we might have hoped. London has ended up with lots of common and thus arguably boring species and a handful at best of the rarer species seen in havens of clean air. West Dorset, for example.

We certainly found plenty of lichens in the hour and a half we spent wandering around the cemetery. Most of them by far were on the gravestones, mausolea, memorial furniture and architectural constructions, those on trees being relatively scarce. Most of those on stone formed flat, spreading patches, firmly attached to a headstone or other construction. They were prolific but few in number of species. Lichens on stone are relatively difficult to identify from a photograph, with even my lichenologist friend Bryan not being prepared to hazard anything more than a shortlist. Nevertheless, I am prepared to hazard that the one pictured is *Lecanora muralis*. I will revisit lichens when we get to The Drift, Tryfan and Seil.

The Plants of Brompton Cemetery

As to the plants, on our brief visit we recorded forty species, including trees. This was just a small subset of what was actually there, but it was encouraging. Brompton Cemetery had suffered the ravages of time and a certain amount of neglect until recently, with Brambles, Ivy and self-seeded native tree species, plus, no doubt, Sycamore, left to do their worst. Sterling work has since been undertaken to rectify this, leaving a neat, but not too neat, vista, full of wildlife. The avowed aim was 'all green open space to optimise biodiversity and wildlife habitat'. A noble ambition that has been achieved to a commendable extent. Several of the more open areas of grass, for example, have been converted to meadow-like conditions by the simple technique of sowing some appropriate seeds, and cutting and removing the arisings once or twice a year. 'Arisings' (what you throw on your compost heap after mowing your lawn) are removed to reduce fertility.

The current count for tree species is sixty, with over 600 trees present. Some of these were planted in the original grand scheme of 1840, notably the Irish Yews, Boxes and Limes. Irish Yew, *Taxus baccata 'fastigiata'*, is a cultivar of the standard Yew which seems almost compulsory in graveyards all over Britain. Yew, and the other funerary tree, cypress, which was also present, earn their keep through their sacred reputation, long lives and evergreen nature. Long-lived is a useful property as falling or fallen trees cause serious damage. Evergreen brings to mind permanence and is marginally more cheerful in such a setting during the winter than are bare branches.

Yew wood is the finest of all our native furniture timber, and I have a stack of thick boards left over from my furniture-making days, covered over carefully at the bottom of our garden. I plan to make some Windsor chairs with them. One day. Timber aside, there is one use of Yew that is of interest to the forager: the berries are edible, fruity and very sweet, but *only* if you do not chew or swallow even a single pip, as those are deadly poisonous.

It was lovely to see some **Box** trees, *Buxus sempervirens*. They usually grow in cemeteries, private gardens and only occasionally in the wild. As with Yews, I always feel the urge to wield a chain-saw and take some home. I *have* wielded my chainsaw on several occasions over the years (with permission) and have accumulated about 400 kg of it to use on a variety of carving and tool-making projects in my dotage. It has taken up a great deal of room next to the Yew over the last thirty years, and D has asked when my dotage is likely to arrive. Boxwood is beyond woody compare, being extremely fine, like a tough ivory. A tree 150 years old will be only six inches (15 cm) or so in diameter. The timber is rock-hard and yellow-cream in colour. It is also the devil to carve unless you keep your chisels extremely sharp, but the detail obtainable is superb. As for its strength, I still have a mallet I made from boxwood with a riven ash handle I made thirty years ago – it is the best mallet ever made, in my opinion.

The ubiquitous London Plane was inevitably present, but the commonest tree was the **Broad-Leaved Lime**, *Tilia platyphyllos*, which formed the main 'aisle' of the cemetery. I once cut up a fallen lime tree, hoping to use the wood. I had some of it planked up, but it rotted away quickly, even under a lean-to. Most of the rest I kept for firewood, though you might as well try to heat a house with wet blankets. It smells unpleasant too.

Dominating much of the open areas were **Cow Parsley**, *Anthriscus sylvestris*, and Green Alkanet, both of them attractive but large and overbearing plants that can come to a compromise between themselves but exclude the smaller plants that would have added variety. Cow Parsley, at least, suggests that the soil is too rich. One way to keep it under control is to cut it early, and there are several ways of reducing soil fertility, none of them particularly easy. Still, bullies that they are, these two plants gave a splendid display – the umbelliferous white flower of the former and blue Borage-like flowers of the latter against the green.

I found some **Common Sorrel**, *Rumex acetosa*, just coming into flower. This common perennial of permanent grassland and hedgebanks spends most of its time as a basal rosette of fruity, edible leaves. In summer the basal rosette largely disappears, and a central red flower spike grows to about two feet high, a few clasping leaves attached along its length. Beneath some of the trees there was the unrelated but similar-tasting **Wood Sorrel**, *Oxalis acetosella*, just coming into flower.

The most unexpected species was **Corn Chamomile**, *Anthemis arvensis*, a now uncommon weed of arable ground. It was in the unlikely environs of Chelsea, no doubt courtesy of a 'cornfield' mix that came in a sack. It certainly loved it in Brompton Cemetery, with some lush growth. I am confident that the authorities made great efforts to avoid the trap of buying the right species from the wrong place, but failure to take care in sourcing wild plants has been a considerable problem over the years. Ecological *forms* from abroad can find themselves being planted or sown in Britain, but they are not necessarily adapted to our climate, or are otherwise noticeably different from the indigenous form. This may not be a problem (except for the purist), but sometimes they will flower at the wrong time and miss their preferred pollinating insect – and the pollinating insects miss them. I have mixed feelings about the admittedly beautiful displays on roundabouts and verges in and around towns that have been planted by the local authority. I presume these are meant to look natural as well as pretty, but in truth they are just pretty.

We did not see many of the other deliberately and reportedly planted species such as Cranesbill, Knapweed, Cornflower and Common Poppy, but we were probably too early. However, **Ox-Eye Daisy**, *Leucanthemum vulgare*, was there and **Springbeauty**, *Claytonia perfoliata*. The latter species is quite common in Britain but with the odd distribution of the London area, East Anglia, Edinburgh and Inverness. Elsewhere it is scarce. Springbeauty has the appearance of having been designed by someone who had heard about herbaceous plants but never seen one. It consists of a couple of diminutive leaves at the base and a stem terminating in a saucer-like green disc from which the flowers appear. The disc is actually two fused leaves. The whole aerial plant is edible in salads and sometimes grown for that purpose. Whether or not this plant was in that seed mix I do not know; it is not impossible that it was a local. **Meadow Cranesbill**, *Geranium pratense*, however, is not much of a townie, so no doubt it was sown, as was **Tansy**, *Tanacetum vulgare*, a common and very bitter plant in the Asteraceae, and which was just coming into yellow flower. It is worth mentioning that some of the plants that are there today were probably there before the establishment of the cemetery or came from seeds subsequently imported via such vectors as hay for the horses leading funeral processions.

I discovered one species I had never seen before and did not even know existed. What I did know, because of its chive-like leaves and smell, and white, five-petalled flowers, was that it was an *Allium*. Later research found it to be **Neapolitan Garlic** (or, less romantically, False Garlic Weed), *Allium neapolitanum*, a garden escapee originating from South America. I did not try any, but one of my foraging friends told me it is edible and good, with a strong garlic flavour. With my knowledge of the trouble caused by Three-Cornered Leek and Few-Flowered Leek, my second thought after 'Can I eat it?' was 'Is it invasive, like its two boorish cousins?' Apparently it isn't, or at least not in Britain, not yet.

Our unimpressive animal count was three: Jackdaws, a Grey Squirrel and an unnamed ant. A more serious survey than our casual stroll would find many more; indeed, I've heard that two hundred species of moth live there and several bat species. Brompton Cemetery has, I think, had considerable success in turning a place of the dead into something bursting with life.

London Pubs

There was little that was new to us along the rest of the Old Brompton Road, so we stopped for lunch. I think I have just about won the long-standing and very minor dialectic concerning the matter of where to stop for a break. D says let's go to a café, I say let's go to a pub, she says but I want some coffee, I say you can get that in a pub, she says you can get coffee in a café, I say yes, but you can't get beer. We went to the Zetland Arms; built in 1840, it is very much a London pub. My grandfather's brother, the ever-cheerful Uncle Tom, owned a London pub that I remember well. At a time when children were not permitted in pubs at all, I was allowed to play with the billiards table, provided I was nowhere to be seen by opening time. Uncle Tom ran it with his wife, my Auntie Hilda, who was a sweet woman and not to be confused with my horrible Auntie Hilda (of whom I have written elsewhere), who lived in Lowestoft.

I wondered where the name Zetland came from, and after a thirty-second search discovered that it was probably a reference to the marquess of Zetland. Considerably more peculiar, though nothing to do with the naming of the pub, is that Zetland is also what you call a cross between a male Zebra and a female Shetland pony. How such an unholy union could ever have occurred I do not like to think about.

Pubs were still operating safety measures, and the Zetland Arms was well practised in making it as painless as possible, with table service provided without fuss. I still rather missed leaning on the bar to order drinks and wondered if this life-affirming pleasure would be lost for ever. At least there were no dreaded floor arrows to follow. For me, these were among the worst burdens of Covid-19 restrictions, as following simple instructions is something I have always found impossible. In some places I had visited, the less well-considered arrangements of arrows had me going around in circles awaiting the arrival of a professor of topology to release me from my predicament. I do not think I was alone in this. Now I can lean unsteadily at the bar as once I did, and treasure every moment.

Kensington Gardens and Hyde Park

Apart from more street trees and some attractive, if common, lichens growing on the coping bricks of a low wall, there was little new to see until we were past the queue of twenty-somethings alongside the Natural History Museum waiting for their first Covid-19 vaccination, and inside Kensington Gardens.

Our walk was to take us past the Albert Memorial, then north for a while along West Carriage Drive. Then left to explore a little of Kensington Gardens and then eastwards on to Marble Arch along the northern extent of Hyde Park. Our walk thus explored a very small proportion of garden and park, and the number of species I found was correspondingly fewer than a complete survey would have achieved. Still, I was pleased with the fifty or so we did find in the hour and a half we were there.

Kensington Gardens and Hyde Park formed a single Royal Park until William III claimed 26 acres of it (later expanded) for Kensington Palace and grounds. They were deer parks and, until the 1950s, pasture for sheep, with a few remnant patches of grasses and herbaceous plants that were typical of those that might have been found in medieval pasture. The sheep, incidentally, were reintroduced stock, used as woolly lawnmowers with a troublesome exhaust.

Both parks have a botanically chequered history because of their position. They have suffered people walking all over them, dogs and being used as venues for military displays and popular music events. Perhaps worst of all has been the inclination by those who managed them to turn them into one big and well-tended garden, where every fallen branch is removed and every blade of grass lives in fear of the rotating blade. This tidy-mindedness takes a dim view of the wild plants we so cherish now, and should any repair to damaged turf be required or a new sward laid, commercial seed mixes were used without thought to history or suitability. But they are havens for the town-dweller and even an over-managed park will at least have trees that will host a multitude of insects and fungi. Parks in general are superb habitats in which to find wildlife that may engage your attention, as they are often of sufficient age to have developed a stable ecology and to have accumulated those species that take time to establish, such as fungi and lichens. Whenever I visit a town, I always take a wander around any park in the full expectation that I will find something that lifts my spirits. The London parks, you will be pleased to hear, have more recently made near-heroic efforts both to be diverse and to reflect native flora.

During the Second World War the parks were effectively trashed, with allotments being established (Dig for Victory), a few air-raid shelters, military camps, anti-aircraft installations and radar stations constructed. It wasn't all bad, though, with Carraway, *Carum carvi*, Heath Cudweed, *Gnaphalium sylvaticum* and Fowl Meadow Grass, *Poa palustris*, making guest appearances in the turf covering the air-raid shelters.

Between 1947 and 1949 D. H. Kent surveyed the parks and found about 140 species. This is not too bad (plants can survive a great deal of disturbance, owing to their seed bank) and only a touch fewer than the 180 species that were recorded in 1871 by J. B. L. Warren. A great deal of tidying up followed the war, and about 200 species were very carefully recorded by D. E. Allen between 1958 and 1962. Surprisingly, over half of the species he found had not been recorded previously by either Kent or Warren. Such comparisons must be viewed with caution, however, as different methodologies and opinions on what counts as a species make them unreliable. Over thirty species recorded earlier were *not* seen by Allen, but these were, for the most part, aquatic plants that had suffered through wartime habitat loss.

Now the parks are managed with a view to natural history, with carefully considered cutting regimes introduced, such as 'rotational', where areas are left uncut every second year to permit the overwintering of invertebrates, and the planting of *suitable* trees, shrubs and herbaceous plants rather than whatever takes the park warden's fancy. Selected grass species are sown as seeds. None of this is easy; of twenty-two herbaceous species planted as shrubs in 2001 only seven survive.

The Wild Plants of Kensington Gardens

My observations started well, just inside the entrance. There was a Hawthorn and Hazel hedge, not unlike those seen in Dorset, except that this London hedge was newly planted and thus lacking the age necessary for a species-rich hedge, or nearby sources (that is, other species-rich hedges) of potential immigrant species. Nevertheless, just at its base there was a group of **Small Nettles**, *Urtica urens*. This looks just like the familiar Stinging Nettle, excepting that it is smaller, obviously, and with more rounded leaves. Less common than the Stinging Nettle, it is nevertheless found throughout most of lowland Britain, with a slight preference for the east, and London something of a stronghold. It was accompanied by the **Small-Flowered Cranesbill**, *Geranium pusillum*.

A little to the north of this was an area of grass with one of the most distinct 'mushroom' rings I have ever seen. There were no mushrooms present, but the grass formed a lush, dark green ring marking where they might (or might not) appear later in the year, formed by the release of plant nutrients by the ring of feeding mycelium. Not having my DNA testing kit with me, I can only guess at what mushroom we might expect. My money is on the Horse Mushroom.

A little further along, the result of careful management could be seen in a lush area of grass, scattered with thousands of Ox-Eye Daisies. One of the grasses was **Soft Brome**, *Bromus hordeaceus*, its elegant flower heads still closed. Not so long ago it would have seen the lawnmower several times by now. In some places the grass had been cut to form broad pathways but left uncut underneath the trees and sometimes between them. There are many introduced ornamental grasses that decorate gardens and parks, but our own grasses are beautiful too. Nevertheless, it is only when examined under a lens that their exquisite detail can truly be seen.

Some of the trees in Kensington Gardens show considerable age. As any individual tree ages, it becomes more replete with life (i.e., parasites), as well as more appealing. Some of the **Sweet Chestnuts**, *Castanea sativa*, are magnificent, with lumps and bumps, holes from fallen branches, massive bases and huge trunks. The lumps and bumps are the result of unusual growth patterns, generally known as 'sphaeroblasts'. They come in two very different flavours: one is where the usually straight grain that one would expect in a tree (and demand, if it were for furniture-making) is replaced by a tight, swirling pattern. The bark that covers such bumps will be typical of the tree as a whole. In dead trees, when the bark has fallen away, the swirling pattern becomes visible. The other sphaeroblast is the burrs often seen on many species of tree as they age. These are a response to damage of some sort — mechanical, perhaps, or from attack by a virus, fungus or invertebrate. Such damage causes rapid growth in the form of a multitude of shoots, to form a vaguely spherical bump, covered in a very *rough* bark. Burrs are quite striking to look at and, with the intricate patterning revealed, exquisite when cut.

My normal response of disapproval to showy cultivars was challenged a little by a Hawthorn in shocking-pink bloom, rather than the white of our native Hawthorns. It was a true beauty both from a distance and close up. I cannot be sure of its identity, but I think it was a cultivar not of our common native Hawthorn, *Crataegus monogyna*, but of the less common **Midland Hawthorn**, *C. laevigata*, possibly 'Paul's Scarlet'. The more common of our native Hawthorns also display pink in their blossoms on occasion, but this is due to crosses with various cultivars; in their native form they are white.

Rust Fungi

Brambles find their way into every corner that is left alone for a week or two, and so it was in Kensington Gardens. Here I noticed scores of tiny, cream-coloured dots on a bramble leaf. Although I had never seen it before, or at least, not noticed it, it should have been fairly simple to work out what it was called. With such fungi generally being specific to a single host, the vast field of 'what it might be' is reduced from one in a thousand to one in three, or maybe ten. Unfortunately, brambles host about fifty such 'micro'-fungi and I took only a photograph with nothing to look at under my microscopes at home. Despite this and going with the notion that the word 'common' is an encouraging thing to read in an identification book, I am plumping for the rust fungus, **Kuehneola uredinis**.*

Peter Pan

Close to the splendid statue of Peter Pan is a garden of wild plants that shows every sign of having been almost entirely planted with natives: **Comfrey**, *Symphytum officinale*, **Common Vetch**, *Vicia sativa*, various Campions, a garden escapee in the form of **Honesty**, *Lunaria rediviva*, Yarrow, a Forget-Me-Not of unknown species, a solitary **Foxglove**, *Digitalis purpurea*, a **Wayfaring Tree**, *Viburnum lantana*, its relative, **Elder**, *Sambucus nigra*, Dogwood and a sky-blue Iris. Together, they made a lovely display.

A little further north I was delighted to see a 'dead hedge'. This is not a hedge that has died but a hedge made from cut branches, laid horizontally between two rows of posts. Dead hedges are likely to have been the first type of hedge used. When woodland was cleared for agriculture, the materials used for making a dead hedge were readily available in embarrassing quantities. This was used directly in the construction of a dead hedge, with some of the material driven into the ground as two rows of posts and other lengths of timber and some brash laid between them. Such a hedge is quick to build and avoids the wait for a live hedge to grow. They are seldom necessary now, but they provide home for a variety of invertebrates and will eventually be consumed by fungi and bacteria.

* The standard work for this is the substantial *Microfungi on Land Plants*, by Martin and Pamela Ellis, the definitive guide to such fungi, and one that no self-respecting field mycologist would be without.

Near to this, behind some railings, was a sea of eminently edible **Stinging Nettles**, *Urtica dioica*. This too can support many organisms, with the caterpillars of Small Tortoiseshell, Red Admiral, Peacock, Painted Lady and Comma butterflies, two specialist downy mildew species and the striking, bright orange rust fungus *Puccina carcina* all finding a home in its uncomfortable embrace. Our final plant in Kensington Gardens was Garlic Mustard, also known as Hedge Garlic or Jack-in-the-Hedge. It is edible while the leaves are fresh and produces mild versions of precisely the two flavours you would expect.

Grey Squirrels were everywhere, and it is impossible not to like them, even though they have usurped our native Red Squirrel. As is so often the case in parks, they were all very tame, and largely fearless of humans, presumably because we are a soft touch for food. I have noticed that urban Grey Squirrels are considerably larger (or at least, *fatter*) than their country cousins. Squirrels are edible, and there are a couple in my freezer – though they were not collected from Kensington Gardens.

The Short Walk through Hyde Park

We turned right around the Italian Gardens to walk the short distance to Marble Arch. Fallen trees are difficult to justify in any park that aspires to be tidy, but Hyde Park has at least one. As many species feed off dead trees as off live trees, and the invertebrates that rely on dead wood become, in turn, food for birds. The fallen Beech was in a sorry state, its bark coming away to reveal numerous holes made by the wood-boring larvae of insects. I used to see these in my stacks of furniture timber – sometimes fat, white larvae that looked most definitely edible. One does, however, have to draw the line somewhere.

The surviving stump displayed the enormous bracket fungus, the **Southern Bracket**, *Ganoderma australe*. This species is discussed at length in the final chapter, when I found a particularly fine example in the New Forest. Also attached was the extremely common fungus **Brittle Cinder**, *Kretzschmaria deusta*. It is mostly this that causes the strange black lines one sees in split Beech logs known as 'spalting'.

We were nearly at our destination, but I noticed a dense white vista of a 'meadow', the white being Cow Parsley flowers. As with Brompton Cemetery, the soil here may be a little too rich. Marble Arch came into view and a selfie was duly taken. You will recall that it was chosen as a destination because it was there that my grandfather met my grandmother. She had been in service for one of the nearby large houses, her remuneration being 35s a year – £1.75 in translation. Even then this was next to nothing and only made feasible by the full board and lodging that came with it. Perhaps with her eye to better things, she spotted my grandfather in his guardsman's uniform and thought him worth a try. He was always a quiet and shy man, while she was a fiery and passionate redhead, so I imagine that she 'accosted' him. They were married for fifty-five years, with only my mother born to them. Shyness and passion do not go well together. We retired to a pub to toast their lives.

The Drift, West Dorset

ANCIENT HEDGEROW, CHALK DOWNLAND
AND WATER MEADOW

THREE MILES

5 AND 11 JUNE 2021

The Drift

God gave all men all earth to love,
But since our hearts are small,
Ordained for each one spot should prove
Belovèd over all.

For Kipling that belovèd place was his home for the last thirty-nine years of his life: Sussex by the sea. For your author it is the chalk downlands of West Dorset. For both of us our small hearts are entrapped by home – the fate of most people, or at least those who are fortunate. Kipling's second home, in the Sussex Weald at Burwash, is encompassed above and below by the North and South Downs; my part of the world is at the western tip of the same contiguous Cretaceous chalk that makes up so much of southern England. The hill I can see from my office window is the last outpost of this 200-mile rock formation. This vast landscape is sometimes known as the 'Chalk Group' or, much more affectionately to my mind, 'The Chalk'.

Our first home in West Dorset was atop what I suppose I might call the second-to-last hill in the formation, two miles to the east of our present home in the village. D and I moved to our lofty new home over forty years ago on a day in late April with snow 10 cm thick on the ground and still falling. We had no money (and I mean well below the poverty line) and could not afford a car. If we wanted to buy provisions, we would walk to the village – down the hill, through the woods, up the next hill, along the top and down the other side. Walking back was worse as it involved carrying groceries over two ups and only one down. There is nothing quite like a four-mile hill walk to make you shop carefully, and it was here and out of necessity that I developed my foraging skills. The last part of the walk (the 'down the other side') to the village is the titular subject of this chapter. It is known to everyone as 'The Drift'.

The Drift runs north-eastwards from the village, steeply up the hill until it branches left near the top to reach the A37 (a conspicuously Roman road at this point) a mile or so further on. It then continues as an unnamed path down the hill to a neighbouring village to the east. We walk The Drift still and may have done so nearly a thousand times. In the difficult first half of 2020 we walked it every day. Going up and straight back down this steep path is rather trying, so we usually followed it most of the way up, then branched right to follow the top of the hill. The path then turns a sharp right, circles around and down to the road on which we live. As a whole, this walk is known informally as the Horseshoe, though it approximates better on a map to a capital 'D' tilted 45 degrees to the left, the straight part of the letter being the A356 through the village. It is around the Horseshoe that I will travel in this chapter, with a later diversion about ten days later into the contrasting landscape of the valley bottom, the old water meadows.

I have chosen this walk because I know it well and it takes us over the exquisitely rolling hills that characterise chalk downland. The addition of the water meadows is natural, because the two landscapes were worked together in the now lost agricultural practice of sheep-corn husbandry, where sheep would be taken to the water meadow to graze and taken back to the high fields each evening to fertilise what would become corn fields in due course.

The name 'Drift' seemed to me to have a fairly obvious etymology, and instinct was confirmed by the OED, which tells us that it derives from the early English words, *drif* or *drifan* or *drifen*, meaning 'drive', in this case to drive stock from one place to another. Furthermore, The Drift was once (and sometimes still is) called The Driftway, which, the OED explains, is a lane or road along which stock is driven to market or pasture. The Drift is a 'drove road'.

Drove roads exist or existed wherever there is or was stock to drive, which was once nearly everywhere in Britain, as is reflected in the name 'Driftway' appearing on maps all over the country. Many of our modern roads were once drove roads. The best-known, those that have entire books written about them, such as the *Drove Roads of Scotland* and the *Drove Roads of Wales*, extended for hundreds of miles, the stock and drovers that used them travelling great distances to winter pasture or to market at the new industrial towns. The Drift, as with many others, is a more modest affair, a local drove road, serving movement to and from the local hills for watering, pasture and market. Maiden Newton was once a small market town, so stock from the farms and villages to the east would have travelled to it via The Drift.

Quite how old The Drift may be has defied my investigative skills, but it could easily be Iron Age or earlier as there is an Iron Age settlement alongside it, half a mile from the A37. Roads and pathways are the most persistent of human constructs as they gain permanence from use. The Drift was formally established as a right of way in 1833 under the legislation that established enclosures:

A Public Bridleway and Private Carriage Road and Driftway, of
the width of twenty-five feet, leading out of the Maiden Newton
Turnpike Road between Allotments to Mr William Warren and Mr

Henry Petty respectively, and extending eastward over Sheeplands and
Rudder Barrow to the corner of an old inclosure, called Genge's Close,
and passing over the said Close until it enters Maiden Newton Down,
and extending over the same in a north-east direction to the Dorchester
and Yeovil public road.

The above merely states what I have already explained, but it encapsulates a great deal of the history of those times. Now, as then, a bridleway permits the free movement of people with or without a horse, a private carriageway permits the owner of the bridleway (who may or may not own the adjacent lands) to use a wheeled vehicle and a Driftway permits the passage of stock.

The Village and Its Market

This was the only one of these walks I took alone. D understandably decided that taking five hours to complete a familiar one-hour walk, most of which she would spend hanging around while I took photographs, would be no fun at all. I had expected to set off first thing in the morning, but endless distractions, such as finding a particularly beautiful fungus on a log on my woodpile which cried out for identification, held me up until 1 p.m. The fungus was a common ascomycete, **Neonectria ditissima**, a mass of 0.5-mm-diameter dark orange, jelly-like spheres, clustered on the ash bark. Ascomycetes are fungi in the Division Ascomycota, which, along with the Basidiomycota, encompasses most of the fungi that can be seen with the naked eye, plus many microscopic species. Ascomycetes include morels, certain cup fungi, truffles and yeast. You can see what I mean about distractions. We will see a handful of these in later chapters.

There is every reason to expect an early June sky to be bright blue with fluffy white clouds, and for once it was just that, but with a breeze sufficiently strong to make plant photography difficult. It is impossible to step almost anywhere without encountering a plant, especially in June, and I was expecting to find several species as soon as the front door was closed behind me. Unfortunately, such expectations were dashed by D's regrettable glyphosate habit, which had rendered barren the usually productive linear habitat where the front wall of the cottage meets the pavement. Perhaps because it was pretty, one wild plant had survived her destructive instincts: a towering **Ivy-Leaved Toad-flax**, *Cymbalaria muralis*, in full yellow and purple flower, climbing up the power conduit. The first part of its name is from the fancied similarity of its leaves to cymbals, while *muralis* is a clear reference to its fondness for walls. This adaptation extends to the flowers facing *away* from the wall while awaiting pollination, then turning *inwards* to allow the seeds to lodge in any unoccupied crevice.

I quickly arrived at the proud remains of the Market Cross, right in the centre of the village. Proud it may be, but 'mostly missing' is a more accurate description. Its all-important top half disappeared centuries ago and is thought to have been impiously included in the nearby stone bridge over the River Frome. Until about thirty years ago the surviving stump of the cross was situated a few yards away, at the centre of the three-way junction. Here it suffered repeated glancing blows from passing traffic, the worst of which was courtesy of a US truck during the war (it had to be glued back together), and its removal to safety became essential. The pavement was widened, and the 'cross' is now situated on a matching ham stone plinth, the whole protected by a line of short but massive oak pillars. Life always finds a way, and these pillars, all slowly rotting away from the attentions of colonies of Glistening Inkcaps that took up residence some years ago.

Opposite the Market Cross is an exceptionally ugly residential building that was formerly the White Horse Hotel. This in turn was the replacement for an older White Horse which was demolished in 1898. The old White Horse was one of the finest buildings in Dorset, a seventeenth-century masterpiece of thatch, arch and ham stone. The proprietor, Devenish Brewery, chose to demolish this treasure because of its wasteful inclusion of an arch for coaches in the middle, the low ceilings, internal dilapidations and a thatched roof that was difficult to maintain and expensive to insure. The structure itself was deemed, by no less a person than Thomas Hardy (an architect in his early career), to be sound. Many other local notables supported its preservation, as did the Society for the Protection of Ancient Buildings and the infant National Trust. Sadly these protestations were to no avail, and the village's greatest asset was lost. One would have thought that a lesson had been learned, but thirty years ago the companion building next to it, the Assembly Rooms, a slightly later building of considerable charm and importance, was, among much local lamentation, unceremoniously demolished. Where there was once an example of splendid vernacular, there are now four houses that would look better in the suburbs of Slough, and none too exciting there.

The market itself, which was once situated behind these two buildings and backed by the River Frome, is now two car parks and another row of new houses. It too enjoyed a chequered and irregular history. Having once sold typhoid-infected pigs to a farmer from Hooke in 1879, its reputation was already on a knife-edge, so a criticism in 1884 that the saleyard was in a very poor state of hygiene seemed to prove a reprobate tendency. The perfectly reasonable defence was that the market was held only once a fortnight, and so it would have time 'to clean itself', presumably courtesy of a purifying rain. Shamefully, this was dismissed by the authorities. Fortunately, or not, the market continued for a while into the early twentieth century. The market was ancient, established in the time of Henry III (or possibly Edward I, there is some confusion in the records), and it ran on and off for several centuries until it fell out of use in the early eighteenth century.

It was revived in the middle of the nineteenth century and run by an exceptionally lively committee that held a riotous annual and all-male dinner every January in the White Horse. Reading the long, long reports of proceedings is like walking into another world. Speeches and endless toasts were punctuated by 'applause', 'laughter', 'Here Here' and 'cheers', each speech followed by a song from one of the attendees. For me, these meetings are particularly poignant because some of the names are familiar in the descendants I know as friends.

Concerns of the time are little different from those of today: disappointment at this year's barley harvest (it rained at the wrong time), high hopes for the next, the incompetence and ignominy of the government and a general feeling that life for farmer and farmworker was not what it used to be. Competition from abroad was a permanent worry, though not in the case of the newly minted (sic) endeavour of lamb exports from New Zealand, which, it was thought, could never succeed because the additional cost of transport would make it uneconomic.

The market was a small one as the following list of stock for sale in May 1879 demonstrates:

1 Hog Bull
1 Two-year old Bull
4 Fresh Young Barreners
3 Barreners

1 Heifer and Calf
1 In-calf Heifer
15 Fat Calves
20 Fat Horn Lambs
10 Fat Lambs
10 Fat Ewes

Note: a 'barrener' is a cow that has not borne a calf for a year. A hog bull is a male pig with his most treasured parts still attached.

The market is unremembered by any of the old boys I have known from the village. I did, however, get a small taste of what such a market might have been like back in the 1980s at the now closed Dorchester Livestock Market. These took place on Thursdays and the nearby pub, the Great Western, was where the old farmers used to congregate for a lunchtime pint. They would sit in a silent row, dressed in tweed and shiny buttoned boots, a stick in one hand and a beer in the other.

The Church and Its Lichens

I turned to the right, along the road to the church and was confronted by the lovely sight of an inadvertent display of **Common Poppies**, *Papaver rhoeas*, growing in the aforementioned linear habitat between wall and pavement. For so narrow an ecological niche they had done splendidly well. Common Poppies were once considerably more common than they are now. Fields would famously turn blood-red all over, but modern herbicides have eradicated poppies from arable land. Still, sometimes the farmer 'misses a bit', and up they come from their long-lived seed banks, despite not having been seen there for decades.

To my left was the church and the old rectory. The latter has long been a private house, one I have visited hundreds of times, having worked there fitting it out with oak furniture during my cabinetmaking days. It is a magnificent building, but irredeemably creepy. I never worked there past nightfall, and the overall 'L' shape provides blind corners from which God knows what might have appeared once the sun had set. A story was told to me by one of those 'old boys' about the eminently sensible Nan Paulsey, the well-respected nanny to the family living in the house in the middle of the last century. She reported seeing the man of the house, Colonel Wrixon, who looked her way just before he disappeared around one of those corners. This would hardly be worthy of note, but he was presumed to be on active service at the time in the Sudan. Nan expressed her surprise at seeing him and asked how it was that he was home. No answer was forthcoming, but a telegram arrived a day or two later from the War Office, reporting with regret his death on active service the previous day. I have never been one to give credence to such things, or I wasn't, until my maternal grandfather came to say goodbye on the night he died, albeit in the more comfortable context of a dream.

I could not resist a quick visit to our churchyard. The near-permanent nature of the grassland that dominates most cemeteries is a perfect habitat for wild flowers and fungi, and some of my best finds of the latter have been beside or even *on* someone's grave. But this was a dry summer, so there was nothing to be seen. There was, however, an abundance of the group of organisms that churchyards do best: lichens. In fact, the ancient church (circa 1150), situated as it is in a mild and wet climate, built of stones of varying chemical compositions and harbouring some old trees, is one of the most blessed, and in a completely different league from Brompton Cemetery, despite being a tiny fraction of the latter's size. A few years ago it attracted the attention of the British Lichen Society, which organised a field trip to view and record its treasures.

They listed thirty species on trees and seventy on stone. Several of them, notably *Lecanora pruinosa*, are diminishingly rare. *L. pruinosa* is an unassuming disc of white and grey, with occasional green flushes of another algae that sometimes grows on its surface. It is now found almost exclusively on limestone gravestones and is a reminder to never clean them beyond a light dusting and removal of ivy. I have rashly assumed that no one would think of cleaning gravestones, but tragically there is a great enthusiasm for 'respecting the dead' by removing every trace of life that might grace their memorial, complete with a large number of specialist cleaning concoctions and even professional cleaners to do the dirty work for you. Just don't.

I have always loved the technical names used by specialists in any subject. These are not used to impress novices or confuse the general public but simply to avoid long descriptions when talking among themselves. In this case the lichen is described as 'crustose, placodioid'. 'Crustose' is obvious and 'placodioid' means radiating out from the centre. Incidentally, as you have seen, it is not my intention to use common names for lichens. A handful do possess them, but they are mostly of recent vintage. They are completely superfluous in so specialised a subject and a great annoyance to lichenologists – and to me.

Despite (or perhaps 'because of', as the photographs were terrible and mostly grey-scale) my purchase of *The Observer Book of Lichens* in 1966, I have always found them to be all but impossible organisms to identify. My lichenologist friend Bryan has not encouraged me, saying that you really need to know just about everything before you start as many species are 'critical', meaning that they are virtually identical to a closely related species.

Thus chemical tests, electron microscopes, pocket DNA sequencing kits with sequencing software and access to an entire library of academic literature will be required. Still, I can readily identify a dozen of the commoner species and make a reasonable stab at identifying many to genus at least. There is one other lichen of interest at St Mary's that I cannot pass by.

Lichens are really communities, consisting of a fungus that gives the lichen its structure and a photosynthesising organism that supplies the energy. The latter is usually an alga, but sometimes it is a bacterium, more precisely, a cyanobacterium – a group of bacteria that contain chlorophyll. While algae are generally held within the fungal structure, the cyanobacteria are separate and effectively 'plumbed in' to the rest of the lichen, the fungal component. A small collection of one of these, *Sticta canariensis*, was in its usual spot on the top slab of one of the sarcophagi in the graveyard. The fungus is inconspicuous, but the cyanobacterium can be seen as small blobs of dark green jelly, formed from long, intertwined, mucus-covered chains of individual cyanobacteria.

Very few people take even the remotest interest in lichens (beyond attempting to remove them), and I think this a great pity. They are ubiquitous, exquisite and, well, *life*. They should be treasured. For your author, they fascinate because they are extraordinarily beautiful when seen through a loupe and even more so when examined under a microscope, they have many 'behaviours' that raise them beyond mere form and they are, as I have said, profoundly annoying. It is this spur, this 'not knowing', that has driven all my attempts to understand and name the species I see on my walks, and my hope is that you will find them as annoying as do I.

The joy of lichens duly exercised, I must tell you that it is a lovely little church in a lovely setting. Our two daughters expressed interest in attending Sunday school there, so I spoke to the lady who ran it. She said, 'Yes, they would be very welcome to come along to our Sunday school. It's called the "Tuesday Club" and meets every Thursday.'

To the Railway Bridge

Back on the road, I walked towards the start of The Drift. This took me past the slip road up to the railway station on my right. We are extremely pleased to still have a railway station, unlike many villages across the countryside, especially as the bus service is now once a week and strictly 'by appointment only'. The station yard was once employed as an occasional market, and disused stalls to hold the stock for sale were still to be seen forty years ago.

The triangular slope and accompanying ditch to the left of the slip road and the right of my path are now seriously overgrown with either weeds or wild flowers, depending on one's view of such wastelands. There is seldom anything rare or special there, just a magnificent display of nature left untended. Typical of many such areas found on the periphery of habitation, it was a flamboyant mess of **Rosebay Willowherb**, *Chamaenerion angustifolium* (not yet in flower), Docks, **Creeping Buttercups**, *Ranunculus repens*, Cow Parsley, Green Alkanet and various grasses dominated by the substantial and (for a grass) distinctive, **Cock's Foot**, *Dactylis glomerata*. Previously, and for many years, Mrs Elsworth, who lived opposite, kept a tethered and bad-tempered nanny goat on this small patch. I think everyone in the village still misses that goat.

Broad-Leaved Dock, *Rumex obtusifolius*, showed the early stages of rust fungus infection in the form of *Puccinia phragmitis*.

It is visible as patches of purple-strawberry discoloration, with pustules under the leaf when mature. Around twenty species of fungus can infect dock species. Docks are also noted for supporting over sixty insect species. The relatively high levels of oxalate in their leaves make it a challenge to the average insect, so most of those sixty are Dock specialists. These are admirably described in one of the several minority-pursuit books in my collection, uncompromisingly entitled *Insects on Dock Plants*.

The tunnel underneath the railway line is the unofficial start of The Drift. Nothing grows well in this dark and muddy environment (the tarmac stops just before the bridge) save a few **Greater Burdocks**, *Arctium lappa*, Garlic Mustard and a bittercress. All three are edible, but we are in serious dog-walking territory here, so they go unmolested by man, if not by dog. Little to see here, then, apart from some spectacular five-foot icicles in winter, but there is something to hear – an irresistible echo.

The Ancient Hedges of The Drift

Soon after the bridge, The Drift begins its climb up the hill. The land that The Drift and the entirety of the Horshoe pass through is a single farm. I have known two of the three recent owner/farmers. Old Mr Budget, who died over thirty years ago, was something of a character. My only serious encounter with him was inadvertent and terrifying. D and I were walking with friends over the downland farm next to his property when we heard the cracks of a .22, plus the whistling sound of the bullets flying past our ears. Mr Budget was shooting rabbits, while failing to take that most basic of precaution of *not* firing over the brow of a hill. I told my old friend Keith, who then worked on

Budget's farm, about my run-in with his boss. Keith informed me that Budget had 'previous' in this misdemeanour when, a few years earlier, a series of bullets thudded into the bank on Keith's allotment very close to where he was standing.

The first thing to see is the hedge on the left which borders the allotments. I resisted the temptation to visit this hallowed ground. Past the gate and the Elder tree I have raided for years, I am in the true countryside. It was hard to pass the full-flowered Elder, but this was to be a walk of observation, not collection. Elder is in my top ten of wild foods; its flavour in sparkling wine, cordial, panna cotta, Turkish delight and more is incomparable. Collect the flowers by snapping them off where they join the two petioles (stems) of the two adjacent leaves.

Most of The Drift is hedged on both sides and classed as a 'green lane'. It is also, just about, a 'hollow way', a pathway that has become deeper over the years from the erosion caused simply by being used. The bedrock here, unlike the calcareous sandstone of the much more impressive hollow ways near Bridport, twelve miles to the east, is relatively hard, the flint inclusions strengthening the soft and 'rotten' (frost- and water-weathered) chalk that makes up the first few feet of chalk landscapes.

As is typical of most hollow ways, the path is deeply rutted either side of the central grassy/muddy strip, in the past caused by carts, now by modern farm vehicles. For the first half a mile the path runs along and up the side of the hill, a steep slope of permanent sheepwalk falling away to the left beyond the hedge. The overall width of the path is twenty-five feet, though it spreads out to thirty-five feet in places, with a wide and steep bank to the right and lower and sometimes flatter area to the left about ten feet wide. There are no ditches, as any ditch running three-quarters of a mile down a steep hill would form a torrent at the bottom. Excess water is drained via periodic run-off gullies, channelling it down the adjacent slope to the left. On both sides there is a hedged bank.

These hedges change remarkably in character over the entire one-and-a-quarter miles of the Horseshoe. This is a matter of soil quality and of management. The Drift at this point was pure chalk, but the relatively horizontal top and downwards slope has a clay cap which is more acidic. It is almost certainly the case that the various hedges were not there when the Horseshoe was first established. More likely, it was a path over open countryside, sometimes cut through woodland or scrub. Indeed, the mile of Drift that diverges from the Horseshoe towards the A37 is largely hedge-free.

Those first hedges past the allotments are probably the oldest I saw that day if the number of woody plants living there is a true guide. The famous 'Hooper's Rule' was devised by the great hedgerow specialist Max Hooper and published in the classic work *Hedges*, of 1974. It states that the number of woody species found in a thirty-yard section of hedge multiplied by a factor of 110 will indicate its age in years. It is necessary to measure four such lengths if possible, and they must be continuous lengths chosen at random. Everyone rather liked this idea, and it was even incorporated into the 1997 Hedgerow Regulation, which provides a useful, if not comprehensive, list of what counts as a 'woody' species. They should be 'structural', not climbers, and Brambles do not count. They also need to be native plants, so including a garden escapee such as a Snowberry or a Rhododendron, for example, is not allowed. If a plant was naturalised in Britain prior to AD 1500, however, it can be counted.

Overall, there are fourteen species of relevant woody plant in the two hedges that make up the first third of a mile of The Drift. My figure for the age of the left hedge using Hooper's

Rule is 1,200 years. The total list of woody species I counted *overall* is as follows: Oak, Ash, Beech, Sycamore, Grey Willow, Spindle, Dogwood, Hawthorn, Blackthorn, Hazel, Elder, Field Maple, Holly, Wild Privet, Dog Rose, Field Rose, Redcurrant, Dewberry and Ivy. The last five do not really count, but I could not resist mentioning them.

Is the age I found accurate? Hooper was cautious about the reliability of his 'rule', saying that it does not work for any hedge more than a thousand years old (except to suggest that it is more than a thousand years old!), and that it suffers from confounding factors such as how many species were planted in the first place and how many were intentionally planted later. Documentary evidence of the age of the hedgerow must also be considered, he said.

The venerable age suggested by my survey does not seem unreasonable, and not at all out of line with many of the hedges that can be found in the south-west of England. The Drift was probably hedged for most of its presumed long life, and none of the species discovered in the hedge is likely to have been planted after it was first established. The exception to this is the Beech trees that occur intermittently along the hedge, which show clear signs of having been laid as a hedge owing to the relic evidence of laying in the form of (now) very thick and low *horizontal* trunks. These Beeches were probably added later. Most of the other plants would have been self-sown incomers, that being the basis of Hooper's hypothesis. Other support for a venerable history can be seen in some of the herbaceous plants. Yellow Archangel, generally accepted as a species indicative of an aged hedge, is notorious for spreading only a metre or so per century and was probably an ancient woodland remnant. These, I think, are truly ancient hedges.

The Invertebrates of the Drift

The walk along The Drift itself is one of the prettiest I know. By May it is buzzing with life, with half a dozen species of butterfly to be seen, notably the **Speckled Wood**, *Pararge aegeria*, which dances gaily back and forth. By striking contrast, in 2020 I saw a large, flat, segmented creature, about two inches long, making its way across the path. It had clearly been at the back of the queue when good looks were handed out, and it was with some distaste that I picked it up and moved it to safety. I did take its photo first, though, and later discovered it to be an ugly duckling by day and delightful swan by night. It was a female Glow-Worm, *Lampyris noctiluca*, something I had seen near that spot ten years previously – but in her night-time glory. The males are smaller and distinctly a beetle, but the female seems not to have bothered developing beyond a larval stage as her beaux always come to her, attracted by the light.

Darting around that day were several species of hoverfly. Attempts to take photographs failed, and I was at a loss as to which hoverflies any of them were. My invertebrate identification skills do not go much beyond butterflies, a few ant species, the more common beetles and highly distinctive species such as that lady Glow-Worm and the evocatively named Common Cockchafer. Years ago I took my butterfly net into an abandoned bit of weedy pasture near the village and dragged it through the grass to see what might be there. In this one sweep there were easily twenty species of insect and spider and, overwhelmed by the joy of the moment, I determined to learn everything about all of them and more. Sober consideration followed quickly, and I decided that my deep interest in fungi and only marginally lesser interest in the flowering plants was more than enough to occupy my time.

Any serious survey of a terrestrial ecosystem will find more invertebrates than anything, easily accounting for 90 to 95 per cent of species in any one area. Even taking an interest in one speciality – hoverflies for example – will consume all of your time. A casual observer may (not *entirely* unreasonably) think that there is only one species of hoverfly, but there are 250 in Britain alone. Even a specialist in wasps will study only one group of wasps as there are a remarkable 7,000 species in Britain and perhaps 100,000 worldwide, spread out between seven 'superfamilies' containing a total of twenty-five families. If you are interested (and you shouldn't be), much invertebrate identification involves examining the private parts of the organism in question under a dissecting microscope. I mention all this to remind you how much more diverse ecological communities are than a mere counting of plant species and the few visible fungi and invertebrates would suggest. My guess is that counting the plants and multiplying by eighteen would give a reasonable estimate of species numbers.

With so very much to see, to find, the minor tragedy of natural history is that you can't know everything. Still, I have managed to identify a few invertebrates on this walk over the years, and that day I was pleased to identify a spider with reasonable confidence. It was **Tetragnatha montana**, an orb-web spider with an unusually thin abdomen and the laconic habit of stretching its legs forward and aft, in which pose it looks like a twig. There was also the familiar cuckoo spit, the white froth seen on stems, and that day found neatly nestling in the centres of three whorls of leaves on a Cleaver plant. The froth is produced for protection by the nymph stages of the froghopper, **Philaenus spumarius**. I also saw a snail.

Slugs and snails (but not puppy dogs' tails) are another problem for the wannabe naturalist. I asked D for the *Collins Field*

Guide on the subject for my forty-sixth birthday, thinking that it would solve all my molluscan problems. It didn't. There are 250 of the damnable things in Britain, and most species look exactly like at least ten or twenty others. The word 'common' in any book of identification is a siren call to the novice, but I am going with that for today. The yellow-with-brown-stripes snail I found looked like one of those disgusting boiled sweets called 'Winter Mixture' that seemed to have formed a major part of my grandmother's diet. It was **Cernuella virgata**. This is a highly polymorphic species, don't you know, so I am sticking with it.

Smut Fungi

Now a third of the way up The Drift, I was back on safer ground with a fungus, a 'micro-fungus'. It was the smut fungus **Microbotryum violaceum**. This is a fungal parasite of campions, most commonly, as in this case, Red Campion. If you have seen this plant, then you will know it is not red but the very essence of 'pink'. The colour pink had no separate name until the early eighteenth century, the colour sense of the word deriving from the plant of that name, the plant possibly owing *its* name to the serrated edges of the petals which are 'pinked', as in 'pinking shears'. The pink of these particular plants was spoiled by a sooty dust, formed in the centre of the flower and contaminating the petals. This dust is the spores of the smut fungus that infects all the aerial parts of the plant. Since the spores are produced only on the reproductive organs of the male plant and spread to the reproductive organs of other plants (of either sex), it is classed as a sexually transmitted disease. If spores infect a female, the fungus employs biochemical trickery to change it to a male plant.

Smut fungi are not clearly to be seen all that often, *M. vio-laceum* being one of the most common and conspicuous. Rust fungi can, however, be found everywhere. Some of these associations with plants are non-exclusive: that is, the fungus can grow on several species of plant, but sometimes they are host-specific. Lose the plant and lose the parasite. 'Parasites' they always are, but again they are *life* and must be honoured along with everything. The much-maligned Common Ragwort, *Jacobaea vulgaris*, for example, is host to twenty fungi plus nearly a hundred invertebrates.

Trees and Shrubs

The hedgerows were in full, luxuriant leaf: a tangle of **Ivy**, *Hedera helix*, **Honeysuckle**, *Lonicera periclymenum*, **Black Bryony**, *Dioscorea communis*, **Greater Stitchwort**, *Stellaria holostea*, and Stinging Nettle. The flowers of the last of these were in splendid bud, and I was pleased with the photograph I took of them. On the slope to the right and flatter area to the left there is a plant that often causes confusion. It is comparatively low in growth habit and looks like a Bramble that has yet to make the big time. The 'blackberries' it forms are pale from a layer of 'frosting' (pruinose), and with fewer, larger drupelets. It was the **Dewberry**, *Rubus caesius*. Although it looks like a blackberry, it is taxonomically closer to the Raspberry and has similarly soft spines but with a trailing habit. It fruits sparsely and unreliably, sometimes with only two or three drupelets on a single 'berry' or 'aggregrate of drupelets', as they are more properly and less conveniently known. This, however, is the best place for the plant I know, producing hundreds of large and very juicy berries. It is probable that I should not have told you this.

Scattered shrubs or small trees occurred all the way along this section of The Drift hedge. **Dogwood**, *Cornus sanguinea*, a tree typical of chalk hills, was in flower, the sprays of four-petalled florets bright in the sunshine. This was June, but the plant can look even prettier in the winter. *Cornus* is simply the plant's name in Latin, but the source of *sanguinea* (bloody) is only revealed in the brilliant reds of the young stems once the leaves have fallen. The timber of Dogwood has few uses – skewers and toothpicks being among them – and the berries are inedible. It is for these failings that it earned its canine epithet, as did several other useless plants, such as Dog's Mercury.

Prettier still, and not *quite* so useless (historically at least), is **Spindle**, *Euonymus europaeus*. We find this on some of the walks we take, and it is surprising that so few people have even heard of it. The tree's attractive appearance comes from its four-lobed flowers and fruit capsules, which are respectively bright pink and bright orange and with both colours persisting at the same time. Such colour matching would be a domestic horror but is vibrant against the greens of the hedgerow. D had been sufficiently taken with the tree to have collected some seeds a year previously and planted them in the late winter in a pot. I had little faith in them germinating, but all twelve of the seeds she planted grew. I thought the seedlings looked a little 'spindly', but then they would, wouldn't they? In 2022 these seedlings, still in a pot, became covered in the nursery webs of dozens of caterpillars and the leaves seriously threatened. I collected some Spindle branches from The Drift, put them in water and carefully transferred the larvae from the seedlings to the leaves of these fresh branches. This seemed like a doomed enterprise, but I was eventually rewarded by the mature moths that duly appeared. It was the Spindle Ermine Moth, *Yponomeuta cagnagella*, and the much put-upon Spindles survived, just.

The tree's Latin name means 'the European of good name', though I know not why. The common name is explicable through its reputation for being used as spindles in spinning. Geoffrey Grigson in his invaluable *The Englishman's Flora* expresses some doubt over this, but there is less doubt about its tough timber being used for barrel hoops, with a late nineteenth-century Scottish newspaper affirming that this was the case.

The twisting, entwining stems of Black Bryony draped over much of the hedge and their translucent, *Art Nouveau* leaves shone in the sunlight. It is a splendid plant that is almost ubiquitous in old hedges. Three months later it will look lovely once again in the gay form of metres-long strings of green, orange and red berries. The plant is poisonous, as is its very distantly related and less frequent namesake, White Bryony, *Bryonia dioica*.

Perhaps the most striking plant along this stretch, and one I find curiously irritating, is **Tutsan,** *Hypericum androsaemum*, a species of St John's Wort. I like garden plants in gardens, but Tutsan looks very much like an introduced garden plant in the wrong place – an old English hedge. Mild support for my views on this plant comes from *The History of the British Flora*, by H. Good, which does not include it, despite five other *Hypericum* species being recorded as native. It is generally described as 'Eurasian' in origin, which hardly narrows it down. Against my hypothesis are the long list of common names reported by Grigson, and various early opinions on the plant's effects on physical and psychological well-being. My guess is that it came here with the Romans.

The plant is certainly striking, with the geometrically inclined flowers, bright colours and large berries which look like red and green apples that turn black on maturity. It thrives mostly in the south and west. On part of the plants the developing flowers were distorted and covered in a silky web with a larva rearing its head out of it. It may have been a species of beetle in the genus *Chrysolina*, on the principle that they are associated with St John's Wort, but there are over four thousand species of beetle in Britain so I troubled it no further. I always look into the uses of plants, and my eye was taken by the following, originating with Pliny (again via Grigson): *Also it dystroyeth and drywyth awey the fowle lust of lecherye if men drynke it.* Perhaps my low opinion of this plant is justified after all.

Ferns and Cheats

Not mentioned so far are the large numbers of ferns to be seen. The most striking and common was the **Hart's Tongue Fern**, *Asplenium scolopendrium*, notable for not being fern-like as generally understood. Back in the winter, when they were not so entwined in the rampant vegetation of spring and summer, they were a great temptation to the gardener (D, in this case) as easy pickings to fill up a bare patch under the apple tree. Wisdom prevailed as the removal of entire plants feels wrong and is, in fact, illegal. One of the fronds carried a single, mature and unimaginatively named **Common Green Shield Bug**, *Palomena prasina*. Shield bugs are tricky to identify because the already dimorphic sexes develop via a number of stages (instars). A superb online 'poster' designed to aid the enthusiast, shows several British shield bugs in all of their stages, the Common Green Shield Bug having no fewer than fourteen forms! Fortunately, there are only sixty-nine British species, which is, at least, better than wasps, with seven thousand. Shield bugs are not a type of beetle, being scattered over several Families within the Order Hemiptera. Beetles are in the Order Coleoptera.

Despite this difficulty, I have identified several shield bugs over the years using an easy and shameful cheat which works for many other groups of organisms. I happened to know the Common Green Shield Bug, but had I not, I would enter 'green shield bug brown patch UK' into a search engine and look at the images that appear. Similarly, 'red mushroom with white spots UK' would turn up the Fly Agaric, and for 'yellow butterfly UK' you would see all the yellow British butterflies and you would be able to spot your Clouded Yellow among them. It is necessary to be as specific as possible, so 'brown toadstool UK' would not be enough as there are about two thousand species of brown toadstool in the UK!

There were a few 'fern-like' ferns too, the most dominant of them being the **Male Fern**, *Dryopteris filix-mas*. This is a common and impressively large and elegant fern. The question that comes to most people's mind is why it is called the 'Male Fern', a name that reappears in the specific epithet, *filix-mas*. It originates from the misunderstanding of how fern reproduction operates, combined with a touch of anthropomorphism. It was called the Male Fern because there is another, smaller and more graceful fern which looks rather like it. This was dubbed the 'Lady Fern' and named formally *Athyrium filix-femina*. Both Latin specific epithets go back at least to John Ray in the late seventeenth century. Which species was named first is not entirely clear, but the Lady Fern has reproductive structures (spores) 'borne inconspicuously along the leaf margin and ... concealed in a manner deemed "female"', so maybe it was she.

Herbaceous Plants

There were scores of smaller herbaceous plants fighting their way through the mass of larger plants, but with one dominating – the **Bluebell**, *Hyacinthoides non-scripta*. *Non-scripta*, meaning 'with no markings', differentiates it from the hyacinth of Greek mythology, which was marked by the tears of Apollo. Bluebells prefer the lack of competition that comes in the depths of a wood but will grow happily along hedges, sharing the space with other plants. Bluebells will even grow in open meadows and pasture. This would seem to be an indication that the meadow or pasture was woodland until fairly recently, but it is not necessarily so in Britain. In the coppice woodland I once walked through to get to the village forty years ago, the Bluebells were and still are breathtaking. One in two hundred was white, and one in a thousand was pink. Everyone knows that it is illegal to uproot Bluebells, though it is legal to pick the flowers – but not sell them. Taking a few strays from the edge of the woods, or from a hedge, will do little harm. More serious damage is done by walking over them and vastly more from the loss of the woodlands in which they thrive. More trouble comes in the form of the invasive Spanish Bluebell, *Hyacynthoides hispanica*, which can displace its cousin. The even worse concern that the two will hybridise and the native become extinct has been largely laid to rest by a study that found the invader and its hybrids with the native are considerably less fertile. Britain is, nevertheless, something of a stronghold for the exquisite Bluebell, with nearly half of the world's population growing here. We must treasure it.

Ribwort Plantain was conspicuously in flower, as was the shocking pink of Common Vetch and Cow Parsley's later-flowering lookalike, **Rough Chervil**, *Chaerophyllum temulum*. The five pink petals of the inevitable Herb Robert could be seen everywhere. The delicate appearance of this plant belies a strong heart as it is nearly always in flower, even in the depths of winter. Any plant with the word 'herb' in its name sounds encouraging, but it is not used for flavouring because the smell is simply 'musty'. Few of our native plants beyond roses and daffodils have poems written about them, but Herb Robert has been lucky. I think. Here is a snippet:

> *Herb Robert, straggling through the hedge,*
> *Where dancing sunbeams quiver,*
> *Is peeping o'er the grassy ledge,*
> *Of every sparkling river.*

There is much more, but too much of a good thing and all that. The author is unknown, which is probably for the best. Fortunately, there is a much better (and *shorter*) poem in Cicely Mary Barker's much-loved *Flower Fairies* books, accompanied by one of her many enchanting illustrations.

The Acid Top

Leaving the horizontal continuation of The Drift and forking right to continue the still upward path to the top of the hill, I was in slightly different countryside. The multitude of hedgerow trees and shrubs that I had passed gave way to two hundred metres of arching **Hazel**, *Corylus avellana*. Each tree was in Hazel's habitual form of multiple stems, the whole looking like a linear coppice overdue for cutting. It is clearly a planted hedgerow, though with no obvious sign of it ever being laid. The path followed a much gentler slope than before, and the chalk is now capped with clay. **Raspberries**, *Rubus idaeus*, prefer these acid conditions and were in the broad, low vegetation to the left. Collecting Raspberries from the wild is a delight, but they seldom appear in sufficient quantity to warrant a basket. These are on-the-go snacks.

The path emerges into an almost level, open countryside, with a hedge only to the left. This hedgerow is dominated by Blackthorn, its habit of producing sufficient runners to create an emerging woodland in evidence. It was too early for the sloes, of course. **Mugwort**, *Artemisia vulgaris*, a substantial plant found in hedgerows almost everywhere, was also there, large and proud. It too is a foraging favourite, with highly aromatic leaves which make it useful as a herb. Lucid dreams are associated with a bedtime tea of Mugwort leaves or flower heads; just don't overdo it.

The herbaceous buffer zone between the path and the ploughed field to the right contained **Bush Vetch**, *Vicia sepium*, running the spectrum of lilac, and ruderal species (pioneering weeds) were everywhere. The common **Scentless Mayweed**, *Tripleurospermum inodorum*, formed a large patch next to the maize field, and the related **Pineapple Weed**, *Matricaria discoidea*, took advantage of its favoured habitat, the muddy ruts of farm vehicles. The first of these two members of the Asteraceae (Daisy Family) is more scented than you would imagine, with hints of its cousin, Chamomile. The second plant fulfils expectations entirely.

The Trouble with Maize

At the end of this stretch I reached my highest elevation, of 105 m (345 ft) above that of my doorstep, and the path turns sharply to the right. The hedge was now flipped to my right, and to my left (east) I looked over a maize field, beyond which is a wood and then the magnificent downland of Hog Cliff nature reserve, where we once lived. Slightly more interesting plant life persists on the margin of the field and the margin of the path, a forlorn barbed-wire fence separating the two. The scene here was dominated by Foxgloves, a sure sign of an acidic soil.

Thirty years ago the maize field was permanent pasture, or at least a venerable ley. A ley, if you did not know, is a sown pasture that is kept three of four years, then ploughed and resown. Sometimes it is left much longer to become a permanent ley or pasture. It is planted with a mix of good fodder grasses plus various herbaceous plants, each of which will have a useful talent: clovers, vetches, sainfoin for nitrogen fixation and chicory for its deep roots, which can penetrate the 'pan' and are able to bring nutrients to the surface. A 'pan', I need to tell you, is the hard and troublesome layer formed in soil at the maximum depth of the plough. A 'panbuster', incidentally, and to explicate even further, is a tractor-drawn machine that quickly removes a pan, and a machine that one of my old friends, Alan, a worker on a neighbouring farm, used to talk about with great animation. Think of spreading out your fingers like claws and dragging them through a sandbox and you will have the idea of it. Ley seed mixes often have useful and encouraging names, such as 'Lamb Finisher', 'Meat and Milk' and 'Permanent Pasture', the last of these perhaps not as permanent as the word suggests, being typically for '5+' years.

This field had been grassed for much longer than this, as I used to find the occasional mushroom there and mushrooms take time to establish. I also recall a deep 30-ft-diameter hole in the field in which an Elder grew and Skylarks sang impossibly above. All gone now, all replaced with maize, though I cannot say for certain what it was grown for and what I write below is merely stimulated by its presence where I stood that day.

Being an efficiency obsessive, I have long wanted to install a bio-digester to produce a supply of methane in my smallish garden. It would involve installing an IBC (Intermediate Bulk Container), a potentially lethal bag to keep the gas in and a lot of pipework and auxiliary guff. The plan is to use domestic, garden and any other organic waste I can acquire to produce methane for my cooker. Unfortunately, this project has suffered an executive veto and is now languishing in committee.

Bio-digesters are commonly and honourably used to deal with troublesome agricultural wastes, such as slurry and other organic materials. They are used on an industrial scale throughout Britain and produce methane and fertiliser. For the most part they work very well, especially when the process is carried out on the farm that produces the waste. Growing crops to feed bio-digesters is, however, another matter. Vast areas of agricultural land have now been commandeered in the West Country to grow maize destined for a bio-digester, and the landscape has changed.

Maize has a higher energy yield per hectare than almost any crop, but it does have serious problems of its own. It is generally late-planted and late-cropped, resulting in distantly spaced stubble being left standing for months over the winter surrounded by bare and unstable soil with little in the way of organic fibres to hold it together. While chalk hills are notable for their ability to drain easily, if it is compacted during the heavy cultivation required to produce maize, it drains very badly indeed. This can result in rainwater run-off, taking the soil and wasted fertiliser with it, which is duly deposited into the river. Fortunately, and increasingly, 'cover crops' are planted in some fields when they would otherwise lie bare, stabilising the soil.

The stimulus for the exercise is the production of (relatively) carbon-neutral energy under what I suspect are ill-thought-out encouragements and subsidies by the government – I am seldom one to blame the farmer. It must be open to questions, then, such as whether it does or not, whether it is worth losing the food production value of the land and whether or not it is environmentally damaging. Taking only the first question: an enormous energy input is used to plough, harrow, sow, spray, harvest, plus that required to produce the necessary fertiliser, and, not least, in chugging a dozen miles (and sometimes much more) to a bio-digestion plant. I do not know the answer, though I doubt it is compensated for by the energy created. But I thought someone in the industry must know.

I wrote to a local bio-digestion plant, asking for an interview and quickly received a very polite and pleasant email in return explaining that they were busy (I knew they were busy upgrading, so quite understandable) and that they were concerned about commercial confidentiality. Fair enough. This was my first sortie into investigative journalism and showed every sign of being my ignominious last, but 'faint heart' and all that. I then wrote to the industry association, duly filling out the online form and explaining my concerns in a cheerful way and requesting an interview or, at least, the answer to my questions via email. Unfortunately, after filling in the online information request form three or four times, phoning them up and writing via snail-mail, I received no reply at all. Here you must draw your own conclusions.

The Spinney and Its Insects

Halfway along the field edge, the hedge on the right gains a companion on the left, a narrow spinney of ash and blackthorn that follows the path downhill for 400 m. This is a magical part of the walk, where countless marvels have appeared. The year before there was a massive cloud of micro-moths that whirled around my head. I was tempted to collect a couple for identification but did not have two days spare for the microscopy work that would be needed. There is a superb guide to these creatures (they are not microscopic, just small) by Mark Parsons and Phil Sterling, their *Field Guide to Micro-Moths of Great Britain and Ireland*, but micromoths are notoriously tricky to identify and a project for serious enthusiasts only.

One of the most exquisite of all insects, the **Pearly Green Lacewing**, *Chrysopa perla*, made my list that day. This species is fairly common, but not so much in Dorset, so it was a good find. It truly looks like something made by a master jeweller, and one wonders why it goes to so much trouble. Certainly, the larvae of the Scarlet Lily Beetle, *Lilioceris lilii*, which was ravaging an otherwise magnificent lily in my garden at the time, was not so concerned with appearances. Although the adult beetle is quite attractive, its larvae are not so at the best of times and at the worst of times protect themselves with what is known as a 'faecal shield'. This is exuded from, and carefully positioned by, what is known ominously as an 'anal turret'. Nature-lover that I am, I used a hose to dislodge them.

Hogweed, *Heracleum sphondylium*, was a constant companion on this walk, and one that is worth a second pause to see what guests it might be accommodating. Leaf-miners are familiar phenomena caused by the track left within a leaf by the feeding larva of whatever insect is making a living therein. The track tends to widen as the larva grows. Typically, it will be that of a beetle, a fly, a sawfly or a moth. Identifying precise species from its resulting leaf graffiti may seem like an ambition without hope, but it is not. Insects can be very choosy about which plant they will grace with their presence (host-specificity), and each will make a distinctive track. Although there are no books that I can find to help, there are one or two online resources where the host species is selected, and most of the leaf-mining species are listed and their tracks described and illustrated. The one I found in a Hogweed leaf that day was likely to be (it's not *quite* as easy as I suggest) *Phytomyza spondylii*, a fly.

Near by I found what I took to be a hoverfly, resting on a leaf. I was wrong, of course. Should you wish to take an interest in insects, an essential thing to realise is how very many species look like either a bee or a wasp. This is a prime example, or collection of examples, of Batesian mimicry, named after Henry Walter Bates, an English naturalist who described the phenomenon in the middle of the nineteenth century. The general idea is that if you are not scary in general appearance or cannot be bothered to defend yourself by growing a sting or adopting annoying habits, then look like something that does – a wasp or a bee, perhaps, or maybe an owl. The yellow or orange bands alternating with black or dark brown are common to many wasps and bees and are taken as a warning by just about everything that doesn't want to be stung, thus keeping the wasp or bee safe from predation. The advertising of one's dangerous nature with bright colours and distinctive patterns is known as aposematism, the startling colours of the many poisonous frogs being another example. Avoidance of creatures with these warning patterns is innate and works just as well for a species that is harmless as it does for one that is dangerous.

Groups of insects that mimic bees or wasps include: hoverflies, bee flies and the parasitic flies (all in Diptera), the Wasp Beetle and the Eurasian Bee Beetle (Coleoptera), the Broad-Bordered Bee Hawkmoth, Scorpion Flies (Mecoptera) and the Sawflies (Hymenoptera). There are even a handful of mosquitoes that look a bit waspy. Sawflies are in the Hymenoptera, along with bees and wasps and, from my reading of the various Family trees for the Order, appear to predate their stinging cousins.* This raises the question of whether wasps and bees inherited the black-and-yellow banding from sawflies or sawflies mimicked it later. The fossil evidence is unclear but slightly favours the former hypothesis.

Although mimicry is 'designed' to confuse potential predators, it also causes great confusion in the naturalist who just wants to know what something is. Which brings me back to my putative hoverfly. It transpired that what I thought was a hoverfly was in fact the **Orange-Horned Nomad Bee**, *Nomada fulvicornis*.

There are about thirty species of Nomad Bee in the UK, all with unpleasant reproductive habits, being 'kleptoparasites' that parasitise (steal) the nests of *Andrena* species of bee. During mating, the male sprays the female with a scent from his mandibular glands. This scent assists the female in gaining access to a nest by mimicking the scent of the soon-to-be parasitised bee, or rather, her nest. Single eggs are laid in still open cells prepared by the host using some abdominal equipment of considerable complexity (brushes and hooks are involved) to fix her impostor eggs in place. Once hatched, the larvae destroy the grubs and feed on the food store provided by the host.

We are terribly sentimental about the natural world, with a fondness for the 'good guys'. Watch a documentary about snakes who happen to eat baby turtles and you will root for the snakes; watch one about turtles and you will root for the turtles. Here we find ourselves rooting for the 'good' *Andrena* bee. Goodness, however, is an irrelevance in nature.

---

* Ralph S. Peters, et al., 'Evolutionary History of the Hymenoptera' (2017).

The Chalk, Identification Keys

Apart from the steep downland to my left at the start of The Drift and a little pasture to my right, all of my walk had been through a linear oasis of the semi-natural world with little but monoculture arable on either side. But as I diverted to the right, off of the Horseshoe path and through a gate, I entered a very different landscape, that of Langcombe Bottom. It is itself shaped like a horseshoe within the larger Horseshoe walk, consisting of a steeply sloping, west-facing combe with an arable field at the bottom, carving out the centre. The romance of this view is ruined slightly by the large, rectilinear and highly aromatic sewage works placed, in turn, within the arable field. The grassland of the slopes is unlikely to have seen the plough since the first clearances were made, perhaps in the Bronze Age. It is permanent pasture in its truest sense; this is chalk downland.

Downland such as this has declined dramatically over the years, to the point where only land that is too much trouble to cultivate or has been protected in law or by agreement with the landowner (usually in the form of a subsidy) has been left in peace. Places like Langcombe Bottom have among the highest species-per-hectare ratios of any British habitat. Such reckless destruction has been a tragedy for Britain. The complexities of these ecosystems are astoundingly intricate and diverse, something that even the impressively long lists of their inhabitants can never convey.

I turned immediately left and followed a broad swathe of grass, bordered on the left by the other side of the hedge I had been following and to my right by an area of scrub. This scrub seems to be fairly permanent, as it is marked on maps made in 1900. But I know that the farmer keeps it under control with some serious 'topping' (industrial-scale strimming). Scrub incursion is one of downland's main problems, with loss of grassland species, though there are species-rich scrublands too, especially on chalk. As is typical, **Gorse**, *Ulex europaeus*, is dominant, but losing its primacy to Elder, Blackthorn and Hawthorn. The cool weather that beset 2021 had kept the Hawthorn well in flower, with its candy-floss sprays and heady/ earthy aromas lingering on. Trimethylamine is one of the fragrances on offer, the smell of week-old fish.

Nothing here is particularly rare, but this bordered corridor is another oasis of life. I decided to sit down for a rest and opened another beer. (I forgot to tell you about the first one.) Sitting down for a few minutes is the best way to see insects scurrying through the grass or willing to land on a nearby flower or stem. There is nevertheless a certain amount of frustration as they often land just out of reach of my camera, pose at the wrong angle, hide behind a grass stem or are simply not prepared to hang around for more than fifteen seconds at the behest of a mere human while he focuses his Canon. A few did come close enough to see clearly and to take a photograph good enough for a reasonable ID. One was the **Blackneck Moth**, *Lygephila pastinum*. It is as dull as a moth can be, its delta of buff/grey wings, ornamented with trailing-edge fur, and a delta black mark in the centre of each wing being its chief identification characteristics. Its main larval foodplant is Tufted Vetch, *Vicia cracca*, which I know grows in the hedge.

One of the commonest things to find in a butterfly net after a couple of sweeps is a grasshopper. There are thirty-three species of Orthoptera native to Britain that generally pass for grasshoppers, with only eleven that can truly claim that name. The rest are groundhoppers or bush crickets of one sort or another. The Orthoptera are spread over twenty-five Genera within ten Orders, and are sufficiently distinct to identify with a degree of ease.

One was hopping around me: the **Dark Bush Cricket**, *Pholidoptera griseoaptera*, though it did not look much like one. A glance at this species online, in a book, or on one of those ID charts that are all too easy to buy with your ice cream while visiting a nature reserve, will show you that again I am not being entirely honest about identifying grasshoppers. As with the shield bugs mentioned earlier, they have developmental instar stages.

A familiar and splendid little beetle landed within a couple of feet. Although I knew this common beetle very well, its name had fled my memory, so on my return I tried the trick I mentioned earlier and typed in 'metallic-green beetle with swollen thighs' – it really does look as though it has been working out. Several images promptly appeared of this species, along with its name, the **Swollen-Thighed Beetle**, *Oedemera nobilis*. Spot on.

Less appealing was a flesh fly, a member of the genus *Sarcophagus*. I could have blagged a species name for you, but honesty forbids. There are over sixty species in Britain with little to differentiate them, so it would have been guesswork. Fortunately for any budding *Sarcophagus* enthusiast, there is a superb key available (complete with over a hundred excellent close-up photographs) which enables an accurate determination. 'Keys' abound in biology, with books specialising in such disciplines as wild flowers, ladybirds, trees or micro-moths usually supplying some sort of key; indeed, I have written a couple of small keys myself, for the edible and poisonous mushrooms. They ask questions and your answer leads you to another question or set of questions, and so on until your reach the answer. The answer may be a species or a higher taxonomic rank such as Genus or Family.

Keys in general are the very devil to compose and none too easy to use, but a bit of close observation and patience will generally see the user through. These virtues will need to be complemented by experience and close examination of the morphology of whatever you are studying. For many things (including *Sarcophagus*) you will also need a dissecting microscope, typically magnifying ´40, and for mycology you will need a microscope that can reach the heady magnification of ´1000, though less will do for some characteristics. Also, and for everything, you will need an extensive and exciting new vocabulary. A sample from page 8 of the thirty-seven-page *Sarcophagus* key gives you the feel: 'antero-distally between veins R1 and R4+5 and along crossvein dm-cu and distal part of vein M; hyaline or at most slightly infuscated …'. Such horrors are bread-and-butter to specialities such as the Diptera and almost any other pursuit (curling, for example), and are understood, *need* to be understood, by those interested. It is fortunate, however, that biological morphologies share many of these terms, with 'antero-distal' being known to me as a statement about position (front of body and away from it) and 'hyaline', which I know from mycology and means 'transparent or glassy'.

I continued through the grassy area above the scrub until I came out on to the downland itself. Beautiful as it was, it did not quite compare to other downland I had seen and, since the management has been no better or worse than on these other, more exciting sites, it is natural to wonder why. The answer here comes in the form of a plant that is dear to me, the **Pignut**, *Conopodium majus*. This is one of the smallest members of the Apiaceae (Carrot Family) at barely 40 cm tall. Its leaves are scant, forking and thread-like. It is something I frequently find on the wild food walks I take, and a favourite with my guests as unearthing the 'nut' (it is really a vaguely spherical storage root) takes patience and dexterity. It also has an excellent flavour, akin to a chestnut. It should be collected only occasionally and with care, as it is almost invariably found on biodiverse and often protected sites. I was challenged once for digging some up (the digging done with permission of the landowner). My defence was that it was worth sacrificing a dozen pignuts in a field that contained fifty thousand of them for the cultural experience and understanding that comes from foraging like our forebears. The significance of pignuts for the ecology of Langcombe Bottom is that they indicate a slightly acid soil, a soil that will not happily sustain many of the plants one would expect on chalk downland. I had forgotten that the other side of the combe had no clay cap, but it was too late to retrace my steps. The pure chalk downland I had expected to see must wait for another day.

Germander Speedwells were scattered everywhere. I would not mention again so common a plant were it not for something I discovered growing on it. In appearance, it was a fluffy 'pom-pom' growing in place of the flower head. This incongruous structure is a gall, the species instrumental in its creation the gall midge *Jaapiella veronicae*. A further oddity was on a specimen of the **Creeping Thistle**, *Cirsium arvense*. It was infected with the rust fungus *Puccinia punctiformis*.

It was getting late, and the beer was all gone, so I made my way back to the main road, the straight part of the overall 'D' shape of my walk, and continued home. I determined to complete my walk by visiting the lost water meadows to the south-east of the village in a week or so.

FRIDAY, 11 JUNE

The River Frome

The blue sky I had left behind six days earlier had deserted me. It was a day of grey cloud, but mercifully with no wind to make the photography of plants difficult. Crossing the road opposite to where I had exited the Horseshoe, I climbed over the stile to enter a very different countryside from that I had left, a flat terrain of pasture and small, hedged fields, the River Frome winding through it.

My route south-east was narrowly constrained by the gently curving road to the north-east and the wildly meandering River Frome to the west. At this point the distance between the two was only forty metres, though it widens considerably further south. The fields, although mostly permanent pasture, are not particularly interesting botanically and I puzzled over this. It is likely that they had been sprayed with a selective herbicide that retains only agriculturally useful grasses. But still the field hummed with insect life that lived in the hedges and trees. Selective herbicide or not, buttercups dominated the field, with **White Clover**, *Trifolium repens*, between. The interest of this landscape lies in the edges, the corners and the river. It is to the river that I went first.

The Frome begins its life five miles north, in the village of Evershot, and continues its wiggly path ('sinuous' suggests something more elegant) for thirty miles east before emptying into Poole Harbour. The River Frome is the major chalk-stream in south-west England. It is fed by other rivers and streams and, half a mile away at the north-western edge of the village, is joined in confluence with the exceptionally pretty River Hooke.

The name Frome (pronounced 'froom') derives from the Celtic word for 'fair', a name it well deserves.

The Frome is a trout stream, and I would watch the fish swimming mindlessly against the flow with my daughters when I walked them to the village school, and again when I walked them back. Fishing rights here, as everywhere, are guarded with passion and all too frequently defended in court. You do not attempt to catch trout on someone else's stretch of river. **Yellow Iris**, *Iris pseudacorus*, not yet in flower, were bordering stretches of the bank, with large clumps of **Water Speedwell**, *Veronica anagallis-aquatica*, displaying a thousand tiny pink flowers. **Brooklime**, *V. beccabunga*, another member of the Speedwells, was also there, sitting in the shallow water, its flowers also biding their time in this cool summer. The bright yellow of **Crosswort**, *Cruciata laevipes*, was gleaming in a nearby hedge, and I went in for the sniff. This member of the bedstraws does not smell typically floral, but smells strongly of honey, so a sniff is irresistible.

Brooklime is edible, inasmuch as it will not poison you; it just tastes horrible. It is eaten in parts of the world, notably in Denmark, where wild food has (among the high-living members of society) acquired a style value out of all proportion to culinary worth. I am known for my appreciation of wild food, but some of the restaurant wild food dinners I have endured in Copenhagen and Jutland offend the palate as much as the wallet. But then the company is always excellent, so I pay my share cheerfully and eat with fortitude.

Much more palatable are two plants that are sometimes confused – **Watercress**, *Nasturtium officinale*, and **Fool's Watercress**, *Helosciadium nodiflorum*. 'Fool's' in this case means that it is simply not Watercress, but perfectly edible, with a pleasant carroty flavour replacing that of mustard. Incidentally, the deadly liver-fluke that uses water plants for one of its (tiny) life stages makes these wild populations a no-go area for the forager without various precautions being taken.

I was studying this part of the river from the little bridge that crosses it and noticed the occasional flight of an insect from the calm surface of the water. The swallows, swifts and house martins that would usually have made these short flights shorter still were absent, so every one I saw escaped to freedom. These, of course, were **Mayflies**, *Ephemera danica*. As you may have guessed, I am a great enthusiast for Latin names, and this behavioural generic name is one of the most appealing in both accuracy and poignancy. *Danica*, incidentally, is most likely to be a not very helpful reference to where it was first described. Although there are fifty British species of mayflies, the *Ephemeroptera*, I have plumped for this species without inspection as it is the only one that lives in moving water, rather than stationary. Also, its strategy of recklessly launching itself from the water in this manner is unique. Where were they headed? The May blossom and a mate.

The Water Meadows

As I walked slowly south, I began to encounter remnants of agricultural construction, a culvert here, a brick channel there. Then I came to a well-restored sluice gate. All are remnants of an agricultural practice now lost to us: the water meadow.

The water meadows below Maiden Newton are visible only as faint ridges on aerial photographs and barely visible banks from the ground. Lidar imagery (radar using lasers to detect fine differences in altitude that are mapped out to form a shaded impression of the topography) is slightly more helpful, with the parallel banks clearly to be seen. It was these banks that were flooded for a while in the late winter to warm the soil for early spring grazing of ewes and lambs. This was sometimes followed by a small crop of hay, then rough grazing. All this was long gone, the land left for rough pasture or arable, by the end of the nineteenth century. The last reference to them in use that I can find is an advertisement from 1882: 'Wanted, at Lady Day, a LABOURER who can Mow and undertake Water Meadow Work ... Apply to Mr J. Cox, Cruxton, Maiden Newton.' The sluice gate I encountered that day was the one that controlled the flow into the water meadows at Cruxton.

Water meadows once covered a vast area of flood-plain meadow alongside the Frome from Maiden Newton to Wareham. There is also one water meadow further upstream, alongside the River Hooke. It is sad that they are all gone, as they were among the most picturesque of rural creations. Those for which we can claim some recompense are those that were spared the plough. Many of these have remained attractive to wildlife in a landscape where most lowland is arable. I go into much more detail on water meadows, how to spot them and how they're formed, in *A Spotter's Guide to Countryside Mysteries*.

Getting Lost, Old Fields, Ivy, Lichens and Cowpats

I reached a small bridge and crossed to the west bank of the Frome and a small country road. I saw two women I did not recognise as locals and greeted them. They turned out to be Dutch and clearly the more adventurous yet easily pleased type of tourist. (We don't do exciting in Maiden Newton.) These were the first people I had encountered that day, and indeed two more than I had seen on my Horseshoe walk. They told me they were slightly lost and politely asked me the way to the village. I politely told them, and they went on their way. Within twenty minutes of this conversation I too was lost. My front door was a little over half a mile away and I did not know which way to go. This was a personal best for me, and quite possibly a world record. As I tried to recover my own bearings, I wondered what had happened to those women.

With the winding river, irregular fields and old hedgerows seemingly placed for artistic effect rather than utility, the landscape here is endlessly complex. Nearly back to habitation, I stopped to look at a group of trees I have marvelled at many times. They are ancient remnants of three hedges, forming parallel lines of trees, with a fourth visible as a field boundary in the circa 1900 map but represented in the flesh, as it were, by a single tree. All the hedges terminated to the north-east at a broad curve in the river. I measured all of the fields, and each is one acre in extent. That the one acre was intentional can be seen by the shorter two fields to the north-west being wider to maintain the required area, something that would have necessitated planning. There were also the remnants of a smaller field south of this group, which is marked on the 1900 map as Ham Waste, signifying an area of common land where stock might be grazed. Pondering this and another conspicuously one-acre field that I had found stranded in the open water meadow an hour earlier, I thought it possible they had been payments in kind for the loss of common law rights during the enclosure period.

History aside, these are truly splendid trees, and all deserve a preservation order if they do not have one already. At least two are ancient pollards, and one of the Beech trees hosts more lichen species than can be found in almost any square kilometre of London. I went to examine it a couple of years ago with my lichenologist friend Bryan and he found twenty-four species on this single tree, at least two of which were very rare. Some were so small that having them pointed out was insufficient direction and Bryan marked their location with some coloured drawing pins.

We have, or had, a problem with Ivy in our garden, one that took years to fix, and frankly it will always be with us. It is easy to hate Ivy, but it is among our most successful of plants, quite beautiful in the right place and with a large number of associated species. These species include a couple of dozen fungi, twenty beetles and numerous insects that consume their nectar. Nectar makes honey, and Ivy honey is a rare, late treat for the bees and those who like really weird honey – it tastes of sugar syrup and turpentine. One Ivy had found its perfect home on an Ash tree in one of these relic hedges. It had taken over much of the tree, while still leaving it room to live, and its 'trunk' was a massive ten inches (25 cm) in diameter, almost the same as the tree.

Leaving this last field, I needed to walk through a substantial herd of cows. It is a sad thing that such an experience is rare these days, with so many confined to quarters for the duration, in the south at least. Cows are an essential part of conservation, as it is only through them that grass can be kept to a height that will allow the more delicate plants to flourish. Also, and a much-neglected aspect of cows and conservation, there is the cowpat. These are endlessly fascinating, with scores of specialist fungi dependent on them, various nematode worms and over three hundred insects. I always look out for cowpats on fungus forays, checking for small Inkcap species and the commonest of the fungi on dung, the little orange and nicely named cup fungus, the Cowpat Gem, *Cheilymenia granulata*.

Studying cowpats in the field is a bit odd, so I suggest bringing one home in a bucket and placing it in a quiet corner of the garden. Check every now and then for insects and fungi. At some point you will need to look more closely by taking a bit of it apart to see what has developed inside. I strongly suggest you obtain your cowpat from an organic farm or a nature reserve, as some of the medicines given to cattle can kill any prospective fungi and invertebrates.

There is an excellent little book by a couple of old friends of mine, Roy Watling and Mike Richardson, entitled *Keys to Fungi on Dung*, a great read for the enthusiast, if no one else. There is also a more substantial book (165 pages) keying out and listing most of the invertebrates found on dung. It is called *Insects of the British Cow-Dung Community*. Copies are rare and very expensive (£400 being the top price on offer), but you might be able to find it online as a file. In a particularly eye-catching piece of nominative determinism, the name of the author is Peter Skidmore.

Studiously ignoring everything I passed on the way and making sterling efforts not to become lost, I returned home, my local adventure complete.

Hook to Farnham

ARABLE AND PASTORAL, HEDGEROWS,
WOODLAND AND CHALK STREAM

THIRTEEN MILES

26–28 MAY 2021

William Cobbett

In exploring a sample of the various habitats to be enjoyed in Britain, I felt it would be helpful to take you through an ordinary part of lowland, agrarian countryside. There is no truly typical example of such countryside, but a walk across north Hampshire, I thought, would be near enough. There were two other reasons why I chose it: I was born in Hook, and William Cobbett was born in Farnham. This walk, our longest by far, was therefore something of a pilgrimage. It was to begin at my childhood home in Hook and take us across country to the birthplace of William Cobbett, the William Cobbett pub. OK, three other reasons.

I first read William Cobbett's famous *Rural Rides* forty years ago. It impressed me with its colourful description of the English landscape in the first part of the nineteenth century and the author's ability to digress on a thousand topics while still keeping my attention. His aim was to assess the state of the land and of those who worked and farmed it.

Cobbett was born in 1763 and died in 1835. It is fair to say that he was something of a character. It is also fair to say that he kept busy, delighted many, appalled others, wrote in a colourful and direct prose verging on stream-of-consciousness, that he was courageous beyond the ambition of most, that he valued work highly and indolence as the worst of all sins, that he was a tireless defender of the poor and indefatigable opponent of privilege and injustice. He was wrong as often as he was right. He would frequently change his mind. He liked beer and, it is said, was the best of Englishmen.

The worst of his many flaws was a virulent anti-Semitism, stemming at least in part from his hatred of stock-jobbers and financiers. There is no excusing this, and nothing I can say that might be helpful, so I must put it aside here, neither forgiven nor forgotten. As to what Cobbett actually achieved, he was a defender of the poor, an utterly fearless champion of free speech and instrumental in the long-overdue electoral reforms that followed at least partly from his writings.

Cobbett's career began on the farm, shooing away rooks and helping with the harvest. He worked as a clerk in London for nine months, then enlisted in the ranks of 54th Foot at Chatham in 1783 and was subsequently posted to Nova Scotia in 1785. Here, rather than wasting a minute, he learned the principles of grammar, became clerk to the commander, amassed a minor fortune by undertaking further writing duties and by thrift and, in the first intimation of his lifelong project to expose corruption, collected evidence of precisely that among the officers. He also met his wife.

The story of their romance is worth the telling. He first saw Mary Ann Reid in the company of others, including her father, a sergeant in the Artillery, and was impressed by her beauty and demure manner. Subsequently, on early morning walks, he admired her outside her father's house, scrubbing out a washing tub. The temperatures were sub-zero, and it was barely light, but still she worked. Cobbett quickly determined that she was the girl for him. She was thirteen, he about twenty-four.

Her father was posted back to Europe, so she promised to wait and marry Cobbett on his return. He was concerned that she would need to work in a lowly position during the time they were to be separated and gave her a purse containing 150 guineas to support herself. Their wait was a long four years, and upon their reunion he found her working as a servant girl. Her first action was to return the purse, unopened.

While Cobbett had many adventures, it was as a journalist that he was best known during his lifetime, often writing from his farm in Botley in Hampshire. He published his articles in a series of his own newspapers, the most famous being *The Register*. In these he exposed corruption, gave his opinion on matters of government policy – most often those which affected the rural poor – and became a serious embarrassment to the great and the not so good. If he took a dislike to you, he would write scurrilous articles about your misdemeanours and nothing could stop him, even threats of libel action. Sedition was still a criminal offence at the time (now, anyone can have a pop in writing at the government or even the Crown with impunity), and this was eventually to provide him with two years in jail.

Rural Rides is a great read but not always an easy one, in that the issues of Cobbett's time were not those of ours. While we may have read about the Corn Laws, the Speenhamland system, enclosure and the various protest movements of the time, we may not appreciate their finer points, making it difficult to judge his opinions or even understand them. With our benefit of hindsight, we can, however, see one thing clearly: he was a utopian, not one who looked forward to a bright future but one who looked back to a sun-dappled past. He longed for the countryside of his childhood, the bucolic England of Henry Fielding. Here, farmer and workers would sit around the table every day to eat, everyone had a patch of land they could work for themselves and everyone knew and was content in their station in life, even if it was not so easy to escape from should they desire more.

Nevertheless, he was entirely correct in his assessment of the sufferings of the farm workers, who had lost their small patch of land under enclosure, that they were working for wages instead of for themselves, that they were not allowed to undertake day work if they were in the poverty trap of the Speenhamland system, that food prices were high, that the rural economy was run by and for the benefit of investors instead of yeoman farmers and their workers and, ultimately, that they had lost their self-respect.

Although Hook and Farnham are mentioned in *Rural Rides*, our journey was not one that he recorded there. It was, however, the countryside he loved most, and our walk was, in a small way, taken to honour his memory. Our project was to consider the flora and fauna we encountered, but several of my digressions directly mirror the digressions of Cobbett – that is, they are reflections on the state of the English countryside.

Odiham

Odiham is not quite halfway between Hook and Farnham, but convenient enough for the complex tactical problems of walking, driving and taxis that followed from the overall plan. Anyway, I wanted to spend some time there as I have happy memories of the place. It was there that I watched *Davy Crockett* in 1955 at what I always fancied to have been the Odeon in Odiham, but which turned out to be merely a happy notion subsequently ruined by the cold light of an internet search. It was the now demolished Regal, and no fun at all. In our hotel room there was a historic photograph of Odiham, taken in 1956, which is the last time I had been there. Even more exciting, however, was the copy of *The Castle of Adventure*, by Enid Blyton, that nestled among several other faded volumes that decorated a shelf in our room. Circa 1961 I had borrowed a copy from the school library in Portsmouth and managed to lose it by the time I had reached page 22. I took it off the shelf and continued from where I had left off. I asked Andrew, the hotel manager, if I could take it home. He said I could.

Blyton was a powerful influence on my generation. Even Noddy had an effect. But some of her books contained horrors that haunt me still. My copy of the notorious *Here Comes Noddy Again* had long ago disappeared, but I recently managed to find a copy online that had not undergone the severe revisionist editing that came later. I was disappointed, however, to find it had been scribbled in by a previous owner, a defect not mentioned by the seller. Nevertheless, I kept it, as only one page had suffered thus, the one that caused me distress. Noddy is mugged in the dead of night, stripped naked and left to crawl around in the dark dark wood until rescued by Big Ears. I still tend to keep clear of dark dark woods.

More pernicious is that Blyton was my introduction, at the age of eight, to the British class system. Philip, Jack, Dinah and Lucy-Ann were at boarding-school when they weren't on 'hols', and had rich, eccentric, uncles who owned islands and who did not talk quite like my parents. They were upper middle class, I was later to learn. Although I was thrilled by their many adventures, I realised that their life was not mine; I was lower in the social scale: lower middle class. Well, yes, but not quite. Echoing George Orwell's characterisation of his own family: lower upper middle class (a class also uneasy in its self-regard) our family was upper lower middle class, my father being Secretarial Chief Male Nurse in a psychiatric hospital pushing us fractionally upwards. I am irredeemably somewhere in the lower-middle classes, but I am thinking of buying an Aga. Maybe that will lay Blyton's demons to rest.

DAY ONE

The Ancestral Bungalow

Our taxi the next morning dropped us in the centre of Hook, and I was delighted to see that the newsagent where my mother had worked was still there. Here, in the centre of the village, the buildings are fairly old, with the newsagent's appearing on a map from 1900. The hundred-metre walk to the Reading Road passed the White Hart, a pub that I remember from my five years in the village as a place I was not allowed to enter.

Our house was still there, a small and pleasant bungalow, backed with what I remember as a large garden and a wooden creosoted garage alongside that has subsequently been rebuilt in brick. Bracing myself, I rang the doorbell, thinking as I did it that it was the first time I had stood there since 1956. It was with mixed feelings that I discovered no one was at home. I was disappointed, of course, but also relieved at not needing to face what was likely to have been an embarrassing and possibly unwelcome encounter. But still it felt like home, most particularly because the wall of trees on the other side of the road was just as I remembered, even though they were unlikely to be the same trees. The fields behind the house were now mostly gone, but apart from that, little had changed in sixty-five years.

Leaving my first home at the age of five left me with a rare treasure. Every memory of my life there is set in time and place. Many are still with me, each a bright snapshot of an event — in idle moments I have counted about seventy. I do not know if other people find this, but my memories always come with a sense of orientation, as though each one had a compass reading attached in the metadata. Regrettable as it was, my leaving Hook at the age of five has protected the memories of that time from those that came later.

We turned back to the A30 and crossed the road opposite the church of St John the Evangelist and found some **St George's Mushrooms**, *Calocybe gambosa*, in the roadside grass. It is a great find for anyone who baulks at picking wild mushrooms, as it is an excellent edible species that deigns to appear early in the year, long before any dangerous lookalike makes an appearance. It even has a strong smell of raw pastry to help with ID, though some are deterred from eating it because of this. It is off-white all over, robust and unmistakable.

We wandered around the cemetery for a while and I casually looked for names that I knew, notably that of Miss Lunn, who had shown me how to form letters in pencil at her dame school. There was no one. Onwards then, to begin the walk proper.

Bartley Heath, Forget-Me-Nots and Wastebaskets

After a short walk through a leafy housing estate and down a path alongside the railway tracks, we emerged from a tunnel underneath the line and followed the narrow road for two hundred metres to find ourselves on Bartley Heath. This, together with Hook Common, makes up a National Nature Reserve where several rare plants, moths, fungi and birds can be found but were not, for the most part, found by us. The scene was one of birch and young oaks, plus some large open areas of grassland and scrub. The land felt old, having in all probability spent its life as a damp wasteland where nothing much would grow, suitable only for rough and poor grazing. Its wild nature was slightly diminished by the susurration of the M3, which has an intersection proudly cutting the common into eight separate plots. It is easy

and tempting to make such damning comments about nature re-
serves, but in an area where land prices are so high, we should be
grateful that they exist at all.

The day was fine and bright, but we had not realised until
then just how wet the ground was to be. Treading around muddy
paths and on occasion splashing quickly through unavoidable,
three-metre-long puddles was to be our fate for the three days of
the walk.

Although we did not see all that much, one species
brought redemption. It was the fungus **Helvella acetabulum**.
Counterintuitively, *Helvella* species come in two very distinct
forms. One is simply a brittle but rubbery fertile cup; the other
is a contorted, vaguely saddle-shaped fertile membrane sitting on
top of a vertically ribbed stem.

Why are such dramatic differences found within a single
genus when so very many almost identical species appear in
wildly different Genera, Families, Orders or even Classes? It is
due to the principle that underlies the system of classification.
Until surprisingly recently, species were often classified
according to morphology (what they looked like) rather than
how they were related phylogenetically (tree of life). This
resulted in many 'wastebasket taxa' into which species were
thrown simply because they looked similar.

When my interest in mycology was first aroused, there was
an enormous Order called the Aphyllophorales. The word
means 'not bearing leaves' or, in context, 'not bearing gills like
most mushrooms and toadstools'. Amusingly, some species
within the Aphyllophorales *did* have gills! A few other groups
that 'didn't have leaves' were already residing within one or
another Order, and so were excluded from the Aphyllophorales:
the puffballs, stinkhorns, certain jelly fungi, rusts and smuts.
The Aphyllophorales, then, uncomfortably accommodated

The Drift, West Dorset

The Drift

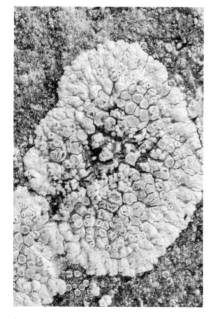

Lecanora pruinosa
(courtesy of Bryan Edwards)

Male Fern

Red Campion infected by a smut fungus

Stinging Nettle in flower

Tutsan

Hogweed seeds

Langcombe Bottom

Pignut

Rust Fungus, *Puccinia punctiformis*

River Frome

Water meadow sluice gate

Lichen-rich Hazel

Hook to Farnham

Bartley Heath

St George's Mushrooms

Helvella acetabulum

River Whitewater

Root flare

Looper Moth larva

Yellow Archangel

Neglected Hazel coppice

Wintercress. A weed of cultivation

A long walk through the woods

Bugle

The grandeur of the arable landscape

everything else – all the weird stuff that did not seem to belong anywhere else. By the 1990s there had been a massive reshuffle, with almost every Order moved around or dispensed with entirely and the Aphyllophorales consigned to ignominy. It transpired that even what were thought to be the better-behaved Orders were, in truth, wastebasket taxa, so they too underwent extensive revision.

Most mycologists knew all along that a serious review was long overdue because they spend much of their time looking down microscopes. In mycology, at least, relationships within species are most clearly seen in microscopic structures (with fish, it is skeletal structure) rather than the surface-level similarities observed by the naked human eye. My own observation here is that fruiting-body textures (brittle, rubbery, fibrous and so on), themselves deriving from and reflected in microstructure, are often excellent guides to family relationships within the larger fungi as they are often conserved within any grouping.

The examination of morphology at the microscopic level is much more informative of how species are related in mycology than in botany, allowing differentiations and connections to be revealed. This enabled the cup form and the saddle-on-a-stick form to be linked by their micro-structure, despite their obvious large-scale differences.

Should you be interested, *Helvella* species are not edible. This is because of the chemical gyromitrin, which is easily me-tabolised in the body to monomethylhydrazine (MMH). MMH is a rocket fuel, which is enough information to dismiss it from the mind of most people as something they would want inside their body. It is also known to be carcinogenic in small quantities. Larger quantities result in 'Gyromitrin syndrome', which produces a list of progressively unpleasant symptoms, with death being at the end.

Alongside the broad path was a plant I knew all too well. It is a non-native and seriously invasive plant that is able to take over any area of land on which it finds itself. It occurs in southern England, the Midlands and is otherwise coastal. **Three-Cornered Leek**, *Allium triquetrum*, is also known as Three-Cornered Garlic, reflecting its flavour and smell. It has snowdrop-type leaves and flowers but is easily distinguished by its pungent nature and the green line ornamenting every petal. The flavour is pleasant enough, and the lower parts of the stem usable as leeks if you like your leeks to be the diameter of a pencil and tasting of garlic. Eat as much as you can. Please.

The dominant plant in flower on Bartley Heath was the common **Wood Forget-Me-Not**, *Myosotis sylvatica*. The name 'Forget-Me-Not' has been on my list 'things to look up' for about fifty years. Not wishing my dying words to be 'Damn, I never did find out how they got their name', now is the time, and it is to the great Geoffrey Grigson in his *The Englishman's Flora* that I turn. It is called the equivalent in French and German and derives from a romantic and exceptionally brief German story. A knight walks by a river with his ladylove and picks some Water Forget-Me-Nots that were growing in the flowing water. Evidently being of a clumsy disposition, he falls in and, as his last act, throws the flowers to his love with the words, *Vergiss mein nicht*. Coleridge, knowing of this story, incorporated it in his 1802 poem 'The Keepsake' with the lines 'That blue and bright-eyed flowerlet of the brook, / Hope's gentle gem, the sweet Forget-me-not!'

Big Fields, Plastic Mulch

Beyond the gate was a footbridge over the M3. I had never stood on a motorway bridge before and did so then with a strong and irrational urge to run for it before something hit me. Before we followed the bridge on its helical path back to ground level, we stopped to enjoy the view. Hard to our right was more of Bartley Heath, while ahead and to the left was a vista of what, in part, we had come for – hundreds of acres of intensively farmed land.

In the far distance I could see the telltale glint of what might have been the now ubiquitous plastic mulch. It consists of long strips of thin, clear film, rolled out in adjacent rows to cover the soil around plants. This is done to reduce chemical inputs, conserve water, raise soil temperatures, act as a buffer against the surprises that can be sprung by the weather and generally improve yields. It fulfils all these aims, with a 30 per cent increase in yield being reported, though barely 5 per cent is claimed for wheat production by one of the suppliers. It is expensive to purchase and to lay, requiring specialist equipment, and expensive to remove after harvest, but evidently it is worth the cost. The land is ploughed and harrowed flat, then kit is brought out to draw up a low ridge and lay the film from rollers, and then coulters are used to cover the exposed edges to keep it in place. Planting occurs later, through a hole pierced through the film.

That they are an eyesore is unquestionable, and they look even worse after strong winds have ripped them away and torn them to shreds, something that can happen occasionally. Whether or not they are or can be environmentally harmful (and one must suspect, at least, that they can be) is a question that has occupied the minds of manufacturers, farmers, researchers and writers of reports.

There are two types of material used for these mulches, polyethylene (polythene) and the more expensive biofilm or biodegradable materials (BDM), which are made from harmless cellulose. Polythene is easily recyclable in general, but in the particular instance of a field it is almost impossible because of soil and organic contaminants, which can account for 40 per cent. Often it is just consigned to landfill, though some is inevitably left behind, where it remains and contaminates the soil. BDMs, by comparison, degrade relatively harmlessly in the soil through consumption by the micro-biota or other means within two or three years.

It seems clear-cut that BDMs are better, if a little more expensive, but research has found that, overall, there is little difference between them if *all* ecological influences are included. One of the more influential of these inclusions was the net release of carbon dioxide, the environmental effect of which was monetised to allow the comparison. Since the environmental cost of CO_2 is completely impossible to calculate (from mildly positive to utterly catastrophic), it feels as though the scales have been weighted against BDMs. I would undoubtedly go with BDMs, and most farmers seem to have gone with common sense and agreed.

The slight, and sometimes not so slight, increases in yield encouraged by 'plastic' mulching are just another of the many improvements made during the extraordinary agricultural revolution of the past sixty years. In the thirteenth century a farmer could expect 650 kg of wheat per hectare, while today it is nearer to 8,000, a twelve-fold increase. In Cobbett's time it was around 1,200 kg per hectare.

Cobbett would have been astonished at the near view from our vantage point on the bridge. The geometric perfection of the plough lines and lack of any sign of a turning plough team at the end of each run would have been something completely beyond his experience. Modern ploughs can be lifted on the turn, whereas horse- or ox-driven ploughs cannot. It is unlikely that he would have been too surprised by the lack of hedges. Hampshire is no Devon or West Dorset, but rather the open country of the open field system. Enclosure would have introduced a few hedges, with most of the area enclosed in the seventeenth century, and with Odiham almost completely enclosed by private agreements by 1779. The earliest map I can find is circa 1900 and shows each of the three fields immediately below my vantage point as being five in number, and I can only assume that they would have been hedged. Not much has changed.

As a farmer, rather than be dismayed by the conspicuous lack of wildlife in those fields, Cobbett would have been mightily impressed by the efficiency of farming on display. He might not even think of the flowers of the fields at all. For him, they and the birds in the hedgerows were a given, like the air he breathed, and he would assume them to be near by still, just not in these well-managed fields. Cobbett was no Gilbert White. Cobbett's interest in the countryside lay in its support of man. Nevertheless, once the damage done to the flora and fauna by technologies beyond his dreams was drawn to his attention, I am sure he would have been as horrified as we are.

I feel I must come clean about my view on farming. When I was first introduced to the excesses of agriculture over forty years ago, I responded with despair. Every ploughed field I passed was like passing a funeral. All around me was loss, and I began to think of the human race as a bane upon the earth. This is something one sees in the young, and sometimes not so young, and I understand how they feel. Nevertheless, the current fad for seeing environmentalism through the foggy lens of a yet-again resurgent millenarianism is unhelpful and, to my mind, slightly embarrassing. Although I still rile at the ploughing of chalk downland that had been replete with herbaceous plants and rare fungi, and farmers who insist on intensively farming every last corner of their land (though such efficiencies of scale may free others to allow nature in), I have come to accept the obvious. We need to eat if we wish to live, and these farming practices are essential for our well-being and that of those for whom it is a livelihood. Human beings have a right to take what they *need*, but excess in production to fill these needs must be avoided wherever possible.

If I ever get upset about something I see, I will either write to complain or express my concerns to anyone prepared to listen, but eventually attempt to put any of the resultant loss, sad to the point of tragic though it may be, into perspective. The Earth has suffered multiple global catastrophes over the billion or so years since life first appeared, and the loss of a meadow, wood or bit of chalk downland is barely worth a mention. I also consider that nothing beyond the splendid variety of life happened before our arrival and that we are the most interesting things ever to appear. This is not hubris, but a mere statement of fact. We make the Earth self-conscious for the first time in its history, a shining light in the vastness of uninteresting, *insensible* space. If this pre-Copernican view fails, which sometimes it does, I look at a photograph of the splendid Sombrero Galaxy and wonder what wonderful things might be happening there.

The Wet Wet Wood at Bartley Common

We made the return to *terra firma* down the helical slope from the bridge to re-enter Bartley Heath. There was little that was heathery about it, just a young and very brambly oak wood. As mentioned, the ground was very wet, and the fact that it was permanently so was indicated by a profusion of the tussock-forming **Pendulous Sedge**, *Carex pendula*.

Nestling at the bottom of an oak were **Creeping Cinque-foil**, *Potentilla reptans*, and **Common Toadflax**, *Linaria vulgaris*, neither of which was in flower and both of which were therefore none too easy to identify. Identifying unfamiliar plants from vegetative characteristics only (i.e., without their flowers, with only stem and leaves to guide us) is a matter of experience. Ordinary floras help to varying degrees, though most will show only the flower in any great detail. There is, however, at least one book that tackles the problem head on, *The Vegetative Key to the British Flora*, by John Poland and Eric Clement, but it is just that, a 'key' (plus some useful photographs of leaves), and requires knowledge of a vocabulary that may be unfamiliar, a considerable amount of effort and bucketloads of time.

The most eye-catching find along the narrow and muddy path alongside the wood was attached to D's coat. Ignoring her pleas of 'Get it off me, get it off me!', I took a photograph. It was an innocent 'inchworm', a creature not known for attacking large vertebrates. Inchworm larvae 'walk' by lifting their front end, then their back end to catch up, forming a perfect Ω. This is such an impressive and efficient form of locomotion that one wonders if larvae that require the difficult manipulation of too many legs wish that they had evolved the same trick. Many species exist with larvae of this form, all (as far as I know) in the Moth Family, Geometridae, the Looper Moths. Although some of these look very much like twigs (another trick they have learned), some are brightly coloured or have other distinguishing features. D's caterpillar displayed none that would enable me to tell it from any of its equally drab cousins.

We had not carried any beer that day on the strict understanding that we would find a pub. We left the wood and, joy of joys, found one called the Derby Inn. I have found many things that have engaged me in pub gardens, and in that of the Derby Inn there was a good-sized oak with multiple burrs running up its trunk. They were not the large burrs that are sometimes seen but shallow specimens, which when cut would display a mix of straight-grain timber decorated irregularly with thousands of shoots. As my former Devon timber supplier would have said, 'Got some nice oak 'ere, John. Tis a bit pippy, mind.'

There was also a bright-purple patch of **Ground Ivy**, *Glechoma hederacea*, the Latin name meaning 'mint that is a bit like ivy'. Indeed it is a species of mint (as suggested by the square section of the stem), but with almost no minty aroma. It is instead bitter and was once used as a primary flavour for ales before hops were used. This provides the plant with its most suitable common name, 'Alehofe'. It first appears in the works of the first-century Greek physician Dioscorides, who referred to a plant useful in treating hip problems as *chamaikissos*, which means 'ivy of the earth'. One of the problems of naming in botany, both with the scientific names (Latin) and common ones, is that many derive from those used by the ancients. Unfortunately, it is often difficult to know precisely which plant they had in mind when they provided a name for it. Many 'translations' of words presumed to name a plant merely give 'a plant', and, if you are lucky, they will make an educated guess of what it might be or at least what sort of plant: for example, 'water plant'. In this case it is generally accepted that Dioscorides was indeed writing about Ground Ivy, as this mint and Ivy share their creeping, spreading nature. This is a bit of a stretch in my opinion, but it may be so. Incidentally, it is one of the many plants that once found its way to the apothecary's shelf, used in lotions and potions to cure or alleviate any number of minor ailments, such as sore eyes, mild tinnitus, indigestion, headaches and 'sores and ulcers in the privy parts'. OK, not all of them are minor.

The River Whitewater

Two or three hundred metres south of the pub we followed a track that led to Newlyns Farm Shop. Just before the shop we stopped for a few minutes on a small bridge over the River Whitewater. Like all rivers in relatively flat terrains, it meanders aimlessly and is linked to innumerable tributary streams, drainage ditches, ponds and, in this case, water meadows. I thought it to be close in appearance to the chalky River Frome I know so well from my forty years in West Dorset. The River Whitewater, however, runs over a bedrock of London Clay. But less than two miles to the south-west it completes a run of a mile and a half over the Seaford Chalk Formation, thus explaining its similarity to the chalk streams I know.

The riverbed was dominated by a Water Crowfoot. The **Chalk-Stream Water Crowfoot**, *Ranunculus penicillatus* was in full flower, with thousands of blossoms to be seen, their centres a bright yellow and their petals pure white. I wondered if they might have given the river its name. Two other substantial plants were visible from the bridge: **Water Mint**, *Mentha aquatica*, and Fool's Watercress. Water Mint is common in damp habitats throughout most of Britain and is easy to find. It makes an excellent herbal tea, if you like such calumnies on the reputation of tea and, with lemon, makes one of the best sorbets you will ever eat. Fool's Watercress is also edible – but I wouldn't bother.

One more plant species was visible from this beautiful and bountiful spot: real Watercress. Not much, certainly, but enough to identify and to indicate that there will probably be more.

This is, of course, edible, being exactly the same as cultivated Watercress. Sadly, unless collected from a place far from, or at least upstream of, cattle and sheep, and/or washed in a chlorine-based salad-sterilising solution, or just cooked, it can be lethal. Reckless picking or preparation can result in the consumption of one of the life stages of the liver fluke, *Fasciola hepatica*, a common species in rivers and streams where grazing animals form a host. The stage of life (liver flukes are overburdened with nine of these) that it spends on a water plant is called the 'metacercaria'. If consumed by a large mammal, it will eventually develop into the adult form, a large, flat, slug-like creature which rolls into a tube shape inside your bile ducts. The organism is a species of Trematode. As you might imagine, the condition can prove fatal.

Following a tastier route, D and I left the Watercress. We don't always get out much, so we thought a quick visit to the super-posh farm shop would be pleasant. It was, and well stocked. I had recently learned from my chef mate, Gelf, about a cheese called Old Winchester. He had given me a taste while we were hosting a dinner together, and I thought it among the best I had ever tried, not too far from a fresh Parmesan I bought in Italy years ago. One does not see it often, but the farm shop had some and was happy to accept the ransom of a not very popular king in exchange for half a pound of the stuff. I fancy I came out of the transaction very well. Leaving the farm shop, we had the main road to cross to make our way westwards. Fortunately, there was a tunnel that took both us and the river to the other side.

The Water Meadows

Before us lay a peaceful scene of permanent and wet pasture, with the River Whitewater wandering through it to our left. In the distance there were trees, behind which the upper reaches of North Warnborough could be seen. Alongside the river was an unusually shaped oak tree. Most tree trunks are wider at the base, but this oak had taken it to an extreme, with a fine example of 'root flare'. Visibly, it was not so much the roots that had flared but part of the trunk, which spread out like the base of a wine glass. I suspect that it was a response to the tree's close proximity to the river in an already wet habitat. Here the roots need to be higher than usual to allow them access to oxygen. This results in shallow and potentially unstable rooting and a requirement for a more than usually substantial base.

The level ground, which rose slightly to the south beyond the river, was likely to have been a water meadow until the beginning of the twentieth century. The markings as seen on the Lidar image are faint but follow the typical herringbone pattern of water meadow banks and ditches; a little further upstream they are unmistakable.

Near the river, swans set the bucolic scene to perfection, and in the drier part to the north were hundreds of thousands of **Creeping Buttercup**, *Ranunculus repens*, a plant typical of poached and damp pasture. It, and the Meadow Buttercup, *R. acris*, are the commonest of our twenty-seven species plus hybrids and varieties of *Ranunculus*. A commonplace question, usually posed during picnics later in summer and early autumn, is 'What it the point of wasps?!' 'Picnic' wasps, however, are useful in many ways, and I would ask instead, 'What is the point of a buttercup?' As witnessed by this patch of pasture, buttercups can claim an entire landscape but, crucially, neither cattle nor sheep welcome them as they are bitter and poisonous. Yes, they are very pretty, especially when they appear in their thousands, and yes, they supply pollen. Pastoral farmers, however, hate them as they reduce the value of pasture (though in hay, their acrid and toxic nature is much depleted).

People's determination that individual species must have a purpose, perhaps benefiting the general habitat and their fellow organisms, or *us*, is an echo of the religious concept of providence and is not necessarily true. Many just *are*.

Cor! Basingstoke Canal!

Across a bridge and up a small incline we arrived at something I had always wanted to see close up: Basingstoke Canal. My grandfather, for whom I provided a pocket biography in the chapter on London, moved to Basingstoke in the early 1920s to become a mental health nurse. He was there for thirty-three and a third years. Some of his upbringing had instilled Catholic values into his soul, and I never heard him swear, beyond 'blimey'. He did, however, have a gentle maid-of-all-works swear word (phrase, in fact) which seems to have been his own invention. When surprised or dismayed, he would say, 'Cor, Basingstoke Canal!' Like his static electricity denial, we were never privy to how he arrived at the notion.

To honour his memory, I exclaimed, 'Basingstoke Canal!' as we walked through the gate. It was no disappointment, with life everywhere, both in and around the slow-moving water. The canal was completed in 1794 and closed in 1932, late enough for my grandfather to have seen it in full operation. Efforts were made to restore this exceptional treasure in the later twentieth century, and it was reopened in 1992, albeit with a few bits missing. The Basingstoke end has mostly been lost to navigation, partly because of the Greywell Tunnel a mile to the west of where we stood. The tunnel was known to be the home of a vast number of bats, many of them packed so tightly into crevices that bat surveyors were reduced to counting the ears and dividing by two. The bats won against those who wished to reopen the tunnel.

For once we just walked, with few stops. We continued past a swing-bridge, eventually to arrive at King John's Castle, also known as Odiham Castle. It is, or was, octagonal in floor plan, but its appearance now is of a wedding cake left out in the rain for a month. It was utterly exquisite still, and looking its best on that bright June day. From what I could see, it was constructed of sand, lime and a billion pieces of flint.

Footpaths

We returned to the bridge and crossed it to begin a zigzag walk through arable and pastoral fields. A few **Willow Brackets**, *Phellinus igniarius*, graced a hedgerow willow.

The first path crossed diagonally through a field of young corn. It was well used and very clearly defined. Such neat and clear paths proved to be common in the area, much more so than in West Dorset, where footpaths are often ploughed over and not reinstated every year as they should be. Rather than battle my way through where I think the path should be, I will follow my own path between rows of crops or simply follow the edge of the field. I wondered why things were different near Odiham. Partly, it is the larger population wishing to use the paths, partly that the more precipitous countryside where I live is less inviting, and partly, I suspect, down to demographics. The dominant ethnicity in the environs of Odiham is Farrow & Ball, and the obstruction or disrepair of footpaths is not tolerated. People power. We had spoken to few people that day, so were (moderately) pleased to be addressed by a woman who appeared to be in charge of some horses. Sitting comfortably in the sunshine next to the footpath, she spoke of the trouble she had suffered during lockdown from an excess of people going for a walk. I commiserated and, perhaps foolishly, explained our quest. She listened with interest but expressed further concern that books about the area might encourage people to visit more often and trouble her horses. She told me of people leaving gates open, dropping litter that her horses might attempt to eat and feeding them sandwiches and crisps. I was interested to hear that even feeding them grass from just out of their reach could dangerously upset her careful rationing and give them some distressing gastric problems. Walking along a footpath is not a challenging accomplishment, so I often wonder how it is that so many people get it wrong. By the way, and if you did not know, the rule with gates is not necessarily to close them, but to leave them as you found them.

We were soon back in civilisation on the outskirts of Odiham, where we found **White Bryony**, *Bryonia dioica*, clambering up a roadside hedge. I am always thrilled to see this plant, the only native British member of the Squash Family (Cucurbitaceae). It should not be confused with Black Bryony, *Dioscorea communis*, also a climber but very distinct in leaf and flower. Both bryonies produce seriously poisonous berries. I was looking at a White Bryony in a hedge a couple of years ago and noticed the structure of the tendrils used to attach the plant to hedgerow trees: long, thin, with a tip that will curl around and cling to anything it touches. However, the thing that gave me a fizz of delight was the helical spring halfway along the tendril's length. This was obviously to allow a little give during windy weather or when the climber and the climbed upon diverged through growth. But they were not just simple springs but a left- and a right-handed spring linked together by 4 mm of straight tendril. This is sophisticated engineering, and I wondered what biochemical wizardry had been used to create it. Quite why it produces so sophisticated a spring took me some thought and even a little experimentation. A single spring, stretched to its full length, will twist the tendril because both ends are fixed. Two, opposing springs, however, if stretched out will leave the tendril untwisted and unstressed. If you have ever wrestled with a poorly coiled hosepipe you will know the type of problem I have in mind.

We were nearly back at our hotel, with just a few more species to entertain us: some **Hollyhock Rust**, *Puccinia malvacearum*, on an untidy collection of Common Mallow by the roadside, a group of Spear-Leaved Orache near the petrol station and a collection of brilliant red galls on Sycamore leaves, probably those of the gall mite *Aceria cephalonea*. Satisfied with our day, we retired to the bar.

DAY TWO

Arable Fields and Hedges

It had occurred to us that we had not walked very far during the eight-hour trek of the previous day, managing only four and a half miles. Farnham was easily twice that distance from Odiham, making it impractical in the single day we had optimistically planned. Aiming for the intermediate village of Crondall was the only option, and relying on a taxi to take us back to the hotel when we arrived. We decided on an early start, and were on our way by eleven.

We headed south out of Odiham and reached a fifty-acre field of young corn. We took the (very well-defined) footpath in an easterly direction. The path backed on to domestic gardens, and I made a cursory list of the plants to be seen in (and likely to be typical of) such circumstances. There were a few, large, standard Beeches and Sycamores, the odd Yew, plus Hawthorn, Blackthorn and Hazel. There were also a few escapees, such as the Snowberry and several 'weed' species, such as Cleavers, Docks, Stinging Nettles, White Deadnettle and the obligatory frothy white of Cow Parsley. Together, they effectively formed a new hedge, one that was not there in 1900, the subsequent houses having encroached into the field.

More interesting to me than this new hedge, and something of an education, was the field itself. One always imagines such modern monocultures to be devoid of all but their titular form of life, but it is not so. We were lucky with the dry, warm and sunny weather, as the object of my fascination would not have been visible on a wet day.

Arable fields have become more complex entities with the new agriculture. Some of the complexity is a matter of efficient farming; some comes from efforts to reduce its impact on wildlife. Occasionally, these come together. More or less permanent and maintained 'conservation headlands' have been set up around many arable fields. These can be grass strips and/ or strips sown with a mixture of grasses and wild flowers, or left unsown to allow any existing cornfield flora to continue or re-establish. The strips may sometimes be sprayed, at least at first, to remove any pernicious weeds. These strips protect the adjacent hedge or wood-edge from any over-close disturbance of the plough, and from insecticides, herbicides and fertiliser. What lives in the strips will provide pollen and nectar and an overwintering ground for invertebrates. A 'sterile strip' is a very

Tryfan

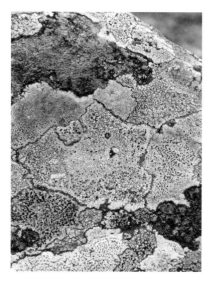

Rhizocarpon geographicum

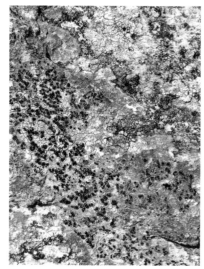

Most likely *Porpidia macrocarpa*

Common Spotted Orchid

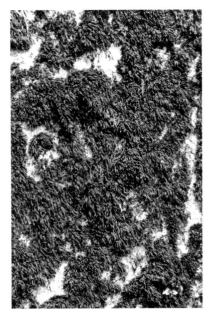

An *Andreaea* species of moss

Polytrichum commune, a moss

Round-Leaved Water Crowfoot

Round-Leaved Sundew

Pellia epiphylla, a Spleenwort

Parsley Fern

Maidenhair Spleenwort

The towering rocks to the south

Hare's-Tail Cotton Grass

Cwm Idwal from the south

Cheviot Hills

The College Valley

Acid grassland of the valley bottom

Purging Flax

Odynerus spinipes

Ewe and lamb

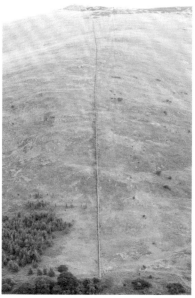

The one-mile wall

'Sheep scrape' and roots

Sheep's Sorrel

Bird's-foot Trefoil

Peltigera lactucifolia

College Burn

The wooded valley and its Gorse

narrow strip of land between the conservation headland and the crops. These prevent weeds spreading from the now verdant field boundary to where they are not wanted. There are also strips which are *effectively* sterile: the multiple tram lines across fields, along which the narrow-wheeled equipment needed for drilling and spraying is repeatedly driven, thus avoiding too much damage to the crops. These tramlines also occur *around* fields, some distance from the field boundary, and are generally wider because of frequent use.

It was in one of the sterile strips that I found a great deal of unexpected activity: that of solitary bees. It was a delight to see that they can colonise so ephemeral a habitat as a ploughed field, but then the sand dunes on Hayling Island can hardly be described as having permanence. I spent twenty minutes watching them going to and fro with pollen for their nests, all of which were situated beneath hundreds of tiny holes in the dry, bare and flattened mud. Solitary bee identification is a taxing pastime, with both males and females to contend with, doubling the number of forms they take to 440. I have a few books on bees, but this would have required me capturing one and killing it to examine under my dissecting microscope. Although I have done such things, this time I did not have the heart. All I can say is that it was a 'mining bee', possibly placing it in the genus *Andrena*. There were also a large number of ants scurrying around these nests, but I could not discover what relationship, if any, they may have had with the bees.

Pastureland and Hedges

We left the field at its north-western corner and entered a much more pastoral countryside: a complex of fields that had been left unploughed for at least twenty years. I could make this calculation because mushroom rings visible in a 2020 aerial photograph could be seen in one taken in 1999. Even twenty years ago these rings were already quite large, and it may be that they have not seen the plough for centuries. There was one field, south of the field whose northern border we walked along, that *had* been cultivated fairly recently, the mushroom rings of twenty years ago now gone with the plough. If you want to know why the field at the end of your road fails to produce mushrooms, this is why. I always tell people it is like expecting apples after someone has cut the tree down.

I can only guess how these fields are used: pasture, certainly, and we saw some sheep in the field to the north of us, but a couple were ungrazed and likely to be meadows from their vegetation, with the grass **Timothy**, *Phleum pratense*, conspicuously present. A meadow is more a matter of usage than a 'thing'. If an area of grass is cut for hay in midsummer and the grass and herbage dried for hay, then it is a meadow. If it is not cut for hay but just grazed, then it is pasture. Even a meadow can (and probably will) be pasture for part of the year when the 'aftermath' is grazed. Nevertheless, it is only long use as a meadow that will favour the many species associated with 'true' meadows.

The term 'permanent pasture' often means what it says. At least some of these fields were poorly drained, and the one that lay immediately south of us had a stream running through that began at the southern end of the field in an area of rush pasture. The stream, barely more than a ditch, drains into the canal a mile to the north. This is permanent pasture because it is too wet for anything else and too much trouble and expense to drain, as, it seems, was another that was dotted with many tussocks.

The first hedge we saw in this area, to our left as we entered, was new, as it is absent from a circa 1900 map. The older hedges contained several very large and truly magnificent oaks, some of which showed signs of ancient pollarding. Agricultural pollarding (quite different from urban pollarding) was a way of keeping a tree useful, under control and out of the reach of grazing animals. The branches of a youngish tree are cut a little way above where they grow from the trunk and at about head height. They will grow into a number of straightish branches that will be periodically cut to provide fuel or timber for construction or tools, then left to grow more.

The process, if done with skill, will maintain a regular supply of timber without needing to cut the tree down. It also prevents it casting too large a shadow, which would otherwise slow the growth of grass or other crops. Considering the repeated assaults wreaked on pollarded trees, they remain remarkably healthy, and will often outlive any unmolested companions. The ancient trees thus created are wonderful places for certain species of lichen and fungi, some of which demand equally ancient habitats. I found one large bracket on one of the old oaks I saw, but it was from last year, blackened beyond my powers of identification.

High up in one of the hedges, and indeed trailing along the ground, was a plant that has a special place in my heart, and one I had been confident of finding that day or the next. It was God's gift, the **Hop**, *Humulus lupulus*. My expectations had been raised because Farnham, now only five miles away, was once famous for its hops. While it is a fairly common plant throughout most of Britain, hops are found most frequently where hops are, or once were, cultivated, with descendants of escaped cultivated varieties producing hops of indeterminate quality. The seventeenth-century antiquary and writer John Aubrey mentions Farnham's hops and hop fields, writing of there being three hundred acres of hopyards in the area. A near-contemporary, Richard Bradley, writes of three types grown, but with more names than helpful details. The names he provides for three varieties are the 'master/good/manured/garden' hop, the 'unkindly/Fryer/male' hop and the 'wild or savage hop'. I presume that the one I found was the savage variety.

Lanes and Hedges

Exiting this venerable area proved to be more difficult than entering. Walking now in a south-easterly direction, we followed the path that would take us to a country road. The path led us close to a house and soon we saw the road, 100 m south along the drive to the house. Unfortunately there was some highly prominent signage to the effect that this was absolutely not, not one little bit, a public right of way. The right of way, it indicated, sent us to the left, into a wood. We duly entered the wood. It was densely overgrown, extremely muddy and virtually impenetrable. Twenty minutes later we staggered onto the road, ten yards from the entrance to the aforementioned drive.

Now on the road, we had to decide whether we needed to turn right or left. Sunny morn had given way to overcast afternoon, my compass of choice hidden behind a blanket of cloud, and we were still recovering from our pointless and difficult diversion. I had also left my actual compass behind, and the one on my mobile phone I considered to be overly imaginative and playful. I did not know which way to go and, after some difficult discussion with D, went with my instinct. In her notes for the day, she records it thus: 'At road turned right by mistake. Walked along a while then turned back (should have turned left).' I am sure you can fill in the implicit expletives, punctuation marks and appellations. Once the mistake had become clear half a mile later, words were spoken for a brief period, then no words were spoken for thirty minutes.

Our period of quiet contemplation took us in an east-south-easterly direction along a narrow country road. It was hedged irregularly, sometimes bordered by a wood and sometimes with nothing but a ditch and a wire fence. As so often happens with wire fences, brambles will claim them and become the nursery for a successional hedge, complete with standard trees if left long enough. This was still a highly pastoral countryside, with permanent pasture and cattle all around. The ancient habitats of the roadside provided a wealth of species to distract me from the canine residence I was still occupying.

Our second St George's Mushroom of the trip was found in a roadside patch of grass and surrounded by **Barren Strawberries**, *Potentilla sterilis*. This is a plant that bears its discouraging nature in both names. It looks like a strawberry plant, but never comes up with the goods. To prevent subsequent disappointment in a plant you spotted out of the strawberry season, just look at the leaves. Both Wild Strawberry and Barren Strawberry have leaves with serrated edges. The difference is that the single serration at the tip of a Wild Strawberry leaf projects past its neighbours, while that of the Barren Strawberry does not. This, of course, is a shamelessly anthropocentric take on an innocent plant, as it is fairly uncommon and an indicator of a varied habitat.

Along the wooded stretches, venerable plants such as Yellow Archangel and the familiar understory plant **Dog's Mercury**, *Mercurialis perennis*, could be seen. The latter plant is moderately poisonous and has been eaten by mistake by some in the past, though what they could possibly have mistaken it for remains a mystery. The ubiquitous Wood Avens was present too. It is not really edible, but if you uproot one and scratch the part where stem meets the root, you can smell cloves.

Arable Fields and Conservation

After three-quarters of a mile we came to a footpath through the middle of a seventy-acre field of corn. This was a large field, matched by most of the cornfields in the area. Hedgerows may be lost in the pursuit of the efficiency that comes with size but, as it happens, not in this case. The field is the same as it was in the circa 1900 map, as are most of its neighbouring fields; indeed, some were larger over a hundred years ago. Also, the adjoining eighteen-acre field of 1900 is now a patch of woodland. The presumption of lost hedges is a mirage here, and what may well have been a relatively barren arable field in 1900 is now a wood.

Similar observations can be made for most of the nearby fields, so we should not be appalled by at least some modern field sizes. I remind you that this was once 'champion' country, countryside of the old open-field system where enormous fields were the rule. In Devon, for example and by contrast, small fields have always been the norm because it was 'wooded countryside' barely touched by the open field system.*

Hedges both ancient and immediately post-enclosure would have been substantial constructions because they were needed to contain stock, most likely in rotation, so all fields would need to be stockproof. With the arrival of artificial fertilisers, rotation was no longer an essential practice and arable fields no

---

* The exception is the extant Braunton Great Fields, a few miles to the west of Barnstaple.

longer required stockproof hedges, so they were either removed or suffered various forms of neglect. Hedgerows can never be so vibrant with life when repeatedly flailed and stranded in a desert of intense arable. They are, above all, edge habitats, where interactions exist between the hedge and its surroundings. The life cycle of an insect, for example, may involve both field and woody hedge, and birds may perch and nest in hedges while feeding in the fields. In an intensively arable landscape that lacks such things as conservation headlands and other helpful interventions, hedges are surrounded by a lifeless nothing.

Modern agricultural technology has removed the many species of plant that easily survived the plough before the invention of herbicides. Until very recently poppies could be seen as bloody splashes in most cornfields, only to disappear with improvements in spraying technology. Many of our cornfield flowers bear their habitual home in their names: Cornflower, Corn Marigold, Corn Spurrey and Corncockle, with the last of these regarded as extinct in the wild in Britain. Incidentally, all of the traditional 'weeds' of cornfields are annuals that can grow and set seed before the crop is taken.

In William Cobbett's day such concerns did not exist. The countryside was in no way natural, but the 'inefficiencies' of the time allowed space in and around fields for plants, invertebrates, birds and mammals. My Wiltshire-born grandmother told me of harvest time, when the field was cropped around and around, leaving a rabbit-rich circle of corn in the middle, the escaping rabbits duly dispatched with dog and gun or caught with 'long nets'. Cornfields, therefore, were also good habitats for mammals – well, they were up to the point when their beneficiaries became pie-filling.

Until the agricultural revolutions of the mid-twentieth century, farmers and landowners, having inadvertently produced an infinitely varied and appealing countryside, considered themselves to be its unquestioned custodians. Most people would have agreed. But farming is hard, and any innovation that improved production made it a little easier and the rewards more worthwhile. Frequently, these innovations meant freedom from poverty. It was with the wartime of the 1940s and the post-war drive for food production, accompanied by cheap fertilisers and relatively cheap access to equipment that could quickly uproot hedges, fill in ponds and bulldoze scrub, that things went wrong.

Much was lost during the war and in the post-war years, much of it paid for by UK governments that understandably put food security first. As the excesses became progressively more obvious, however, the idea of farmers possessing 'inherent stewardship' of the countryside became seriously questioned, though this seems a little unfair considering that farmers were once forced by law to plough meadows and remove hedges. Public concerns reached a height during the absurd subsidies given to farmers via one of the more egregious of the excesses of the (now) European Union's Common Agricultural Policy (CAP). This continued in its most virulent form from the UK's accession in 1973 until the late 1980s. Famously (at least for those around at the time) the policy gave rise to butter, beef and grain mountains, the mountainous landscape complemented nicely by wine and milk lakes.

This appalling excess was due to paying farmers for as much as they could produce, not what they could sell on the open market. Not that the EU was ever an open market in the global sense; it was a protectionist trading bloc. With such largesse on offer, it took a strongly principled farmer or manager to refuse it. Many fields that had been left undisturbed and species-rich for centuries went under the plough, and many hedges that were inconveniently positioned or simply took up potentially productive land were grubbed up. It almost goes without saying that the larger farms gained disproportionately more than those that were smaller, nearly 80 per cent of the subsidies going to 20 per cent of the farmers. William Cobbett, champion of the yeoman farmer and his labourers, and outspoken critic of those who invested money in farms they had never seen, and certainly not worked on (those hated stock-jobbers and financiers), would have been appalled, but hardly surprised.

Unforeseen consequences are waiting in the wings to scupper all but the best-laid plans, but there was little that was unforeseeable in the mountain and lake debacle. In case you think such excess is a thing safely in the past, it has not entirely disappeared, with a 2018 report of a 380,000 tonnes of surplus skimmed milk powder being stored in the EU.

Most farmers are now well aware of the conservation issues they face, and considerable efforts have been made by them, conservationists, charities, government bodies and government departments to increase biodiversity of farmed landscapes. A confusion of incentives, disincentives and suggestions have been applied over the last fifty years or so, not all of them helpful, with 'unforeseeable' consequences repeatedly rearing their less than beautiful heads.

One recent problem was that of farmers cutting down healthy, species-rich trees which masked the aerial view of pastoral fields for which they were receiving conservation subsidies based on the area of grassland visible from above. Another is the EU's 'fifty-tree rule', where fifty trees in a hectare are too many for farm subsidies and too few for forest subsidies. My all-time favourite of these came with the rules governing the earlier declarations of an SSSI. Before one of its 1985 amendments, the 1981 Wildlife and Countryside Act, under its government body the Nature Conservancy Council, could notify a farmer (or anyone else) of a proposal they had made to declare an area of land an SSSI. The proposal ran for three months, during which time the area of land was left unprotected, with no penalty for any damage. Many less scrupulous farmers would then proceed to do as they would with it, removing any chance (or point) of it being declared and protected.

Some policies to either reduce agricultural production or increase biodiversity were expensive but lacking in ambition. The EU's 'set-aside' policy, which ran from 1988 to 2008, encouraged farmers to leave certain fields fallow, or leave parts of arable fields uncultivated. This certainly took land out of production and perhaps provided pollen for foraging insects, but only ruderal species of plant grew there, only to be ploughed up again within two or three years. If any of these barren plots or strips had been left unploughed and managed with a yearly cut or some other thoughtful intervention, they might now be full of species of much greater value. It is an egregious lack of foresight here that annoys: nature takes its time in re-establishing itself, with some ecosystems requiring centuries to achieve their high degrees of complexity and interest.

With Britain, for good or ill, now free of the CAP, the British government has spoken of a new concept for agriculture, that of 'public money for public good'. Whether or not this will actually be enacted, or will fare better than previous schemes if it is, I have no idea, though at the time of writing the prospects are not encouraging. Nevertheless, I am cautiously optimistic, in that it takes as its principle an embracing stewardship of the countryside, with agricultural production more or less integrated with conservation. More than this, both public and landowner are increasingly aware that nature conservation is an essential and not a luxury. The sudden appearance of people with the capital and desire to own or invest in rewilding projects has been an encouraging surprise, especially as they frequently occur in what is the last place people might be expected to establish such projects – the expensive, fertile lowlands of southern England.

Encouragingly, the field I stood in that day had a 3-m-wide strip of grass with a few common plants, plus a 30-cm sterile strip, separating it from the crop. In a field we saw soon after, a much wider conservation strip could be seen, with several wild flowers on display, surrounding a field of oilseed rape.

Back in that particular arable field in Hampshire, my thoughts turned not to matters of loss but to the rolling, sweeping grandeur of the arable countryside. I felt uncomfortable with such sentiments and wondered why I felt so in awe. Like so many things, it may have been an early memory, in this case walks beside fields of corn with my father when I was a child in Hook.

Crondall

We walked alongside hedges, over ditches and across more arable fields for over a mile. There were still weeds of cultivation to be seen: the occasional Ox-Eye Daisy, Cranesbills, Shepherd's Purse, *Matricaria* species (chamomiles), Field Forget-Me-Nots and a striking pink mustard plant challenging the planted rape. Skylarks were singing above the corn and rape, and I wondered yet again where they find the energy.

Eventually we made our way into the pretty village of Crondall. Although it is close to Cobbett's birthplace in Farnham, he only mentions the village in passing two or three times, with his only relevant comment being that the hops grown there were of poor quality. In fact, we found some more hops near the large playing field by which we entered the village, though I cannot vouch for their quality. After a very great deal of asking people and making a serious nuisance of ourselves in the village shop, we managed to find a taxi prepared to take us back to Odiham.

DAY THREE

Beans, Aphids and Bumblebees

We drove to Farnham after paying the bill at the Bel and the Dragon and saying goodbye to our new best friend, the manager, Andrew. A taxi dropped us back in Crondall, just where we had left off, opposite a small house that would make the romantically inclined weep with affection. It was of brick, oak and tile, and had seemingly accreted over several centuries with never a plan, and settled to the point where not a single component was orthogonally oriented.

Exiting Crondall south-south-easterly, we passed the familiar plants that are seen in such semi-rural locations. Whereas the previous day had brought a discovery of Barren Strawberries, this day we found **Wild Strawberries**, *Fragaria vesca*. They were in flower but not yet in welcome fruit, and accompanied by a few Bluebells and Primroses clinging to the last of a cool spring. Nothing looked inviting, as May had turned aside its merry face and presented one of greyness and tears. Having employed too much optimism in our interpretation of the weather forecast and not wishing to burden ourselves with suitable clothing 'just in case', we became progressively wetter for the first three miserable hours.

The landscape had none of the romance of the day before, with a field of beans being our first arable encounter. These were broad beans, or, more likely, fava beans. They are both *Vicia faba*, simply different varieties. While broad beans will be harvested fresh, the smaller fava beans are allowed to mature completely while still attached to the plants, the whole plant harvested by a specialist combine harvester.

As you will know if you have ever grown broad beans, they are, like all the vetches, good nectar sources for bumble and honeybees. Only the Long-Tongued Bumblebee, *Bombus hortorum*, can reach the nectaries from the front of the flower, employing its 15- to 20-mm-long 'tongue'. But bumblebees with short tongues will gain access by biting holes at the base of the flower. This sneaky fix has earned them the title of 'primary nectar robbers', while other species using a hole made by the bee are known as 'secondary nectar robbers'. Unfortunately, the poor weather ensured that these squadrons of Apoidea were grounded.

Less attractive than the various species of bee is the Black Bean Aphid, *Aphis fabae*. These were no trouble to the beans in the field we saw that day, the well-spaced plants having avoided the close conditions that embolden them – or maybe they had been sprayed. My limited experience of growing beans suggests that pinching out the affected tops is enough, if messy. The other 'technique', suggested by many, is to encourage ladybirds. Quite what might encourage them more than a hundred thousand aphids waiting to be eaten, I cannot say, but ladybirds do not necessarily have an easy time with this seemingly vulnerable aphid. I have been unable to find any research specific to the quartet of *Vicia faba*, *Aphis fabae*, a ladybird and a bacterium, but there is research with parallel species suggesting that *A. fabae* may have a plan. The bacterium, *Hamiltonella defensa*, is harmlessly, indeed beneficially, endemic (the technical term for an organism with this mode of living is 'facultative symbiont') in the ubiquitous Pea Aphid, *Acyrthosiphon pisum*. The North

American ladybird, *Hippodamia convergens*, is a predator of the aphid, but will obviously consume the bacterium with its prey. The bacterium, once inside the ladybird, significantly reduces the latter's reproductive success. This sounds more like revenge than defence, but aphids are almost invariably clones, so the effect is to protect a genome, rather than an individual.

In a more direct approach, one that *is* observed in *Aphis fabae* on *Vicia faba*, the aphid delegates its defence to the jealous ants that feed on the honeydew the aphids produce. More direct still, but effective, is for a threatened aphid to simply drop off the plant to which it is attached. It is a little risky in that it must then climb to the top of another bean plant, but far less so than being inside a ladybird.

While on the subject of aphid defence strategies it is worth revisiting the Sycamore Aphid we found outside the Hotel Lily in London. Unlike most aphids, it has functional wings and long antennae. They space themselves carefully, about two antennae-lengths apart. If an aphid is troubled by a ladybird, it will twitch its antennae against those of nearby aphids to signal that something is amiss. The signal is quickly passed to fellow aphids on the leaf, who then fly to safety.

A Rolling Countryside, and Not Getting Lost

We followed the footpath diagonally across a fallow field, in what was now rolling countryside, to the far corner. 'Fallow', does not entirely describe this field; 'an interesting mess' would be more appropriate. Messiness is generally 'a good thing' with plants, and there were many to be seen between the patches of bare earth. The dominant plants were **Cut-Leaved Cranesbill**, *Geranium dissectum*, a stitchwort, **Wood Spurge**, *Euphorbia amyg-*

daloides, and Forget-Me-Not, plus some Common Sorrel and various twisted and discoloured thistles that looked as though they had been sprayed with herbicide four days previously.

We continued due east between heavily wooded hedges and then alongside a plantation of oaks. Our path then zigzagged south-easterly across open arable land, Farnham visible in the distance, before entering the southern end of a fifty-five-acre wood. It was largely hazel coppice, with many standard oaks and Beeches. The path descended steeply and muddily. Some kind soul had provided the rudiments of steps, so there were no slips. I wished it had been later in the year, as it looked like promising autumnal mushroom-hunting territory.

Being so cold and wet, we paid little attention to the landscape and its natural treasures, the day having become gruelling rather than a pleasure. Three things did brighten the grey of the last hour or so: some tunnelling in the form of tiny, linear spoil heaps on the bare ground of the cornfield (possibly ants), the lovely woodland and hedgerow plant, **Bugle**, *Ajuga reptans*, and a **Dryad's Saddle**, *Polyporus squamosus*, in the coppice. The Dryad's Saddle was attached, as ever, to an old Ash tree. It is one of the commonest of our fungi, often appearing relatively early in the year. I must receive a dozen photographs of this species every year, accompanied by a request for its name and always with the question, 'Can I eat it?' in there somewhere. Yes, you can, if you pick it in its infancy and enjoy an overpowering flavour of raw pastry.

We exited the wood across an embarrassingly patchy field of corn and found ourselves on a country road. We did not know which way to turn. I have never liked carrying maps with me, especially on wet days, as wherever you go your path will inevitably and unhelpfully cross the four-way fold. I much prefer online maps and bring a battery charger to keep them permanently active on my phone while walking. Unfortunately, my map app chose that moment to update itself and then demanded the re-entry of my password. This was not going to happen, so we had to guess which way to go. After the embarrassments of the previous day, I left the choice to D, who (slightly to my disappointment) guessed correctly. We went left.

Our south-easterly zigzag continued across fields and through more woods. The woodland path was narrow, straight and downhill. I am always pleased to be able to introduce common, easily identified species of plant and fungi to people on my walks as it gives them the chance to show off to their friends. I found one of these along the narrow path, growing on a dead Elder. It was **Elder Whitewash**, *Hyphodontia sambuci*, one of the very many fungi that form nothing more than a white powder on a dead branch but the only one to appear on dead Elder. This is simple enough to remember, and easier still if you recall the Latin name of the tree, *Sambucus nigra*.

The William Cobbett

Farnham, or at least the new-build outskirts of the town, was before us, at the bottom of the grassy hill below the woods. We made our way to our destination, The William Cobbett. Given that it was Cobbett's home turf that we had intended to explore, this was an obvious destination. However, it was so named not simply because of his Farnham origin, but because it is in this building he was born. Here he spent his early formative years, learning the arts of farming from his farmer-cum-landlord father. I had seen it before from the outside and had dark thoughts about what it might be like inside. Probably, I thought, a pub that had been repeatedly 'improved' over the years and was now a sterile mess of red plastic upholstery, sticky, brown-varnished furniture and full of out-of-town and elderly visitors like us.

But it was not so, and I could not have been better pleased. It was indeed a mess, but one of magnificent chaos. Everything was colourful, but with no colour gaining dominance over the thousand that jostled for attention. Every inch of the walls was covered in posters, brasses, boots, souvenirs from Benidorm, bottles, vintage fag packets, photos and trophies of pool championships and postcards of ladies' bottoms (also from Benidorm). The charming bar staff were also a riot of colour, and barely visible against the equally riotous background. In a reminder of the times, there was a printed portrait of William Cobbett that showed the great man wearing a face mask.

We fell, exhausted but content (and by then mostly dry), into some partially collapsed armchairs beside a small coal fire. I had a pint or two of the local IPA, and there was a not so hearty fruit juice for my driver. D and I spoke about Cobbett and what he might have thought about his countryside now compared with what it had been in his time. Our consensus was that the modern world would have been incomprehensible to anyone from that time, that he would have considered the undoubted loss of wildlife sad but no more than that and that he would nevertheless have approved of modern farming methods and be astounded that the serious poverty he knew among the rural poor was very much a thing of the past. People, more than countryside, was where his heart lay.

I chatted to the bar staff for a while, hearing about the female ghost that made a nuisance of herself in one of the gaming rooms. When we left, we discovered conclusive proof, as though such were needed, that we were in the perfect pub: they had security staff. Cobbett would have been proud.

Tryfan

MOUNTAINSIDE AND WET UPLANDS

THREE AND A HALF MILES

14 JUNE 2021

Snowdonia

My first job beyond grocery delivery boy was as an extremely junior scientific officer at the Royal Aircraft Establishment in Farnborough, Hampshire. All of us junior SOs and apprentices lived in the YMCA hostel situated to the south of the runways. A notice was pinned to the board offering a guided trip to Snowdonia, including a bit of climbing. My friend Martin and I put our names down and, as it turned out, were the only ones to do so. I was eighteen, he was seventeen and the year was 1969.

We packed and dressed as best we could from the instructions provided; with genuine waterproofs and fleeces a decade or so in the future, it was barely sufficient. A pleasant man in the familiar mould of scoutmaster, who was to be our guide, picked us up outside the hostel. With him was another lad who was joining us, called Andy. We arrived in Snowdonia late at night and stayed in a godforsaken and freezing-cold stone cottage, perched on the side of a mountain. The next day was to be a gentle stroll up Snowdon. I had been hoping for something a little more exciting than the three miles of sloping rough ground over which we walked as it was very boring. Unfortunately, my desire for excitement was soon granted as the terrain became steeper and steeper.

There is one thing I have not yet mentioned about this trip – it took place in mid-December. Soon, the refrozen snow was two feet or more thick, and we were roped together and shown how to use an ice axe should one of us suddenly shoot down the mountainside. Within an hour Andy, in front of me and behind the leader, did indeed shoot down the 45-degree slope. We all dug in our ice axes and leaned into the thick snow, as instructed. He dangled a little before we pulled him back up again. We were terribly pleased with ourselves, felt a little safer after that and duly made it to the top.

The next day it was Tryfan, which contrived to be even more terrifying. The path followed a vague spiral around and up to the top. The day was freezing cold, with a bitter wind, and while there was little snow (it had blown away), the narrow, sloping rock path was covered instead by ice. I was utterly certain that I was going to slip and fall, never to be found, but by a miracle we all survived intact with just a few scratches, almost all of which were earned while taking the quick way home down the scree slope. Thinking back to the whole adventure, it seems unbelievably risky and would never be allowed today without, appropriately enough, a mountain of paperwork, and probably not even then.

I had always planned to visit the three UK countries that are within Britain and, inspired by my original trip, it seemed like a good idea to visit Wales as an opportunity to explore upland ecologies. Since we had managed Tryfan on a particularly cold December day, Martin and I thought we would manage it easily enough in June. Yes, we were a little older by half a century, but we were fit and healthy. However, this proved too optimistic, and Martin regretfully dropped out and D volunteered to take his place. She and I had stayed in Snowdonia for our honeymoon (also in a snowy mid-December), and she recalls the small amount of climbing we did with horror. It was a foggy day, so little could be seen until we reached a ridge where the mist suddenly cleared and what looked like a 25,000-ft drop came into view. She closed her eyes and refused to open them again until I had led her by both hands back to level ground. Knowing what the mountains were like, she said that there was no way she would climb to the top of anything higher than a small stepladder and a reasonably safe and gentle walk would have to do, hence our total climb being a paltry 120 metres, with Tryfan still towering above us.

The Trouble with Lichens

We parked in a roadside car park 300 m above sea level, with Tryfan to the east-south-east. The first thing to strike me was that I was out of my depth, or more accurately out of my height, because what surrounded me, even in the car park, was an upland flora. Such a flora was almost completely new to me: daunting, yes, but that is the excitement we all enjoy when we explore. I knew I would need to take some very clear photographs of any 'difficult' species for identification later, many of these photographs destined for the attention of my highly knowledgeable friend Bryan. I did, however, manage to identify over half of the plants we saw on the day, which was not too bad. The second consideration was how very many lichens there were, growing on the rocks that were all around and untroubled by the contaminated air of civilisation beyond that contributed by passing traffic. Away from the road, they were troubled not at all.

The big plan was to walk the half-mile to the National Trust Ogwen Cottage Ranger Base, then follow the well-marked Cwm Idwal walk. As such, it is the only walk in this book that follows a complete and designated path. The marked walk is a mere two and a half miles and consists of a thousand-yard walk from the National Trust Base to the lake, a mile-and-a-half walk around the lake and the thousand yards back again. Adding in the walk to and from the roadside car park and a half-hour private excursion (not a euphemism) of mine up a steep path on which D flatly refused to join me, it amounted to three and a half miles. It took us seven hours to complete what a determined walker could manage in one and a bit.

A walk always begins for me the moment I step out the door, be it front door or car door, and so it was that day. The first organism I found alongside the road was a lichen. Its stylish colour palette was similar to that of a wasp: lemon yellow tessellations with black dots in their centres. Encouragingly, not to say, miraculously, it was one I already knew, **Rhizocarpon geographicum**. I am (just about) happy to tell you that it is sometimes known as the Map Lichen, because its colonies arrange themselves in a map-like pattern. It is common (hence my knowing it) and is to be found on hard, siliceous rocks. On the next rock I found the large, vaguely circular plate of **Pertusaria corallina**, a greyish, though often pure white, crustose lichen covered with minute projecting structures known as isidia. Isidia are vegetative propagules that can detach to established new colonies. All of the lichens I looked at closely that day were growing on rocks, and it is these that are the most difficult to identify. They often require the application of various chemicals which will (or won't) induce a colour change in the lichen. Sadly, even with some good photographs to help, many more from that day remain unnamed.

There are two terms among the painfully substantial number used in the study of lichens that could be easily confused. They are 'lichenised fungi' and 'lichenicolous fungi'. The first is simply a more formal term for 'lichen' as we would normally understand it: that is, a fungus that constitutes the structural body of the lichen and forms a symbiotic relationship with a 'photobiont' that supplies food for itself and the fungus. The photobiont will be either an alga or (more rarely) a cyanobacterium. Lichenicolous fungi, however, are lichens that parasitise other lichens (or lichenised fungi, if you now prefer). Lichenicolous fungi possess no photobiont, preferring to take a free ride on a lichen that does – they are straightforward parasites. In fact, they do not parasitise the fungal component of lichen; they just 'steal' the products of photosynthesis from the photobiont of the other lichen. Despite this difference, both are considered to be lichens because they both rely on photobionts. In the case of *R. geographicum* the parasite (lichenicolous fungus) we saw that day was *Lecidea insularis*.

Plants along the Roadside

My fourth success of the day was less impressive, an attractive group of the **Maidenhair Spleenwort**, *Asplenium trichomanes*, growing in the crevices of the wall above the roadside pavement. Spleenworts are ferns in the Family Aspleniaceae, which includes about seven hundred species worldwide, all in the single genus *Asplenium*. This is an enormous number of species for one genus, especially as they are spread all over the world, from the tropics to northern temperate zones, and with a variety of lifestyles – terrestrial or epiphytic and from the forest floor or riverbank to mountainous ravines. There is one on my flint-and-brick garden wall. The various species within *Asplenium* also take on a dizzying variety of physical forms, from the one shown in the photograph here to several with very round fronds and some with 'classic' fern shapes, such as that of the Male Fern, and some with fronds that look like fennel.

Frequent attempts have been made to split it into at least three informal subgroups. Unfortunately, that seemingly final arbiter, DNA analysis, had proved until recently of little use in confirming any particular relationships that might make a family tree possible. A more recent study by Ke-Wang Xu et al. has, however, clarified matters, if only for those that are found in Australasia. The paper places the many species of *Asplenium* into groups (clades), based on DNA sequences from six plastid markers (plastids in this case being the chlorophyll-containing structures inside plant cells). There were around a dozen of these, which suggests that the genus *Asplenium* could be divided into around a dozen named genera. Whether or not this will happen, I do not know. Biology is messy.

Our only gall of the day was busy making a considerable mess of a **Rowan**, *Sorbus acuparia*. The leaves were densely covered in cream spots created for the gall mite, **Eriophyes sorbi**, its name (as is often the case) reflecting that of the tree. Filling most of the gaps between the profusion of lichen-covered rocks, **Western Gorse**, *Ulex gallii*, and Bell Heather could be seen; the gorse now turning to seed. There were a few more common plants behind the wall alongside the path: Common Sorrel, Herb Robert, Cuckoo Flower, a ragwort, Holly and Ash. Then there was a poppy. It was the bright yellow **Welsh Poppy**, *Papaver cambricum*. It would have been gratifying to think that the specimen I found had ancestors going back to Snowdonia's prehistory that had never left, and very likely it did, but the Welsh Poppy, pretty and easy to grow, has been adopted in a million gardens and escaped back to the wild beyond these mountains. While it is called the Welsh Poppy, it is a common species of uplands in Western Europe.

The Conservation of Snowdonia

The start of the 'official' walk comes with its own wrought-iron entrance gate, situated between two thin rock pillars that mark the gap through a drystone wall. It depicts some of the geomorphology seen on the walk, though I could not make head or tail of it on the day. Still, it is a magnificent piece of craftsmanship. The 'mountain gate', as it is sometimes called, was made as a tribute to the life of Evan Roberts, a man whose life spanned most of the twentieth century. He was a naturalist from the area, who, as well as working in the nearby quarry, spent his life recording the rare plants that can be found there.

Without the benefit of any education beyond the local school, he was a self-made botanist, learning to identify plants with almost no reference material. A couple of visiting botanists of (then) greater repute were kind enough to send him the three-volume set of Bentham and Hooker's *Handbook of the British Flora*. He was to discover the locations of plants that had not been seen for decades and sought to protect them.

Protection has certainly been a necessity, as the area has long been overgrazed. It was designated as a nature reserve in 1958, and during the 1960s and '70s experimental plots were fenced off to see what happened when grazing was removed. The much-maligned practice of grazing is of great benefit in rich soils, allowing delicate and generally shorter plants their chance to grow. In poor soils of such places as the Cwm Idwal area, however, delicate plants already do well and sheep will eat almost everything, not hesitating to consume the last living specimen of a particular plant species. Even more robust species such as heathers, Rowan and Holly had suffered. Freed from the organic lawnmower that is the sheep, plants that had not been seen for years returned and the natural balance of the right plant in the right place developed rapidly.

Encouraged by the results of the experiments, grazing was banned completely in 1998, and the landscape transformed into a riot of plant life. It is now a National Nature Reserve, an SSSI and a RAMSAR site, the last deriving from a meeting in Ramsar in Iran, where an international convention was signed to protect wetlands. Only one problem remains: feral goats, which are prepared to eat more than sheep, are famously accomplished mountain climbers and almost impossible to eradicate by any method that does not involve a helicopter gunship.

The Path to the Lake

It seemed unlikely that we would find any of the great rarities discovered by Evan Roberts, but we continued in hope. I thought I had one almost immediately, but disappointment set in when I discovered what it was from the little flora I kept in my bag for emergencies. It was **Round-Leaved Water Crowfoot**, *Ranunculus omiophyllus*, and I had never seen one before. The five white and well-separated narrow petals told me it was likely to be a Crowfoot, and the lobed leaves told me which one. It is very fussy about where it lives, with a strong preference for rocky, upland, western regions, but also the lowland heaths of Dorset, New Forest, Surrey and the Sussex Weald. Most counties boast not a single specimen.

An insistence on finding rare birds, plants, fungi and so on is overrated, in my opinion. This is especially so with groups such as the Eyebrights and Sea Lavenders. Slight and ambiguous differences, usually associated with mere regional variety, are accepted as sufficient to differentiate a species or at least a subspecies or variety. My principle of being pleased with whatever I find was immediately rewarded with an exquisite display of **Common Spotted Orchids**, *Dactylorhiza fuchsia*, a plant known from every county. Here it was in grass on the thin peaty soil, with rocks all around. It was close to the path, but not a single plant had suffered at the foot of a careless walker.

The path went south and then around to the west. A booted, bobble-hatted and charming lady of a certain age noticed my prone body in the mud and, for once not assuming a fall or intoxication, asked what I was photographing. I mumbled something about rushes and then proceeded to relate the entire story of our project to publish the tale of our eight biological walks. She listened with patience, while looking at her watch as discreetly as she could. When I graciously allowed her to speak, she told me she was trying to catch up with the nature warden, who had received reports of a rare plant being found at Devil's Kitchen, a place we were later to see on the far side of the lake. She rushed off and we followed, but I became distracted by my next find and lost sight of her. Eventually we reached the lake and could see the warden disappearing into the distance and beyond all reach. Having lost hope of ever finding out which of the several rare species he (and she) was hoping to see, we stopped for lunch.

We sat in the grassy area at the northern end of the lake, about fifty metres from the very distinct beach. Lakes are forbidding places, and I have never understood why people swim in them. They are always just above freezing point all year round, whether in Devon or the Shetland Isles, and host any number of evil creatures determined to drag you under. I viewed the lake as eight hundred by three hundred metres of death. There is a legend of the ancient prince of Wales, Owain, prince of Gwynedd, being murdered by drowning in this lake, and it is said that birds now refuse to fly over it. Which brings me to the bird.

I hadn't noticed many birds that day, not that I ever do, but the medium-size bird flying around us as we ate our lunch flitted here and there (avoiding the lake, obviously), and every now and then landed on a rock just a little too far away to get a decent photograph. I took a couple of shots anyway with my 100 mm lens and studied the slightly blurry images back at the hotel later. Not being much use as a spotter of birds, I gave up and I had to ask Bryan when we got home. It was a **Wheatear**, *Oenanthe oenanthe*, a species I should have recognised because I have written about it before, admiring its euphonious and tautological Latin name. It is uncommon in Britain now, but another Dorset friend told me that it was once trapped on Portland in 'wall traps', taking advantage of its habit of nesting in holes in walls and cliffs. One year, over 7,000 were captured. The Portland name for them is Cobblers.

Two beers, a sandwich and one and a half packets of chocolate orange biscuits later, we proceeded anticlockwise around the lake, the rocky, grassy, heathery and precipitous slope to our right.

The Sundew

There is one plant that I know so well, and have known for so long, that on arrival almost anywhere I can tell whether or not it will be there. My decades of experience with fungi can similarly allow me to guess what mushrooms might be found in any particular place – there are some habitats that look exactly *right*. So it was that day with a group of **Sundew**, *Drosera rotundifolia*. I first found it in the 1960s while out with my friend Peter Marsden and his slightly eccentric father, who had suggested the trip. In proper Lara Croft mode, we had set off to raid tombs near Petersfield in Hampshire, armed with a small trowel and a toothbrush each. In fact, they were barrows we were to raid. Even at fourteen I could see potential problems with this venture, such as 'Are we allowed to?', 'Surely this is a job for a team of professional archaeologists?' and 'If there had ever been anything to be found it would have disappeared years ago.' But we went anyway – and found nothing. What *was* there was the Sundew. I was entranced by its strange appearance, particularly the blood-red sticky hairs that covered the leaves. I dug one up (at least I wasn't tomb raiding) and took it home. Mr Marsden, a schoolteacher, told me of its habit of catching flies in its sticky and syrup-topped hairs, the leaf subsequently curling around the trapped fly and digesting it. The point of this unusual behaviour (how wonderful that plants can have 'behaviour') is to obtain mineral nutrients that were missing in the poor, wet soil. Naturally, I put my specimen in a pot and fed it flies. It was dead within six weeks, possibly from indigestion.

Drosera rotundifolia is the commonest of three British species, the others being *D. anglica* and *D. intermedia*. There are also two hybrids, *D.* x *obovata* and *D.* x *eloisiana*, which are crosses of *D. rotundifolia* with the other two non-hybrid species respectively. About thirty-five years ago D and I were taken by our old mycologist friend John Keylock to an exceptionally boggy area in the very boggy New Forest. Here he showed us all five growing together.

There were occasional tiny ponds in the wet area that supported the Sundews, and it was in one of these that I saw one of our water plants. It was a **Water Starwort**, named, I presume, after its star-like rosette of leaves which break the surface. Its Latin name is often rendered as *Callitriche stagnalis* agg., the 'agg.' meaning that it is one of an impenetrable group of near-identical species, and *Callitriche* meaning 'beautiful hair'. As an aggregate it is a fairly common species throughout much of Britain, but, like so many other organisms I encountered on these walks, I was delighted to find it as I had never knowingly seen it before.

Mosses

I have not been very forthcoming on the subject of mosses. They are almost as impossible to identify in the field as lichens, and not particularly easy back in the lab either. A few of the more common species will become familiar with a bit of effort and experience, but for most you need a loupe or dissecting binocular microscope at least to be sure of obtaining an accurate ID. You will also need some serious specialist books, but even these can be insufficient, and you will find yourself online, searching for academic papers. One online resource that will certainly help is that of the British Bryological Society, which offers truly exceptional support for those wishing to identify bryophytes. I consider this largesse highly commendable, and a fine rejection of the ivory tower nonsense of former times.

There is one further problem for the neophyte moss-spotter: liverworts. Many liverworts are unlike mosses in appearance, but many others are dead ringers. Even the British Bryological Society agrees that it is difficult to tell one from another. Next to the group of Sundews we had found were scores of tiny 'leaves'. It was a liverwort, and the only reason I knew this was that, despite superficial appearances, it was clearly not a flowering plant and did not look like a moss.

Mosses and liverworts plus another related group, hornworts, are all bryophytes. All reproduce using spores, and some can form clones when they 'bud off' a minute part of themselves which will then grow. Some have thought hornworts to be evolutionarily closer to the flowering plants, but more recent work has supported the long-held view that the three groups are close together on a separate and ancient branch from the tree of life. The UK, densely populated and long industrialised as it is, has few claims to international importance in biodiversity, but bryophytes (and also lichens) are exceptions, with the UK hosting an impressive 767 mosses, 298 liverworts and a paltry 4 hornworts. If I find a hornwort on my travels, I will let you know.

The moss-like liverworts are known as 'leafy liverworts', their thalli (leaves) being very thin and narrow (often only one cell thick). The one I found had thalli in the form of small, green plates, and is a 'thallose liverwort'. This seems to be the wrong way round to me, but let us stick with it. I cannot be entirely sure, but it looks like a common liverwort known to occupy damp mountains – **Pellia epiphylla**. Tell me I am wrong if you dare. I was to find another liverwort that day, this time sitting on a rock. I had to give up on that one, and showed its photo to Bryan. In appearance it is vaguely reminiscent of a pile of bronze-coloured maggots. Its name is **Gymnomitrion crenulatum**.

Geology and Plants from a High Vantage

Owing to my very minor career as a television personality, strangers sometimes recognise me. Just such an encounter occurred halfway along the western bank of the lake. I am a little ashamed to tell you how much I enjoy these, but I always think of the Teacher of Ecclesiastes: 'Vanity, vanity, all is vanity.' I might have ruined the moment by my uncontrollably garrulous nature, telling them all about *Drosera* and, yet again, our mission to write a book about our walks. 'Nice enough chap, but boring' is what I imagine they might tell their friends when they get home.

It was at about this point that I had intended to climb to Devil's Kitchen, where the rare plant had reputedly been discovered and a place well known for its rarities. It is a famous, high ravine, the kitchen reference being to the smoky mist that forms as the air cools when channelled upwards. Had I been on my own, I would have shot up there without a second thought, but D always has my best interests at heart and reminded me of my age and that my bones are not what they used to be and would take months to mend, if they ever did. It was not so much the broken bones that concerned me, but that I would never have heard the end of it had I broken one.

We reached a broad, wetland area at the top of the lake, dominated by rushes. Had I brought waders, I would have spent a couple of hours seeing what else I could find. Next time, perhaps. Passing the wetland, we were in the south-east 'corner' of the lake. Here was an opportunity to go higher and enjoy the private excursion I mentioned earlier. I followed a much steeper path than those we had walked so far and went up the mountain by ninety vertical metres to take in the view northwards over the lake. It was, of course, quite stunning, and my thoughts inevitably turned to that which was most conspicuous, the geology. I am not in the slightest qualified to describe or explain it in all but the most superficial way, so I sent some of the photographs I had taken of the rock formations and individual rocks to my good friend Eddie, an exceptionally talented and engaging geologist with an enthusiasm that will fill your entire day if you do not hit him with a stick.

Also of great assistance was the remarkable BGS Geology Viewer, provided free to anyone with an internet connection and courtesy of the British Geological Survey. Here it is possible to zoom in and out through two layers of interest – the bedrock geology and the geology of the superficial deposits. It is possible to do this with just the bedrock, just the superficial deposits or both. Thus one is able to determine the geology of any spot in Britain, with the caveat that not all superficial deposits have been recorded.

The timescales involved in the creation of Snowdonia are vast, 450 million years ago marking their genesis. The formations that now make up Snowdonia began 40 degrees south of the equator and made their way 53 degrees north. Very slowly. On the way, they underwent the adventures of vulcanism (some of it beyond anything seen in human history, with a sixty-metre-thick layer of pyroclastic debris to be found a few miles away), quiet moments as a seabed (ripples can be seen in some of the strata) and the usual compression, faulting and tilting that form the everyday, or every millennium, experience of geological entities. The overall topography of Snowdonia is, however, created by the process of glaciation, and it is to the multiple ice ages that we owe so glorious a landscape.

This tale of the movement, moulding and sculpture of the Ordovician and Cambrian formations that make up Snowdonia is a very broad picture with a thousand intricacies left unsaid, but what the walker wishes to know is the name of any particular rock or formation, what type it is and only then how it came to be. From my vantage point above the lake I was surrounded on three sides by the steep slopes above Cwm Idwal, and only to the north over the lake was the view a distant one. Immediately to my left was the scene pictured here, its hollowed and windowed stratifications with the feel of an Indian temple minus the monkeys. This is part of the Lower Rhyolitic Tuff Formation that forms much of the area, created during the Ordovician period. Its layered nature is caused by alternate marine sediments and deposits of red-hot volcanic ash. The two terms 'rhyolitic' and 'tuff' deserve a brief exposition. Rhyolite is the most silica-rich of rocks that are formed during volcanic processes; 'tuff' is any type of rock formed from volcanic ash.

To my right was the same formation but tilted to 45 degrees by tectonic forces, though I could only see the incline clearly an hour later and further north. This particular spot is much loved by climbers who literally learn the ropes on this relatively safe slope. I fancy that anyone who could manage a staircase could quite easily walk up it on all fours but would simply keep going all the way to the bottom at the very first slip.

A little later in the walk I found a couple of rocks that did not seem to my untutored eye to belong with the geology in which they found themselves. One was a lump of quartz, made up of millions of crystals. During tectonic compression, silica minerals, such as those found in sandstone, preferentially dissolve and re-precipitate in zones where there is less stress. These crystals probably formed in the hinge created when strata folded, or in a mass of rock that has split apart to leave an open joint.

The second was the most stylish of all the rocks we saw that day, a grey-green-blue slab, delicately ornamented with the finest of striations. It is known as a volcaniclastic siltstone sequence. During less explosive times the volcanoes would spit and splutter many times and the individual pulses of fine ash would settle on the sea floor in these exquisite layers. I was delighted to hear that my geologist friend (who penned the last sentence) was familiar with that very rock and has spent many a happy hour relating its story to his no doubt entranced students.

On my way up the path there were more plants to delight me. The most exciting find was a fern that did not look quite like a fern. It is called the **Parsley Fern**, *Cryptogramma crispa*, the common name reflecting the appearance of its fronds. The odd thing about it is that its fronds come in two flavours, one reminiscent of flat-leaved parsley, the other with much narrower fronds. It is on the latter form that the reproductive apparatus is constructed, the former type of frond being sterile. It is quite a rarity, or at least it is very restricted in its range, insisting on strictly lime-free upland regions in Snowdonia, Cumbria and the Scottish Highlands.

Near by was a **Lady's Mantle**, *Alchemilla* sp. I can get no closer than 'sp.' (a short but fancy way of telling people you haven't got a clue), as it is a genus containing seventeen British species that are virtually identical to one another. Their leaves are similar to those of the common mallow, but a little thicker, paler and more sharply toothed. Identification comes down to counting the lobes (indistinct leaflets), how sharp the sawtooth edge of the leaves are and whether the leaves are hairy or not. If they are hairy, you will need to know where the hairs are positioned and if they are 'erecto-patent' or just plain old 'patent'. (Me neither.)

When I returned from my energetic trip up the mountain, I found D talking to a charming young couple. We chatted pleasantly about their trip, which involved a tent, not a pleasant hotel. D was horrified, her camping days being very firmly behind her. She was even more appalled when the young man kindly showed us his legs. They looked as though they had been shot at with a .410 at thirty paces, but his injuries were caused by midges, not pellets. I hadn't seen a midge all day, but they are certain to be there.

The Walk Back

The relatively narrow, half-mile walk northwards along the eastern side of the lake found a few more plants. **Wild Thyme**, *Thymus drucei*, is common, with catholic tastes when it comes to acceptable habitats. British thymes (there are five true species and one hybrid) are dwarf evergreen shrubs, often taking 'dwarf' to the extreme of being 1 cm or so tall. Wild Thyme is the most common. I was expecting to call it *Thymus polytricus*, but C. A. Stace, who writes the definitive work on British plants, the *New Flora of the British Isles*, uses the name I give above, mentioning that there are constant arguments about what it should be called. Finally, one would imagine that Wild Thyme would behave itself and smell of, well, thyme. It does, but the bouquet is usually very slight and requires a serious rubbing between fingers for it to smell of anything at all.

One patch of thyme was artistically complemented by the blue of **Common Milkwort**, *Polygala vulgaris*, and next to it, the **Dog Violet**, *Viola riviniana*. We had no doubt passed many **Bilberries**, *Vaccinium myrtillis*, on our walk, but here they were close to the path and sporadically bright with flowers.

We completed our heroic circumnavigation of Cwm Idwal and rejoined the path back to the National Trust base. Although I had noticed it on the outward journey, I thought it time to pay some attention to the beautiful cotton grass that was living in the boggy area alongside the path. There are only four British species, but still they need to be differentiated if one is to take a botanical expedition seriously. How helpful, then, that the species I had found was distinguishable at a glance. With this plant there was no need to whip out my loupe to determine the answer to such imponderable questions as 'Are the calyces *densely* whitish-tomentose with eglandular hairs or *sparsely* whitish-tomentose with eglandular hairs?' With this cotton grass I could clearly see that its flower heads grew singly, not in clusters. The species was the **Hare's-Tail Cotton Grass,** *Eriophorum vaginatum.* This species, like several others we found that day, is restricted almost entirely to western uplands and lowland mires. Here it populates wet areas that are intolerable to most plants, using various physiological tricks to keep its roots aerated. Most of the roots are cheerfully abandoned over winter as the anaerobic conditions rot them anyway. When growing, the plant sports air channels called 'aerenchyma' within its roots and stems. Also, it always grows in tussocks, enabling the roots to sit high in the soil. If you are worrying about the specific epithet, *vaginatum*, it means 'sheath', a reference to the 'leaves' (technically, 'lamina'), which, instead of behaving like normal leaves and flapping about, remain as a sheath around the stem.

'Cotton grass' is the usual name for *Eriophorum* species, though they are not grasses but sedges. They are not cotton either, so it is not the most useful of names, with the alternative of 'Bog cotton' going at least halfway to redemption. Attempts have been made to use the 'cotton', but it is far too brittle.

We saw several other grass-like plants that day, most of them represented near the cotton grass. These are often ignored by most people, but worth a look close up, especially at the emerging flower. Among them there was **Carnation Sedge**, *Carex panicea*, **Star Sedge**, *Carex echinate,* and **Spike Rush**, *Eleocharis palustris*. If you have trouble telling a rush from a sedge, or either from grasses, there is the well-known rhyme about their stems: 'Sedges have edges, rushes are round, grasses are hollow right down to the ground.'

An Unwelcome Late Addition to Our List

Happy with the photographs I had taken and the detailed notes recorded by my carer, we walked the now quite short walk back to the car. Our species list was reasonable, but later that evening the count was increased by one. Both of us had acquired a tick or three. I have similarly acquired easily a thousand ticks over my many years of walking. They just hang about on vegetation and latch on to anything that emits carbon dioxide (suggesting that it is an animal) and, more embarrassingly, sweat. I treat them as a mere annoyance but nevertheless remove them quickly and carefully, and check for the 'bulls-eye' rash that indicates infection by the bacterium that causes Lyme Disease, and for any sign of a fever. I guess I have been extremely lucky, or maybe I have caught it but never displayed symptoms. My then young nephew caught Lyme Disease with his first tick bite, though a hefty dose of antibiotic, given early on, prevented illness. I am not one to nag but do check for ticks after any walk in the countryside. Health aside, a species is a species, so the **Deer Tick**, *Ixodes Ricinus*, is on the list.

Cheviot Hills

UPLAND GRASS, CONIFEROUS PLANTATION

THREE AND A HALF MILES

23 JUNE 2021

Kelso

The Cheviot Hills were a complete unknown to us both, but I knew them to be beautiful and exceptionally wild, and I wanted one of our walks to be across heath and acid grasslands of the northern uplands. Such habitats are found in such places as Dartmoor, Exmoor, much of central and northern Wales, the Pennines, Cumbria and Northumberland and, of course, Scotland. When we arrived, it seemed that the Cheviots were unknown to everyone else too, as the place was virtually empty – there were few cars, few lay-bys, few places of habitation and a mere handful of places to park. It looked closed for an unnecessary refurbishment. Our visit was part of a prolonged journey that also included a birthday celebration in Harrogate (that of D), though which birthday I will not say, and a walk around the temperate rainforest on the isle of Seil, described in the next chapter.

We travelled on the third day to Kelso, just over the border in Scotland, our Northumberland destination just a few miles to the south. We arrived mid-afternoon of the day before our walk and, having learned the lesson of not relying on online maps, bought one for the Cheviot Hills. I was impressed by the large, cobbled marketplace and guessed that it must have been used as a location in some period drama or other. It had. It also looked like the sort of place that had once welcomed the occasional and no doubt gruesome public execution. It was a warm evening, and we sat on the hotel lawn with our drinks and enjoyed a family video conference that had been planned. We learned that our first grandchild was to be a girl. While I was writing this book, she was duly born and is the dedicatee of this book.

As you will have learned by now, forward planning has never been my strong suit, so we spent an hour that evening examining our shiny new map to discover precisely where we might go. It was to the car park on the College Valley Estate. Our breakfast the next morning, of 'everything except black pudding' for the ever-slender D and kippers for your author, set us up well for the day.

College Burn

The sixteen-mile journey was a switchback ride through broad arable land that became progressively more pastoral as we neared our upland destination. With our chosen car park being one of the few that were available, we only just squeezed in. Despite this, there seemed to be no one about. We shared out the bags and equipment, D refusing to carry my large tripod on the grounds that she had carried it for miles quite recently without it ever being used.

We were in a valley, our path due to follow the western bank of College Burn for half a mile before a right-turn off the road and steeply up a hill. The name 'College' has no connection with any nearby place of learning, a possibility that is as implausibly modern as, say, 'Municipal Office Burn'. The name appears to derive from the Old English 'col' for 'cold' and 'letch' for 'a stream through boggy land'. The area is thick with 'Burns': Rowhope Burn, Sourhope Burn, Kaim Burn and Calroust Burn, to name but a few. There are also some 'Waters', such as Bowmont Water, and a few 'Sikes', such as Holywell Sike. 'Sike' is a northern term for a stream, from the Middle English 'syke', a stream that runs through marshy ground and sometimes dries out in the summer, much like the southern 'bourne'.

With the burn to our left and relatively flat ground leading to the steeper slope beyond to our right, we began what was to be a mere three-and-a-half-mile walk. I will tell you now that it took nine and a half hours. The first impression of this unfamiliar countryside was almost overwhelming. Deep valleys and massive rolling hills. It was craggy in places, but mostly it was a soft, smooth and rounded landscape. I have seen it every day while writing this book because one of the photographs of it that I took has the rare honour of being my computer 'wallpaper'.

As with Snowdonia, the bedrock is volcanic in origin, in this case andesite, a rock close to the familiar, extrusive basalt that one sees flowing from active volcanoes on television. Here it is known as the Cheviot Volcanic Formation, formed about 400 million years ago, in the Devonian period. The superficial geology of the valley bottoms is 'till', an unsorted material unceremoniously dumped there by glaciers. The stream sides are of alluvial material.

The Low Grassland

The first plant found was one I had not seen before or, to be more accurate, never noticed before. It is fairly common throughout Britain, so I have no excuse. It was slender, with narrow, pointed leaves that clasped the stems in pairs. The flower had five white petals with faint, dull blue lines visible. It was **Purging Flax**, *Linum catharticum*, also known less worryingly as Fairy Flax. As you will guess, it has medicinal benefits as a mild laxative, though it is poisonous in large (unspecified) quantities, so 'mild' may not always be the appropriate qualification.

Next to the Purging Flax, indeed all over the large field, were young **Red Clovers**, *Trifolium pratense*. The Latin name is one of the easier to understand: 'three-leaved and growing in a field'. I have become something of a 'photo stacker' in recent years. This is a technique that enables the photographer to produce images that are in focus for their entire depth of field. One can photograph a nearby plant, the field behind it and the hills in the distance, the in-focus parts of each stitched together by software. It is even more useful for small subjects such as, for example, the Herb Robert, mentioned on page 69 and pictured. This could require twenty or even fifty photographs as depth of field is *extremely* shallow with so-called 'macro'-photography. The images can be stunning in their detail, the profound hairiness of most plants being the most striking revelation, plus the almost invariable inclusion of one or more previously unnoticed invertebrates.

There were two trefoils, the ubiquitous **Bird's-foot Trefoil**, *Lotus corniculatus*, with its sepals the usual brilliant red where they reach their pedicles (stems), and one of a group of mildly impenetrable species with very small yellow flowers, the **Lesser Trefoil**, *Trifolium dubium*. This specific epithet is frequent in biological nomenclature, generally understood to mean 'not typical'. I am not quite sure what that might mean, and the invitation is to believe that the taxonomist does not know what the hell is going on and is prepared to admit it. **Marsh Thistles**, *Cirsium palustre*, were scattered here and there; both its names suggest a damp habitat, something confirmed by the rushes that were present near by.

Other common plants on the gloriously herb-rich area of flat pasture included **Heath Speedwell**, *Veronica officinalis*, **Heath Bedstraw**, *Galium saxatile*, Lady's Bedstraw, Common Sorrel and Pignut. Most of these are typical of acid grassland, though Lady's Bedstraw is unfussy. I did not find (or notice) any rare plants there, but this simply does not matter; it needed none.

I was to learn later of something in that area that was completely invisible on the day: the Hethpool Rings. I have seen several photographs of them taken from the ground, and carefully examined half a dozen aerial photographs at the supplied grid references. Nothing ring-like can be seen from the terrestrial or aerial photographs that might be interpreted as a ring of rocks, just a scattering. I therefore propose Hethpool Rings as the least impressive of Britain's ancient monuments.

Coniferous Plantations

We walked past one of the many coniferous plantations scattered throughout the Cheviots and then left the path to climb the steep hill with the plantation to our right. Such plantations have received a poor press over the years, but if timber is needed, then it is arguably better to grow it here than rely entirely on imports. The 'interesting times' during which this book has been researched and written have made national self-reliance all the more important. But still, coniferous plantations are almost invariably a literal blot on the landscape, their biodiversity poor and, with the exception of Scots Pine, always consisting of non-native trees. Any non-native will automatically arrive with an ecological deficit, as none (or few) of the species that might live in or on it will be waiting for them here. A first-class example is the enormous Leylandii in my garden. It is about fifty years old, during which time only five species have taken an interest in it. One is the pigeons that attempt to nest in it every year, their eggs quickly falling from their perilously situated nests, a presumed wasp that took to making a honeycomb of papery cells on the bark and three lichens. Nothing else: no other invertebrates, no fungi apart from the topical lichens. Despite this serious failing, I have always loved the tree because it is so *big*. D loathes it for precisely the same reason, and I have finally relented. It should be down by the time you read this. I might plant a birch tree instead.

Forestry England and the parallel bodies in Wales and Scotland are much more sensitive than they were not so long ago. Back in the mid-1980s D and I would visit a plantation area of Dartmoor with some friends from Exeter. Although most of the trees were spruces and firs, the car park was surrounded with venerable Beech trees of great beauty and interest to the naturalist. Under pressure (as they were at the time) to grow more trees, these Beeches were felled to make room for more spruce. My friend later spoke to one of the (then) Forestry Commission officers who had some responsibility for the decision. He said that they were a business and that was that.

Of course, there is now a new generation in charge of forest management, the excesses of government policy and over-enthusiasm within the forestry bodies mostly a bad memory. Now, no report on reafforestation or forestry management comes without an ecological assessment and directions or promises to provide open areas for suitable herbaceous species and their dependent biota, buffer zones of native hardwood trees, bat boxes and ecologically productive rotting wood on the forest floor. Well, almost. Still, even with Forestry England being involved, a few valuable habitats have been lost to conifer-planting schemes.

There is a persuasive school of thought that coniferous plantations should be replaced by native-species woodland. I make a plea to anyone who is considering the removal of a coniferous plantation – do attempt to discover what species exist there already that will be destroyed through your efforts. For example, in the Cheviot Hills, Forestry England is very well aware that some of their Sitka Spruce plantations are rare refuges for Red

Squirrels and that any proposed felling and replanting must take this into account. A less cheerful story, though not one that many will shed tears over, is what happened at Powerstock Common, about five miles from my home in West Dorset. I have led fungus forays there for twenty-five years, wandering the footpaths and delving into the areas of Beech and oak. There were also extensive enclosures of spruce and pine. About ten years ago the spruce and pine were cleared and the number of fungi found there dropped by 50 per cent. I was particularly sad to lose a rare and exquisite fungus that looked as though the base of its stem had been dipped in red ink and that used to grow in the scrappy plantation pines. *Tricholoma basirubens* has disappeared from the area for ever.

The entire enterprise of planting trees (native or not) is fraught with the potential for loss rather than the hoped-for gain. If anyone wishes to plant trees to aid biodiversity or capture carbon, knowing what is there already is essential. A report from the Centre for Agriculture and Bioscience International (CABI) questions the evident enthusiasm for planting trees on any grassland. There have already been several reported incidents of people who attempt to do what they think is right by planting trees on their land to capture carbon, but who, because the grassland is of high biodiversity, actually destroy complex populations and communities growing on land that was already making a good fist of carbon capture.

Some are of the opinion that planting trees will capture more carbon than grassland used for grazing. This may be so for a mature forest, but when it is harvested the carbon will (either quickly if it is burned or eventually if it is used for timber) be released back into the atmosphere.

If hardwood trees such as Beech and oak are planted, I would hope that they are managed for timber production. I have bought tens of thousands of pounds' worth of hardwood timber over the years, and there was always a significant difference between, say, German and French oak and English oak. They may have been the same species, but the German and French timbers were vastly 'cleaner', having been plantation-grown specifically for timber. The foresters ensure that the long wait for a crop was worthwhile by removing errant side-shoots before they form side-branches that would ruin the main trunk for timber. On the whole, I preferred English oak because it is more complex of grain – twisted, swirly, pippy, a little shaky and always lovely – but if I did not wish a dining-room suite to twist, split and wander around the house, it *had* to be the boring, straight-grained stuff they grow on the continent.

There is no reason home-grown timbers should be as difficult as I describe; it simply (if expensively) requires good management. On the whole, a well-managed forest will be nearly as accommodating of associated species as one that has been left to do as it will. The reasons for the 'nearly' are the temptation to remove the valuable habitat that is fallen timber and the fact that trees need to be cut in their prime to provide quality timber, long before those species that require ancient trees have time to establish.

The Trouble with Bracken

The walk up alongside the plantation was only four hundred metres horizontally but ninety vertically: a bracing one-in-five climb. We took our time, but then we always do. There were few plants to be seen that were not found in the flatlands we had passed. Except **Bracken**. Bracken, otherwise known as Bracken Fern, bears the Latin name *Pteridium aquilinum*, meaning 'fern like an eagle', and it is often called 'Eagle Fern'. It is a native plant, but no longer of our best behaved – it is not just non-natives that can be troublesome. Its natural habitat is believed to be within woodlands, a difficult belief to maintain with Bracken's current domination of many unwooded parts of Britain.

In woodlands, Bracken lives comfortably with its neighbours. However, when the mixed upland pasturing of sheep and cattle was lost to sheep-only pasture, Bracken was no longer kept under control from the trampling it received from cattle. Abandonment of pasture will also invite Bracken. It is also the case that from prehistory until recently Bracken was collected in vast quantities to be used as bedding for stock, thatch, potato-clamping and packing, and its ash used in glass-making. None is collected now, and it is just a nuisance.

Control is difficult, expensive and consuming of time. Spraying with a herbicide is best, frequent cutting, the bracken roller and bracken sledge second-best. The tempting technique of setting fire to it merely encourages the plant. Even with success at hand, care must be taken on steep ground, as the soil will be bare and exposed to erosion after the demise of its consolidating Bracken.

Nevertheless Bracken, being a native species, does have its associated flora and fauna. Many animals use it for cover, the uncommon Cow Wheat and species of violet can grow beneath the less-dense stands and four rare fritillary butterflies depend on Bracken for their survival. Martin and Pamela Ellis, in their *Microfungi on Land Plants*, list twenty-nine species of microfungi that live on Bracken, though some of these may be found on other ferns. I did not find any of these fungi, the view and a variety of invertebrates distracting me. I wish I had taken more notice, but it is the fate of Bracken to pass unnoticed as a mere nuisance.

Common Names

Among the distracting insects was a hoverfly that on closer examination was not a hoverfly. It took half an hour with my barely adequate photograph and copy of *Britain's Hoverflies* to discover this. I knew that hoverflies have only one pair of wings as they
are true flies, in the Diptera, and that bees and wasps have two
pairs of wings. However, these essential details are not always as
conspicuous as they might be.

After ploughing through a relevant subset of my forty or so
books on insects and the first-class website of the Bees, Wasps &
Ants Recording Society (BWARS) I found it! It was the wasp
Odynerus spinipes. BWARS provides no common name for
this creature, or of any of the species it describes, including the
Honeybee, which it refers to only by its scientific name, *Apis
mellifera* (bee that bears honey).

I have a great fondness for common names, and, unless
writing formally or talking to a specialist, I am perfectly happy
to use them in most other contexts, most particularly the plants.
However, what I do not like are the several thousand names
that have been invented in the last twenty years by the various
societies that take an interest in the various groups of organisms.
(BWARS and the Lichen Society are among the exceptions.) In
part, this rush of invention came from a government directive
asking that all British species for which there is conservation
concern be given an English common name. This, I must
presume, was to make them more accessible to the layman,
who will then, it was thought, feel more inclined to show that
concern. Well, there is some sense in this – who would give a
damn about *Ailuropoda melanoleuca* if they did not know it was
the Giant Panda? Against it, I would argue that most rare species
are almost never knowingly encountered by the layman, and

they would be no more likely to defend the Hogweed Bonking Beetle than *Rhagonycha fulva*. OK, OK, they might – this one sticks in the mind rather. I will try another beetle: the Rufous-Shouldered Longhorn, *Anaglyptus mysticus*. If anything, it is the Latin name of this creature that is the more striking and memorable. I must point out here that I do not know if these two names are newly minted or not, or if the species are rare or not, but they are nevertheless typical of many of the new names. Having found the bit firmly between their teeth, the societies went much, much further and provided a large proportion of the species within their purview with a common name. Partly this was unbridled (if I may mix my equine metaphors) enthusiasm and partly an understandable tendency to consider that all the objects of their desire were in some way threatened.

Now we are stuck with horrors such as the Small Spored White Beak-Sedge Smut, the Stinking Fanvault and the Piggyback Shanklet (all fungi), and the Dubious Bladder Moss, Pointless Screwmoss and Top Notchwort (all mosses). I could go on – and on.

There are, of course, many thousands of common names that have come into existence over the centuries simply because people need them. With the more obscure corners of the natural world such as mycology, bryology, lichenology and the greater part (by a very long way) of the invertebrates, no one needs or needed to call them anything at all because they have and had no impact on their lives. Those for whom these specialities were of great interest, the mycologist, bryologist and so on, already had the Latin names and needed no more than that, and indeed did not wish for any more than that as 'more' would engender confusion.

People often ask me how I remember so many of the Latin names for fungi. I say that I am extremely interested in the subject, and I need to, want to, know the names. A reading of the above may make me seem elitist, but it is not so. I point out that remembering the names of things is easily done by *anyone* interested in the subject. Ask the (mostly) boys in any remedial classroom the names of the players in the Real Madrid squad and they will reel them off without hesitation. It is worth pointing out that many of the names (about half at the time of writing) will be of Latin origin.

My final defence of Latin names and resulting dismissal of some common names is that they provide information that is often missing in common names – the key to where they are placed in the tree of life. That key is the generic name: *Anaglyptus*, for example. Knowing this will enable you to discover its Family, Order and so on. This knowledge leads to further understanding an organism's relationships with other groups and species. Many common names do this too, but poorly and rather randomly. Of Common Sorrel, Sheep's Sorrel and Wood Sorrel only the first two are related other than very distantly.

Odynerus spinipes, does, in fact, have a common name: the Spiny Mason Wasp. BWARS provides a good description of its lifestyle. As its common name suggests, it nests in hard clay or clay-like earth in vertical surfaces such as we found on the occasional risers of our stepped path. It makes several chambers for its eggs, and each egg is suspended by a filament. Around these eggs the mother places collected and paralysed weevil larvae, which she leaves ready to feed her young as they emerge from their eggs. At least one sci-fi movie comes to mind. Of course, *O. spinipes* suffers like everything else from parasites, in this case kleptoparasites (thieves) in the wasp genus *Chrysis*. They certainly cause a crisis for their host, whose eggs are consumed by the parasitic wasp. This does not mean liberation for the paralysed weevil larvae of course – they are also eaten.

O. spinipes, I discovered, has acquired a peculiar trick that may help it spot any thieves: depth perception. In the compound eyes of insects, depth perception is poor to non-existent. However, *O. spinipes* flies in a rapid zigzag manner if it sees anything untoward flying near its nest. This gives it repeated pairs of 'snapshots', which can provide information on depth, just like the two photographs in 3D viewers.

The Trouble with Sheep

Our path turned to the left in a south-westerly direction at the top where the plantation ended. We stopped at the turn, partly for an early lunch but mostly because there was so much to see from this vantage point. Here we were in drystone wall territory, not the small enclosures of the lowlands but the long walls and huge fields of upland pasture.

The wall by our picnic site was of the 'random rubble' variety, a mass of angular rocks with flat sides, all piled up to form a wall three feet wide at the base, tapering to one foot with large capping stones. 'Random' does not do the style justice – every stone was chosen and positioned in its resting place with artistic care. Judging by the lichens with which they were covered, they were old, and indeed looked like the eighteenth- or nineteenth-century Parliamentary enclosures they were, where land held in common was divided into private and usually physically enclosed holdings. Standing at a strikingly picturesque gateway in the wall were a ewe and her lamb.

Sheep have long been a staple of this landscape. If stocked at sensible densities, they can provide a species rich and stable grassland, though it helps if cattle are in the grazing mix. At grazing densities that are too high they can have a seriously detrimental effect on plant life and its dependent invertebrates and fungi. Typical problems are plants never flowering and seeding, a patchy environment caused by the selective grazing of palatable plants, a domination by boorish grasses and rushes such as Matgrass, *Nardus stricta,* Purple Moorgrass, *Molinia caerulea,* and Deergrass, *Trichophorum caespitosum,* and, ultimately, by soil erosion. Now stock levels are generally lower, with fewer sheep, but the damage has been done and recovery will be slow, if it happens at all.

Various UK government initiatives (notably the Hill Farming Act 1946) and EU policies were instrumental in the creation of the problem, and further government policies the solution. As discussed in our walk from Hook to Farnham, in the early days of the Common Agricultural Policy, subsidies were offered on an 'all you can produce' basis. This and similar home-grown policies resulted in the excessive stock densities that caused so much damage. In 2003 wiser counsels prevailed, and area-based support was provided instead. With sheep grazing having had such a bad press, grazing itself has acquired such a bad name that some have even suggested that it be banned completely.

Grazing involves animals that are destined to be consumed by people, and the eating of animals is not to everyone's taste. Should vegetarianism or, much more so, its sister veganism ever become the rule rather than the exception, then grazing will simply be impossible. Allowing sheep and cattle to wander wild and uneaten with no top-level predator (or impractical fences *around* top-level predators, should they be introduced), an accumulation of dead and dying grazers would result. If grazing was no longer practised, 'abandonment', as it is called, then a progression to climax forest would begin, the interesting grassland fauna, flora and mycota lost. A vegan friend of mine agreed that this would, indeed, all happen, but added that the loss of the grasslands so beloved and of their inhabitants would be a price worth paying to remove the evils of carnivory.

My ewe and lamb were evidently keen to have their photograph taken, their part in maintaining biodiversity recorded. My sheep-spotting skills are not what they should be, but I am reasonably confident that they were what one would expect, Cheviots. They lacked all but a hint of the pale chestnut brown that is often, though not always, seen in the breed. But the fleeceless face, pointed ears, distinctive facial markings and lack of horns all seem to fit. Perhaps the pale fleece was down to a cross with another breed. Cheviots, hardy and well protected by their sometimes comically thick fleece, are grazed all year round except in the more sensitive areas of sub-alpine grassland where it is summer grazing only. The all-year-rounders live entirely on what they find, save in heavy snow when supplementary food is provided.

Ancient Fields

Looking from our vantage point, we could see for miles over the hills. To the south across the valley, a single, straight, drystone wall ran from the valley bottom over three hundred metres up the hill. It was nearly a mile long with a shieling (a hut where shepherds lived during the summer) at its base. The wall was striking enough, but what caught my attention was clear evidence to the east of agricultural systems of the near and distant past.

I am very familiar with what are known as 'strip lynchets' as I can see one out of my 'office' window in West Dorset. They are impressive constructions: massive terraces on the hillsides, following the horizontal contours of the land. My local strip lynchets are four hundred metres long and consist of four 'steps'. This is typical of the chalklands of the south, but those before me that day consisted of between fifteen and twenty-five steps. They also looked 'softer'.

It is generally agreed that strip lynchets are cultivation terraces, created during times of 'land famine'. Those in the south are thought to be from around the fourteenth century and a response to the catastrophic climate change that came with the end of the thirteenth century. In this case, it was the climate becoming not warmer but colder and wetter, a usually more dangerous imposition in agrarian societies, at least those in temperate zones. The strip lynchets we saw that day were created for a much earlier downturn in fortunes, the abrupt decline in temperatures in the early Bronze Age.

How they are 'constructed' is explained in my book *A Spotter's Guide to Countryside Mysteries*, but in essence they are the result of repeatedly ploughing field strips that follow the contours of the land. Some of the steeper terraces may have been constructed before ploughing commenced, but those on the Cheviots were most likely the long-term result of that ploughing.

The other ancient system of agriculture was that of ridge and furrow or, in the vernacular of the Cheviot Hills, 'rig and furrow'. These are visible as parallel ridges about ten metres wide, where the plough had heaped the soil towards the centre line of each ridge, with a furrow left between them. These were planted with corn or some other arable crop. These are difficult to date, but they were used from the Middle Ages until early in the nineteenth century.

Great Hetha

We followed the now broad and relatively gentle path further up the hill towards Great Hetha, an Iron Age fort. Halfway up I spotted a 'sheep scrape', a hollow in the soil where sheep (effectively) scratch their backs, its usage clear from the wool in and around it. With the soil dispersed, the roots of grasses and herbaceous plants were clearly visible. Upland grassland plants need deep roots to survive drought, and here they could be seen growing down a full thirty centimetres. Near by was a patch of **Sheep's Sorrel** (presumably named for its fondness for the short grass of sheep pasture), *Rumex acetosella*, in full and brilliant flower. It is much smaller, and less common, than Common Sorrel, and easily distinguished by the bent 'wings' at the base of its leaves.

After gaining another hundred metres in altitude, we arrived at the Great Hetha hill fort, the 'Great' distinguishing it from a lesser one to the east, which we had seen but decided not to visit on the principle of 'seen one, seen them all'. As hill forts go, Great Hetha was middling, but set among a superb landscape. No doubt you will know that the word 'fort' in the context of the Iron Age denotes a place of fortification. These generally involve terraced earth banks which would have sported palisades and are nothing like the toy fort I had as a child (and still have) or the one in *Beau Geste*. Leaving the fort behind us, we made our way down the south-western side of the hill.

The ubiquitous Heath Bedstraw was joined, in patches, by Wild Thyme and by **Tormentil**, *Potentilla erecta*. Tormentil is easy to spot, as it has four yellow petals arranged in a flat corolla – most similarly flowered plants have five. Trailing Tormentil, *P. anglica*, is its only confounder of your ID skills because both plants have a trailing habit. However, the leaves of the latter plant have three leaflets per leaf, and it is much less common.

It was at this point that we were passed by a couple of male hikers who were probably even older than your author. Like most hikers, they appeared to have the hounds of Hell behind them, looking neither to right nor left. Even what was before them seemed of little interest. Perhaps they were retired botanists or entomologists who had seen everything and just wanted some exercise. They passed us by at speed with merely a nod. Ten minutes later we had more luck with a female walker, also of some maturity, who did at least stop to talk for a minute to put us on the right track (we were very slightly lost) before shooting off after the two men.

Considering that this is an expedition to study upland grasslands, I have said very little about the grasses. Most were common, such as **Tufted Hair Grass**, *Deschampsia cespitosa*, **Sweet Vernal Grass**, *Anthoxanthum odoratum*, **Yorkshire Fog**, *Holcus lanatus*, **Smooth Meadow-Grass**, *Poa pratensis*, **Rough Meadow-Grass**, *P. trivialis*, and, inevitably, the ubiquitous **Annual Meadow-Grass**, *P. annua*. Sweet Vernal Grass is one that I collect every year to make a vodka infusion similar to Bison-Grass Vodka. It is like drinking a meadow.

The now uncommon **Harebell**, *Campanula rotundifolia*, was nodding in the gentle wind, just as it does on the chalk hills near my home. Near by was a slightly rarer treasure, one restricted entirely to upland Britain, the **Mountain Pansy**, *Viola lutea*. These come in three exquisite colour forms: violet, yellow and with both colours represented. We saw a dozen of the yellow variety. Three more common flowers were scattered around: **Bitter Vetchling**, *Lathyrus linifolius*, with its distinctive pointed leaves, bright pink pea flower and purple calyx, Bird's-Foot Trefoil, with its flashes of orange, and **Smooth Hawksbeard**, *Crepis capillaris*, with its bright yellow dandelion petals, each of which is terminated with a pinked edge, the outermost backed with scarlet.

Several of the plants we found that day belonged to the Pea Family, the Fabaceae, a Family that provides the occasional botanist with endless frustration. There are nearly a hundred species in Britain, many of which are common, but with some rare members too. They run from the tiny medicks through the clovers, vetches, vetchlings, peas, gorses and brooms. It is tempting to look first at the colour of the flowers, but better to consider their arrangement – loose heads or short spikes, tight heads, long spikes, solitary and so on – and then proceed to a consideration of the leaves – multiple opposite leaflets, trefoil, lanceolate and so on. The above-mentioned Bitter Vetchling, for example, has flowers that droop from one side of a stalk and narrow leaves made up of several immediately opposing pairs of leaflets, and the leaf stalk ends without producing the tendrils found on other species.

Interestingly (well I think so), the trefoils (*Lotus* sp.) actually possess five leaflets, not the expected three: the other two are inconspicuously bent backwards or appear like stipules on the stem. Bird's-Foot Trefoil, incidentally, gains its avian reference from the seed pods, which radiate like the foot of a bird.

As we made our way down the hill along a ridge, we saw a cluster of oaks at the bottom providing shelter for a flock of seventy sheep. I took what I considered to be a good photograph of them, but a representation of this most bucolic of scenes would, I think, have been better in the hands of Constable.

The Valley Bottom

We left the open pasture of the hill behind us and found ourselves on a tarmacked road alongside a drystone wall which was pierced by an impressive sheep gate. The map seemed to direct us through the back garden of a farmhouse, and there seemed to be no other way. Awaiting the shouts of enraged inhabitants, we traversed it in some haste and very quietly. The road had led us south, but now we travelled east across the small stream and subsequently on through another coniferous plantation, one that carpeted the valley bottom and southern hillside.

We were, of course, now in a quite different habitat, or habitats. The landscape beside the stream was one of rush pasture, and the streamside itself provided a different habitat again. The rarer plants of the high hills were behind us, and scores of more familiar plants were now all around. **Thyme-Leaved Speedwell**, *Veronica serpyllifolia*, in seed, Foxgloves, Pineapple Mayweed, docks and thistles, willowherbs by the stream, **Bog Stitchwort**, *Stellaria uliginosa*, Greater Stitchwort, Brooklime in the stream, Greater Burdock, Stinging Nettles and more. The last four of these are edible to some degree, but only one is worth your time. Stinging Nettle is a near-perfect food, topping even kale in the health food stakes. Its flavour is mild and, well, 'green'. Soup, of course, a purée with pasta, perhaps, or maybe a pesto after blanching. I collect a great deal every year, most of it destined to be dried and powdered so that at least some of its recipes can be made out of season.

It is always a pleasure to be able to identify *any* insect, so I was pleased to find that the large, black beetle I photographed on the stony path through the woods was ***Pterostichus niger.*** The creature looks as though it was designed for the Ministry of Defence, with its tough, corrugated wing cases and generally robust appearance. A beetle one could tread on without a crunching sound, I suspect. It is common in woodlands throughout Britain, with two closely related lookalikes.

Although it is avowedly common, **Common Figwort**, *Scrophularia nodosa*, is always a pleasure to see. Its flowers are small but, with their yellows and sombre purples and intricate details, worth looking at closely with a loupe. The name figwort has no relationship to the fruit but derives from an old usage of 'fig', meaning 'useless'. There was just the single plant, and I spent some time later studying the photograph to discover which figwort it was, there being five to choose from. My problem was that I had photographed the tiny flowers (most of them still unopened) and had only inconclusive photographs of the leaves. It is in the leaves that the most obvious differences lie. I brought in the big guns here with another trick for helping the helpless wannabe botanist – I checked to see what had been found there before. This is not foolproof but usually works.

On this occasion I asked a botanist friend who knew the area, but, failing such local assistance, two of the sources I use for my identification trickery are the online lists and maps provided by the National Biodiversity Network Trust and the Botanical Society of the British Isles (BSBI). The former has records for every type of organism – insects, fungi, plants and so on – while the BSBI is entirely about plants. Find the 'search species' page and type in the name you think it might be. Latin names are best, and they seem to cope with the endless synonyms (out-of-date names) that have accumulated like snow drifts for most species.

Just to the side of the path there was a large lichen nestling in the undergrowth. It was a so-called 'dog-toothed lichen'. The genus for this group is *Peltigera*, and there are fifteen species to choose from. The choosing is not easy. They are leafy (frondose) in structure, the upper surface grey, brown or green, the lower surface usually some version of white. The lower surface may also possess long, fine threads known as 'rhizines'. It was *Peltigera lactucifolia*. The 'doggy' reference of the group common name is due to the fancied similarity of the rhizines to canine teeth, and, under the 'doctrine of signatures', where similarity would (erroneously) indicate a cure, they were once used as a doomed cure for rabies. There was a bonus species nestling within the lichen, an attractive liverwort in the genus *Scapania*.

Faith in my insect identification skills (*tricks*, really) was raised when another beetle fell to my talents. It was ***Geotrupes spiniger***, another black beetle but smaller, more rounded and iridescent blue underneath. It is a type of dung beetle, also known as a dor beetle and presumably one of the species that one sometimes sees chopped up in unusually colourful badger poo.

I noticed a Common Dock where the leaf had curled, longitudinally, into a tube. This was caused by the aphid ***Aphis rumicis***, which manages to wrap itself in a protective layer of its dinner. Resting on a length of grass was an insect that proved to be beyond my burgeoning talents. It had waspish markings and two pairs of wings. This put it in the Hymenoptera and was therefore a sawfly, a wasp or a bee. Unfortunately, my camera has misled me somehow, and there was, I eventually discovered, only one pair of wings. This mistake took me on a futile journey through the Hymenoptera and, eventually, a 'phone a friend' moment (Bryan). He told me that it was the **Common Scorpion Fly**, *Panorpa communis*, although it could have been the almost identical *P. germanica* – photographs cannot always be relied on for difficult differentiations. Frankly, I was happy with either and the mystery was solved to my satisfaction. Often, it is good enough to know more or less what something is. Regardless of its true name, it was a beauty, its wings a mosaic of light, creamy grey and some horizontal bands, its body with wasp-like bandings and the tip of the abdomen orange. Mine appeared to be a female. Had she been a 'he', he would have had vicious-looking claws. These are not for war but for love, used to grasp the matching piece of kit on the female's abdomen during mating.

Back along the Burn and Gorse

Out of the woods, we walked the last stretch with College Burn to our right. I glanced at the woodland at the bottom of the hill that ran down to the far bank and wished we had time to explore it. Such extensive streamside native woodlands are quite uncommon in Britain. In fact, the wood did not quite reach the river, as there was a narrow band of Gorse in full flower separating it.

Gorse is one of our unappreciated national treasures. In Northumberland the commonest species, *Ulex europaeus*, predominates, and along that river it was demonstrating its considerable talent for filling any bit of open land. The odd Elder and Willow indicate that it may in time be subsumed in a climax forest. For hill farmers it is a perpetual nuisance that is all but impossible to eradicate. When cut back to ground level, it will spring back rapidly to full vigour within two or three years. It is also a serious fire hazard in that, if it catches fire, it burns with an intense heat and is impossible to extinguish. In fact, it was once used as a fuel, and owners of a garden pizza oven should bear it in mind – it is the best fuel for this fine purpose.

Gorse is a native species of Western Europe, though exceedingly rare in Scandinavia. It seems to have arrived in Britain with Neolithic man, who probably used it for fuel. Later the young branches were used as fodder, made more palatable by being crushed, first using hand tools and in later years with machines such as Messrs Wedlake's splendid Gorse Crusher, made in the mid-nineteenth century. It seems a pity that this practice has gone almost completely out of fashion and the Gorse is burned where it grows or after cutting. I have asked a farmer friend who has a field overrun with Gorse if he could pile some in the corner for me to collect in my pickup. I plan to experiment with it on my woodburning stove.

Gorse is famous for flowering at random times throughout the year, with a notable burst of floral activity towards the end of April. It is believed that there are two types of the Common Gorse, one that flowers mostly in April, one that flowers mostly in the winter. In this way at least one form or the other can seed nearly every year.

Common Gorse supports twenty species of micro-fungi and six galls, which make their presence known as swellings on the stems, artichoke-like structures where the flowers should be or a lump on the spiny leaves. Six galls is not a high number, but the tough nature of the plant makes it a difficult target. I have occasionally found larger fungi on Gorse, most often Witch's Butter, *Tremella mesenterica*, a brilliant orange jelly fungus. Much less commonly I have seen the Gorse Crampball, *Daldinia fissa*. *Daldinia* species are xerophytic, meaning that they like, or at least tolerate, dry conditions. Such desert landscapes do not exist in Britain – unless there has been a fire. So it is that *D. fissa* fruits only after its host Gorse has been partially burned.

Gorse is something I talk about a great deal on my wild food forays, though not with much enthusiasm. The petals can be mixed in a bread dough to make the bread look pretty when sliced: they can be steeped in vodka and sugar for a few days to make a brightly coloured but otherwise indifferent liqueur, or they can be made into an equally indifferent wine that tastes of pea, with maybe just a hint of the same phoneme, but with two 'e's.

The Banana

The formerly full car park was almost empty when we arrived back after our all-day but gentle walk. We drove back to our hotel, calling into a supermarket on the way for some provisions. I left D in the car and collected a few things from the shelves. One was a bunch of bananas that were over-ripe, or 'perfect', depending on taste. As they went through the checkout, one became untidily detached, so I put it in my trouser pocket to eat in the car. When it was time to pay, the lady at the checkout asked, 'Is that a banana in your pocket?' Resisting the almost irresistible response (she did, after all, have me down as a thief and introducing an off-colour joke did not seem wise), I explained. She would have none of it, 'But you didn't buy any bananas!' she said. I pointed out that I most certainly had, whereupon she checked through the receipt and eventually, red-faced but without even a faint mist of apology, said, 'Oh. You did.' I chuckled all the way back to the car, my banana in my hand.

Seil

ATLANTIC HAZEL RAINFOREST

FOUR MILES

26 JUNE 2021

Temperate Rainforests

Advance preparation is everything on projects like ours, so when we were about twenty-five miles away from Seil, I looked to see if there was anywhere we might stay. Fortune sometimes rewards the chaotically inclined, and I found a lovely hotel alongside Loch Feochan, a small sea loch six miles south of Oban. Our hotel, Knipoch House ('Knipoch', I am assured, means 'place of the knolls' or 'hilly place', neither of which narrows it down much in Scotland), was almost perfect, the only issue being one common to all such venerable establishments – it creaked. After a first-class meal (and I am infuriatingly fussy about such things) we had a few drinks and then retired for the night. A little after midnight we were woken by creaking sounds from above. The clientele, I think it is fair to say, were of the elderly persuasion (myself included), so I fancy that the creaks were due to weak bladders rather than embarrassing romantic engagement. With this reassuring thought, we went back to sleep, me dreaming of the Scottish temperate rainforest that was our destination for the following day.

I have visited this rare and variable habitat type only twice before: Holford Wood on the Quantock Hills and Wistman's Wood on Dartmoor. The latter is one of the most extraordinary places I have seen; for Tolkien enthusiasts it *is* Fangorn Forest, albeit in miniature. While I saw no trees that could walk, they all looked as though they might if sufficiently roused. In my mind's eye I see nothing but moss, flowing over boulders and trees. I checked with some of the photographs I took at the time, and it seems my memory is entirely accurate. Like its fictitious counterpart, it was forbidding like no other wood I have seen; the very edge was as far as I felt I could go.

With such limited experience of these habitats and their fame being chiefly down to their lichens, mosses, liverworts and ferns, I knew I would be out of my depth as an observer but had decided to go anyway.

These forests are also famous for their fungi, but it was out of season and precious few of them made an appearance. Still, I was disappointed not to find more than I did. What I did manage to do was identify most of the plants I saw and photograph some of the many mosses and lichens as best I could for identification later.

The word 'rainforest' immediately brings to mind tropical rainforests, but the term refers to any woodland where the rainfall is sufficiently high. More specifically, it should have an average annual rainfall of 1,500 mm or above and should rain on an average of 200 days each year. Of course, a spruce plantation could be planted in such a location, but it would be a stretch to call it a temperate rainforest because all those that are treasured as such are species-rich and venerable. There are several bona fide temperate rainforests in Britain, as would be expected with its prevailing wind coming across an ocean. They are scattered along the western coast, with the greatest proportion being in Scotland, where the climate is optimal. Temperate rainforests come in several flavours, depending on the dominant tree species: Wistman's Wood is an Atlantic Oak Forest, for example. Birch is a common type, but there are also Scots Pine-dominated instances. On that day it would be one of the rarer specialities, Atlantic Hazel Rainforest. I chose this partly because I wanted to include

Scotland and because it involved less travel than going to any of the forests further north, but mostly because I have a great fondness for Hazel woods.

Such forests exist wherever climatic conditions are suitable. The Atlantic variety are also found in north-western France, the north coast of Spain and some of the Atlantic islands of Spain and Portugal. The north-western coast of North America, southern Chile, south-east corner of Australia, much of Japan and New Zealand have their own.

The British rainforests, at least, are remnants of much more extensive primeval forests that grew after the retreat of the ice, ten thousand years ago. Eighty per cent of land where the rainforests once grew is now cleared, or planted with non-native conifers, with just 30,000 hectares of Scottish temperate rainforest surviving. Many were transformed into blanket bogs (very wet and peaty bogs), though whether naturally or from the action of neolithic axes is not known. Thirty-thousand hectares may seem large, but it represents less than 0.4 per cent of the total area of Scotland. Those that survive are not quite what they once were, human intervention having caused numerous problems. Chief among these are plantation conifers and invasion by the dreaded *Rhododendron*. Now that they have been recognised for their impressive biodiversity, programmes have been instigated to remove unwanted species (Sitka Spruce and *Rhododendron* beware), protect what is left and even extend them with a fifty- or hundred-metre circumference around their perimeter (where possible) into which they will be encouraged to extend. I wish these projects well.

The Bridge over the Atlantic

Shamefully late the next morning, we left the hotel and went straight to the pub. The thought here was that we were in Scotland, four days after the longest day of the year, and that we had plenty of time for lunch. The approach to the pub was challenging – it was over a single-lane bridge. No ordinary bridge was this but one that crossed the Atlantic – just a bit of it. Known as Clachan Bridge, or more fancifully the Bridge over the Atlantic, it spans the sound that separates Seil from the mainland. This is excitement enough, one might think, but on the approach attention must be paid to any traffic coming in the opposite direction along the bank visible on the far side to the left, plus a twenty-second pause to await anything already past the point of visibility to cross the bridge first. Failure to do both may well result in an unavoidable head-on collision as the severely humpback nature of the bridge leaves nothing in the driver's view apart from sky.

The pub, Tigh An Truish, was very pleasant, with a small green opposite on which one could sit to drink a pint in peace while watching the activity on the sound and the steep hills of the mainland. The name, I learned, means 'The House of Trousers', a colourful reference to its one-time secondary use. After defeat at the Battle of Culloden, the Jacobite rebellion failed and the brandishing of bagpipes and wearing of kilts became punishable by fines or even transportation. For true Scots leaving the presumably safe haven of Seil for the mainland, the pub was where kilts were removed, and trousers donned.

So pleased were we with the pub that the next day (a day off) we returned. We had visited Oban in the morning and spoken with a charming woman who was minding the shop for the owner. I had thought the shop to be a tourist-only emporium but no, it was the real thing, a shop selling true Harris tweed clothes made to ancient patterns on Harris. We spent an hour and a half there talking, later, to the owner of both the shop and the mill. The woman, while telling us about the glories of Oban, mentioned some sea eagles that had been seen over the town. Never having seen one, I was duly impressed, but even more so when we saw a pair later that day flying over the sound near the House of Trousers.

An Impossible Terrain

My customary lack of preparation made our Scottish adventure slightly more adventurous than it might have been. Having studied the map, I decided there was only one place where we could park without the car being towed away or its integrity otherwise threatened – down near the Cuan Ferry slipway at the southern end of the island. After parking and pleasantly wasting time in cheerful conversation with another pair of visitors, we set off for our destination: Ballachuan Hazelwood. In a straight line it was less than a quarter of a mile away and the blessed lack of a law of trespass meant we did not need to stick to footpaths. Unfortunately, proximity and legal licence do not guarantee accessibility.

We walked back up the road we had driven down and soon turned right along a clear footpath that took us due east, as hoped, then up onto a low ridge that was covered in Foxgloves, several of them pure white. These pale beauties hung from their spikes like so many nightdresses billowing from a washing line. Such dramatic colour loss is down to a loss-of-function mutation (ability to produce the colour, in this case), but it may be that the ability is still there but has just been switched off. Sometimes, unexpectedly white flowers are produced when rare recessive genes are passed from both parents. White flowers where there should be colourful flowers is quite different from plant albinism, which is defined as a partial or total loss of the ability to produce chlorophyl. If the albinism is complete, the plant will die as soon as it exhausts the nutrients from its seed. The healthy white Foxgloves we saw that day were a recognised form, *Digitalis purpurea* f. *albiflora*.

From the top of the low ridge we could clearly see the slipway on the isle of Luing to our south, one that corresponds to the slipway near which we had parked. The islands here are packed tightly together and are known as the Slate Islands because vast quantities of slate were once mined there. Luing and its slipway was only five hundred metres from where we stood, less than half of that distance being sea. Apart from the hundreds of Foxgloves, the landscape in which we found ourselves was a rough pasture of grasses interspersed with White Clover, buttercups, sorrels, Field Speedwells, Tormentil, Red Campion and Rough Chervil, with Bracken dominating in places.

Also from the top of the small ridge we could see Ballachuan Hazelwood on a much higher ridge to the east. Our most direct way to it lay across two hundred metres of ground made up of very rough pasture, peaty mire, ditches that looked like military fortifications and three sturdy fences. On my own, I would have given it a go, but D, a Londoner to the core despite her forty years living in Dorset, would not, and so the only way was north. After five hundred metres this way too was blocked, with the only possibility being south-west, back to the road we had left an hour and a half earlier. Fortunately, our inadvertent diversion was rewarded with an orchid that, while frequent in north-west Scotland, is rare in most of the rest of Britain (or at least under-recorded as it has only recently been accepted as a separate species). It was the deep pink **Heath Fragrant Orchid**, *Gymnadenia borealis*. The back of its flower elongates into a long spur, which requires the long tongue of certain moths to reach the nectaries inside.

That south-westerly path also found an enormous, multi-stemmed Sycamore, completely covered with mosses and lichens. It grew alongside a dyke – the Scottish word for a drystone wall – which was similarly adorned. Among the many lichens we found on the Sycamore's trunk were the leafy, pale green *Parmotrema perlatum*. This is one of the handful of edible lichens, and is used in curries for its earthy and smoky flavours. The second lichen was *Pertusaria hymenea*, also common in Britain but largely absent from the Midlands and much of East Anglia. This species forms a crust of tiny, clustered grey and thick-walled cups. There was also the superficially similar *Ochrolechia parella*, colloquially known as Crottle. On the wall was the trailing lichen *Ramalina cuspidata*, an uncommon and strictly maritime (the sea was close) grey-green branching species and a very gratifying find. We were to see a related species an hour later, *Ramalina fastigiata*. Finally, there was *Hypotrachyna laevigata*, a foliose (leafy) lichen with an exclusively western distribution. I find it difficult to explain my relatively new-found passion for lichens. I assume that it is the intricate beauty, which is only seen through a loupe or under a microscope, that appeals, or maybe it is their complex lifestyle or simply their other-worldly qualities or just that they are difficult to identify. Perhaps you see these things too. I hope so. I trust that this list of lichens found in a small area has not been too tedious. If you were thrilled rather than bored, then the good news is that there are more to come shortly. Believe me when I tell you that you are being let off very lightly: Seil boasts no fewer than four hundred species of lichen.

The Road to Ballachuan Hazelwood

After finding ourselves back on the main road, just two hundred metres north of where we had left it, we walked north for half a mile and came to the road that leads east towards the main entrance to the reserve that is Ballachuan Hazelwood. We had earlier decided not to drive down this road as there was no hint of a car park where one might be expected. Had my research been more thorough, I might have noticed that, while an attempt to park anywhere along that road would have been difficult, Kilbrandon Church, to the left of the main road and opposite the junction, leads a double life as a place of worship *and* a car park to serve the reserve.

The side-road followed a steep downwards gradient towards the reserve and then a further three hundred metres across a wet plain which was, I discovered later, only three metres above sea level. As with all our days of walking, there was much to see along even this short stretch. Here we found two forageable species: the invasive but extremely useful **Japanese Rose**, *Rosa rugosa*, with which I make rose-petal vodka for cocktails and Turkish Delight, Honeysuckle, with which a mead can be made provided you *really* like the smell of Honeysuckle, **Meadowsweet**, *Filipendula ulmaria*, which other people (not me) use to make wines, syrups and alcoholic infusions that all taste like an ointment for boils, and **Cuckoo Flower**, *Cardamine pratensis*, a delicate member of the Cabbage Family with mustard-flavoured pink flowers that are worth eating as a salad decoration. In addition, there was Common Sorrel, the perpetual bad-hair day of the **Ragged Robin**, *Silene flos-cuculi*, **Yellow-Flag Iris**, *Iris pseudacorus*, and numerous rushes, all confirming the damp nature of the soil.

Ballachuan Wood

At last we arrived at the gates of Ballachuan (Tolkien comes to mind again). Once through, we could see the wood clambering up the low hill two hundred metres south across a grassy, rocky and frequently wet area. The reserve that includes Ballachuan wood is around fifty hectares in extent, twenty-seven of which are inhabited by Hazel. The rest is occupied by other trees, including a few Beeches planted in the nineteenth century, as well as willows and birches, or is left unwooded. The unwooded area lies predominantly along a low, narrow strip of grass heath along the entire western edge and Bracken and grass patches on the plateau among the Hazels. The entire eastern side of the wood descends to the sea. It is now owned by the Scottish Wildlife Trust, who, seeing the importance of the site, bought it in 1984.

Purchases of land by public bodies for reasons of conservation are fairly unusual, and less so than in the 1980s. They are often seen as a last resort by the authorities that pay the bill. It was certainly worthwhile in this case, and I would be pleased to see such practices extended or reintroduced. An authority, working with local wildlife trusts or national groups such as, in this case, the Lichen Society, can be very successful in protecting and understanding an area that has biological and often historical value. There are often arguments over how much grazing, if any, should be allowed and over proposed reintroduction of species, but if Ballachuan is a guide, it can work out very well.

A charming display of orchids welcomed us inside the gate – the **Northern Marsh Orchid,** *Dactylorhiza purpurella*, and the **Heath Spotted Orchid**, *D. maculata*, plus several plants that I had never knowingly seen before, plus the usual mosses and lichens. But what engaged me most was a furry, deep-orange coating to a rock. Dismissing the superficially obvious guess that it was a fungus, since fungi other than lichens simply cannot grow on rocks, I was pleased to discover that it was an uncommon alga, a *Trentepohlia* species. It is one of the so called 'green algae', though there was nothing remotely green about it, the chlorophyl hidden and protected by carotenoid pigments, something that also happens with lichens and the reason why some of them are brightly coloured. There are scattered populations across Britain, most of them further north in Scotland.

Among the mosses on the drystone wall and less exposed rock was a liverwort. I mentioned liverworts and the difficulties of identifying all but a few in the chapter on Tryfan. This one, however, I was prepared to make an informed guess at as it had a thallus (leaf-like structure). The thalli were shiny, their surface divided into multiple 'tiles', each with a raised dot in the middle. It was **Conocephalum conicum**, sometimes known as the Snakeskin Liverwort, for obvious reasons.

The unregarded liverworts form a world of barely explored beauty. *Conocephalum* species, for example, gain their generic name from what look like hundreds of tiny mushrooms that cover their surface when they decide to come into fruit: they are in fact cones (hence *conocephalum*) on a stick, and are the reproductive structures. With the liverworts, detail is everything, whether in identification or in the appreciation of their beauty. Their structures are complex and almost absurdly varied, but a loupe or, better still, a 'dissecting' microscope is needed to reveal that detail, that beauty.

A common plant everywhere, though especially so in Scotland, is **Wild Angelica**, *Angelica sylvestris*. I found none in flower, directing my attention to the leaves. I had never before noticed the fearsomely sharp 'claws' that form their serrated edge, though fortunately they are soft. The collectable part of the plant for the forager is the immature seed heads. These are full of angelica flavour and make a pleasant vodka infusion or curry ingredient.

The low, flat area before the small hill on which the Hazel wood is situated contained a couple of ponds linked by a stream to the nearby and almost circular Ballachuan Loch, situated alongside the reserve to the west, which drained into the sea only a hundred metres to the east. One pond was as fresh as a daisy, the other partially dried out and covered with algae. From its general appearance (thick, lumpy and yellow-green) it was the common filamentous algae, *Spirogyra* sp. and known generally as **Blanket Weed**. It is a typical summer species and not something you would wish for in your pond.

In a brackish area beside one of the ponds I saw the flower spikes of **Sea Arrowgrass**, *Triglochin maritima*. The base of its stem smells strongly of cumin, and perhaps it would go nicely with the smoky lichen and Wild Angelica seeds to make a Scottish curry.

The Geology

The entrance to the wood was up a short but steep slope. The bare sides of the ridge rose about fifteen metres above the plain to the west and consisted of some particularly attractive geology. The basis of any terrestrial ecology is a matter of climate and geology. With these defined, the next level is the plant species available that might colonise an area of land and their associated support organisms in the form of fungi and bacteria. Lichens content to grow on bare rocks will also appear and possibly some algae. Those of this list that contain chlorophyll are primary producers of biomass and known in the jargon of ecology as 'autotrophs'. To describe an ecosystem properly, these factors must be known, as it is these autotrophs that delimit the animals and fungi that will subsequently and often very quickly find a home there. The geology provides the canvas on which these organisms are painted, and will allow only those organisms that 'like' the characteristics of the rocks and subsequent soils and subsoils. The pH is of great importance in deciding what can thrive, and that of the rocks at Ballachuan was low – acid. Permeability – in this case it was impermeability – also plays its role.

With Ballachuan, all my untutored eye could see was sedimentary rocks with mysteriously oriented lines running orthogonally to the plane of deposition that were tilted a serious 70 degrees to the horizontal. I subsequently sent a photo of it to Eddie for his consideration. 'Ah,' he wrote back, 'Craignish Phyllite – a six-hundred-million-year-old meta-arenite (sandstone) sequence from Seil!' and added how much he admired my salicaceous photos (I had sent him a few previously). The 'vertical' deposits, he told me, were of quartz that had dissolved under high tectonic pressure and crystallised in the vertical gaps formed where there was negative tectonic pressure (stretching). So now we know.

The Hazel Wood

We entered the wood, leaving the bright sunshine behind us. The Hazel was, of course, in full leaf, so the light was poor to the point of 'gloomy'. There was a path to follow, and we kept to that simply because the treacherously uneven ground and dense growth made it difficult to leave. As we walked further into the forest, I found that I was surprised by, well, the lack of surprises. Superficially at least, it seemed like every Hazel coppice I know in Dorset, except that it was more chaotic, and the trees' multiple stems were of irregular diameters and comparatively crooked. They twisted and branched out in the messy manner of nature left untended: they also carried *much* more lichen and moss. Together, these elements showed that the wood was natural, not (at least recently) managed by man. Such management is known as 'coppicing', where the Hazel would (usually) be cut to ground level every few years, then allowed to regrow with all the new stems about the same diameter and straight. While such management might seem like a sterile way to treat a forest, human intervention when done carefully can actually encourage diversity and interest; indeed repeated cutting over the various five-, ten- or fifteen-year cycles produces a variety of habitats, from a bright open patch in the woods to the close cover of a mature Hazel canopy, and a corresponding variety of organisms. Butterflies and plants that prefer more light, for example, will establish in the newly cut patches for a few years. What you do lose by coppicing are the lichens and mosses. These take a long time to establish, and there is simply not time. Finally, I was pleased to see that the forest was not moribund, that is, displaying a lack of new growth (a problem with some of these ancient forests) – here there were numerous young shoots making their way towards the canopy.

Few things are certain here, but evidence of the hand of man is, nevertheless, clear, and there is no doubt that the existing Hazels found by colonisers were once coppiced. Indeed, 'Ballachuan' means 'settlement by the sea'. Documentary and physical evidence of settlement was recorded in a 2004 report funded by the Scottish Wildlife Trust. Clear evidence exists for Bronze Age and Iron Age habitation for Seil in general, though not for Ballachuan itself. There is little beyond this apart from the settlements in the form of moss-covered foundations and the field systems discovered by researchers. Unfortunately they were coy about dating without more extensive investigation – their remit having been to record what was there, not interpret what they found.

Hazel was an early and major pioneer species when the ice retreated at the end of the ice age 10,000 years ago. The exposed west coast of Scotland has been suggested as a difficult place for climax trees such as Elm, Oak and Lime to establish themselves, though they grow there well enough when planted or when grazing is curtailed. Here it might be the case that the presumably tougher Hazel *is* the climax woodland.

We did not see anything man-made that day, though had we been there when the Bracken was not in flamboyant growth, we would have noticed that some of the open areas are disused arable fields from their telltale signs of rig and furrow cultivation. Numerous consumption cairns (piles of rocks removed from fields to allow cultivation) were also discovered and, towards the south, a jetty. The buildings, now nothing more than traces of mossed-over stone, are within the Hazel itself. Rig and furrow cultivation goes back at least to the Middle Ages, but there is nothing more as yet to enable a precise dating. Such dates do not, however, really concern us; it is what the people who lived there did with the woodland that matters.

Very little, it seems, as, apart from the areas cleared for arable, the Hazel was likely to have been a carefully conserved resource. The authors of the report suggest that coppicing works poorly in the harsh environment of the north-west, with new growth subsequent to the cut being slow and not producing straight 'wands' (as the lengths of Hazel were called). Instead, they may have cut suitable wands *individually*, leaving most of any Hazel intact. This would have provided a more stable ecosystem in which the many rare lichens and mosses found the continuity they require to survive and flourish.

Much as pollarding extends the life of standard trees, coppicing seems to do the same. However, it is difficult to say how long a Hazel might live as it can, eventually, die off in the middle, only to form an external ring of new, vegetative growth. I have personal knowledge of Hazels – an entire wood of them that have barely changed in the more than forty years I have known them. Individual and enormous (some 2 m in diameter), these Hazels are almost old friends. Whatever the age of the Hazels of Ballachuan, they are living components of the nearest we are likely to come in Britain to a true primaeval woodland.

Later, as we exited the wood, we saw a tree other than a Hazel: a Hawthorn, whose branches were scarcely visible beneath their cloak of lichens. Not far away was an Alder, or possibly two side by side. It had seen better days, with bits falling off quicker than they were being replaced. Still it clung to life, while life clung to it. Again, nearly every inch was covered in lichens, this time the common, foliose lichen **Flavoparmelia caperata** and ferns. Its rotten branches showed attention from woodpeckers and wood-boring invertebrates.

The Fungi

Among the first species we found in the wood were two fungi. I took no samples home, so my determinations here are 'field IDs', which can turn out to be quite different once something is studied under the microscope. The first was a small mushroom, 3 cm in diameter, with a dull orange cap and stem, and pale gills. It was not immediately clear what it was but seemed likely to be an exceptionally perfect (hence my hesitation) **Gymnopus dryophilus** (formerly *Collybia dryophila*). This is one of the commonest of all the woodland fungi and, frankly, quite a disappointment.

The second was not much easier from field characteristics alone. It consisted of dozens of 3-mm-diameter rubbery orange discs, each attached to the bark of a Hazel by means of a short stem. In cross-section, it was funnel-shaped. Little disc fungi like this are often in the genus *Hymenoscyphus*, and my guess for this one was **Hymenoscyphus calyculus**. Fungi that form discs are common in woodland, *Hymenoscyphus* alone fielding seventy species just in Britain.

There are two species of *Hymenoscyphus* with which you may be familiar. One, *H. fructigenus*, always grows peaceably on old hazelnut shells, and the other, *H. fraxineus*, is simply notorious. While most members of the genus make a quiet living consuming dead organic matter, *H. fraxineus* spends its time trashing the hotel room, for it is the cause of Ash Dieback disease.

I cannot leave the fungi of Ballachuan without mentioning one that we did not see and that is confined entirely to Seil and its cousin rainforests, the Hazel Glove Fungus, *Hypocreopsis rhododendri*. It is an extraordinary fungus that does indeed look like a glove, albeit with many more fingers than the customary five. Its fat orangey digits crowd out from tree limbs, ready to grasp anyone who dares to come near. It will not surprise you to learn that it is a parasite, but not of passers-by or its Hazel host but of another fungus, common on Hazels, the Glue Crust Fungus, *Hymenochaete corrugata*. This latter fungus does just what it says: it glues together any two branches that are touching, its dull-brown fruiting bodies extending from one branch to another. We didn't see this fungus either, though we kept our eyes peeled for both.

The Lichens of Ballachuan Hazelwood

It is time for the stars of this show, the Ballachuan lichens. These, and those of other temperate rainforests, are of international importance, and many are consummate beauties, the jewels of the wood. We wove our way through the Hazels, and I stopped to set up tripod and camera to attempt photographs as best I could in the low light. While there were many reported from Ballachuan that I did not see, many I encountered but did not photograph and several that I did photograph that were too blurry to identify, I did not do too badly. Of these, I have chosen just two, because both of them are temperate rainforest specialists, insisting on a permanent habitat and the heavy rainfall of the area.

Pectenia cyanoloma is almost entirely confined to Scotland's rainforests, with just one record each in England and in Wales according to the Lichen Society. It is one of Scotland's 'Internationally Important' lichens. Its grey thallus forms an irregular disc of lobes, each concentrically and broadly ribbed. Its apothecia (fruiting structures) are rounded, clustered and red-brown when young. Crustose lichens like this species often have a layer beneath the thallus called the 'prothallus'. This is a mass of fungal hyphae that lack any algal component. The Lichen Society likens (*sic*) it to a carpet underlay. It is usually invisible, but in one of the young individuals I saw it was clear as a fuzzy grey structure.

The second, **Ricasolia virens**, while being *slightly* more common and found in Wales and south and south-west England, is even more attractive. It is large, the specimens I saw being easily 10 cm across, with lobes flattened to the bark. They are a pale but still vibrant green and the apothecia deep red cups with a pale rim. I was delighted with what I had found, as most of their representative specimens were in perfect condition and, for once, I was thoroughly impressed by their rarity.

The Toad and Tautonyms

On a walk largely devoid of animal species, I found a common **Black Slug**, *Arion ater*. Its common name is among the most straightforward I know, as its Latin name derives from the Greek for 'slug' *areíones*, and *ater*, which is Latin for 'black'. The other creature, inches away from the slug and giving the small scene a slimy aspect, was the more memorably named *Bufo bufo*, the **Toad**. 'Tautonyms', as such doubles (and sometimes triples) are called, are allowed under the rules for zoological nomenclature but banned under those that govern the naming of plants, fungi and algae. They are seldom, perhaps never, coined anew; instead they are the result of these rules of nomenclature combined with a change in taxonomic understanding. When a species is assigned to a new genus – something that occurs when an existing genus can easily be divided into two or more distinct genera – its original specific epithet is sometimes promoted to generic status (see *Persicaria* in the chapter on Hayling Island). The rules insist that specific epithets are conserved (kept), so a species ends up with a name with two identical parts. In this case, the original name of the Toad was *Rana bufo*, literally, 'the frog that is a toad'. It was decided that frogs and toads are too distantly related to reside in the same genus, and so the specific name (second name) of the Toad (*Bufo*) was promoted as the generic name for the toad genus. Other examples of this nomenclatural quirk are the Wolverine, *Gulo gulo*, literally 'glutton glutton' and the already mentioned (see the Tryfan chapter) Wheatear, *Oenanthe oenanthe*. I will leave the explanation of *Troglodytes troglodytes troglodytes* (the wren), *Buteo buteo buteo* (buzzard) and, wait for it, *Bufo bufo bufo* as an exercise for the reader.

I have always harboured a fondness for toads, a fondness laced with a touch of pity for so sticky and slimy a creature. When I was at grammar school, my class was instructed by our biology teacher to collect frogs over the weekend for dissection back in class. Derek and I made our way to a field just north of Langstone Harbour and collected what we proudly assumed to be a frog. Just as we had put the creature in a box, satisfied that we would be achieving top marks on Monday, we were accosted by two huge, bearded men, presumably the farmer and his son, whose evident mission in life was to terrorise thirteen-year-old boys. They towered over us with menace and malice on their faces, and the fuss they made would have been justified only had we tried to run away with the whole field tucked under our arms. This was my first encounter with apoplectic farmers, but sadly it was not to be my last, not by a long way. But we did manage to escape with what we still assumed to be a frog. On Monday, Mr Kent expressed severe disappointment in our inability to tell a toad from a frog (it was a toad) and we never saw the toad again. I always wondered what happened to her.

Flowers and Mushrooms

I have said little about the flora of the wood, and it was indeed largely unremarkable as is typical of most, or at least many woods. The canopy excludes light from the forest floor and, with a few exceptions and in the odd corner where the light shines through, only those plants that can leaf up in the spring before the canopy closes over and a few shrubby plants with dark leaves that indicate more than the usual amount of chlorophyll, such as Ivy and Butcher's Broom, can make a home there. A few Blue-bells were to be seen, Red Campion, Cow Parsley, Wood Forget-Me-Not, Bugle, **Woodruff**, *Galium odoratum*, and the odd Wood Sorrel. The two of these plants worth picking to eat (not that I did or would in such a location) were the fruity-flavoured and handsome leaves and stems of Wood Sorrel and the coumarin-rich aroma (the smell of hay) of dried Woodruff, which is used in drinks and syrups.

Unsurprisingly, there were several species of ferns among the Hazels, with **Hard Fern,** *Blechnum spicant,* making a good picture. It is an exceptionally neat and understated species with its narrow fronds which come to a point only at the very tip. I was pleased to see **Sanicle,** *Sanicula europaea,* as it was another plant I had never noticed before, though it made a welcome and surprising appearance in my Dorset flower bed the next year. It is another member of the Apiaceae (Carrot Family), produces bright pink florets and has rounded, deeply indented leaves in a rosette. After two hours in the woods and a pleasant day turning to drizzle (well, it *was* a rainforest) we felt we had seen enough.

The Plants below the Wood

We were now on the narrow, flattish area of wet grassland to the west of the wood and walking back northwards. Much of the grassland was now scattered with Bracken, which made it a walk that was wetter still in the rain. In the Scottish Isles you might come across any number of lovely plants, but the most spectacular plant we saw here was **Marsh Cinquefoil,** *Potentilla palustris,* of which there were several specimens. The colour of the petals, calices, pedicels and even anthers is sometimes described undramatically in books as 'maroon', but 'bloody' is more accurate. It is a common enough plant, but with only scattered outposts in the south-eastern half of Britain. The specific epithet, *palustris,* is a reference to its favoured habitat – marshes.

Another plant lending colour to the grasslands was the bright purple of a **Common Butterwort**, *Pinguicula vulgaris*. This is a truly northern plant and does not occur in much of England south of Sheffield, where there are just a few scattered records. It was for this reason, and the simple fact that it looked like one, that your Southern author originally mistook it for a violet – and spent pointless hours trying to decide which one. It is an insectivorous plant that lures its prey on to the sugary hairs inside its flowers and digests them within the long spur.

We were almost back at the gate to the reserve when we saw some mushrooms that had gone unnoticed on our arrival. They were almost certainly **Field Mushrooms**, *Agaricus campestris*, because of their size, the overhanging skin of the cap and the fragile ring on the stem, but were a little too mature for us to come to any firm conclusion. Colour changes on bruising or cutting, for example, are seldom visible on old fruit bodies and are sometimes critical in identifying *Agaricus* species. The genus *Agaricus*, which includes Horse Mushrooms, Wood Mushrooms, The Prince and several other first-class edible species, is the very devil for the field mycologist. There are forty species plus varieties recorded from Britain, and examining the finer points of a specimen is everything. Two species, incidentally, are poisonous – *A. xanthodermus* and *A. moelleri*, otherwise known as Yellow Stainers. They are not deadly, but from the very many reports of their effects that I have heard over the years, death might well be a blessed relief. I had uprooted one of the Field Mushrooms to examine the ring on the stem and, rather than just drop it on the ground, I fixed it to the top of a fence post with a slender piece of wood that I had inserted in a fissure in the post. This gives it the chance to continue producing and distributing its spores. This is a trick I use frequently when I do not wish to take a specimen home.

Leaving the reserve, we retraced our steps (well some of them) back to the car. I had loved everything I saw that day, but now I was to encounter something not so welcome – **Himalayan Balsam**, *Impatiens glandulifera*. The specimen I found was in bud, and it was with shameful treachery that I admired its beauty. Our final find was the **Woolly Fringe-Moss**, *Racomitrium lanuginosum*, a truly spectacular plant, cascading down a dyke.

It was late by the time we reached the car, and the prospect of dinner seemed faint in that remote area. The hotel restaurant having taken last food orders an hour ago, we were expecting a dinner of crisps, chocolate biscuits and a few extremely mature bananas. We returned to the hotel and asked if there was the slightest chance of something better. There was.

The New Forest

LOWLAND DECIDUOUS WOODLAND
AND CONIFEROUS PLANTATION, ACID
GRASSLAND, MIRE AND HEATH

NINE MILES

18, 19 AND 30 OCTOBER 2021

The Forest and Model Aeroplanes

The dates above for this walk are clear indicators that it did not go entirely to plan. The year 2021, unlike its predecessor, when most, if not all, fungi fruited vigorously, was unhelpfully restrained. I had been convinced that we could do it in a day, but it took three. These were taken in reverse order, but together, comprising a walk that was continuous geographically speaking, if not temporally. If the dates were to follow the path, so to speak, they would run 30, 19, 18 October. D only joined me for the two consecutive days, no doubt because she had had enough the first time.

The overall walk was about nine miles, beginning (geographically) a little south-east of Bolderwood Car Park, and following the forest road towards Emery Down, then through Lyndhurst and south along the Beaulieu Road for a mile. We then went south, deep into the large area of forest that led, eventually, to Balmer Lawn, near Brockenhurst, the last bit of the journey involving some hack and slash.

I know the New Forest very well, visiting it at least ten times a year and frequently staying over in a hotel when I take my fungus forays there. It is for this reason that I returned to the forest for this walk, plus the encouraging fact that approaching 3,000 species of fungi have been recorded there. The New Forest and a few other ancient woodlands, plus ancient grasslands, are where to go if you wish to find the rarer fungi. In choosing woodland, I

271

strongly suggest sticking to those that are native: the oaks, birch, Beech and Scots Pine – the last one preferably in its native range. These are the major trees that form mycorrhizal relationships with fungi that produce large fruiting bodies. There are others worth looking out for, such as Hornbeam, and it was under one of these, in 2022, that I found the rarest British fungus of all those I had seen. The fourth British record and its second location. It was *Hemileccinum depilatum*, a Bolete.

Apart from a few barely remembered visits in the early 1960s, my earliest memories of the New Forest are of autumnal Sunday outings with Peter Marsden, my friend from school, and his parents. Peter's father (and leader of our tomb-raiding adventure – see the Tryan chapter) was a teacher and also ran the Tip Top model shop in Portsmouth. He, Peter and I were all keen model aeroplane makers, and the point of the visits was to fly our creations at the designated model aircraft area near Beaulieu. It was here that I discovered the dry and papery remains of a puffball. I know it was a puffball because Mr Marsden told me – well, he was a schoolteacher. Knowing vastly more about fungi now and with a clear memory of what we saw that day, I can add that it was *Lycoperdon nigrescens*. This was one of the handful of inspirational moments that led to my lifetime interest in fungi. It was the sheer weirdness of these organisms that entranced me, plus the fact that they did not fit at all into my youthful and profoundly ignorant understanding of the natural world – that is, plants and animals.

The New Forest lies within the Hampshire Basin, a formation that stretches from Dorchester in Dorset in the west, to just past Hayling Island in the east. Much of Dorset, notably around Wareham, is almost indistinguishable from the New Forest, being on the same formation and left for heath and woodland. The superficial geology is as simple as it is evident – gravel, sand

Seil

Ballachuan Hazelwood

Drainage ditch in the peat

Mosses indicating the wet climate

Sycamore at its species-rich best

Loch and rocky pasture

An algae – *Trentepohlia* sp.

Rock formation at Ballachuan

Irregular wands of Hazel

The exquisite *Ricasolia virens*

Pectenia cyanoloma

Snakeskin Liverwort

Common Butterwort

Marsh Cinquefoil

Woolly Fringe-Moss

The New Forest

A typical New Forest view

Valley mire

Ugly Milkcap

Saffron Milkcap

Meadow Coral

Jelly Rot

Sphagnum flush

Sweet Gale

Tiered Tooth

Mycena rorida

Relic pseudosclerotial plates

Fool's Webcap

and clay, with the clay being just that little bit *too* evident. This is strictly wellington boot country.

The soil, then, is poor, but it is this, plus a historic need for timber for shipbuilding and a complex system of land tenure, that has saved the New Forest from much human interference, at least the sort of interference that might have turned it into an arable desert. It has its problems, but for the most part it is the biological jewel of southern England. Like one of the great and the good that has received an abundance of honours and acquired too many doctorates, its post-nominals are legion: SSSI, SAC, BAP, SPA, WII, RAMSAR. WII might give you some trouble should you try to look it up: it means Wetland of International Importance, not a games console.

The name New Forest is one with an inherently expired sell-by date. It may have been new once, but that was nearly a thousand years ago, when it was established as a Royal Forest. That it long pre-dates its establishment in 1079 is undoubtable – it was never much use for agriculture. Even with tree cover giving way to grazing and back to tree cover as fashion patchily dictated, it has enjoyed an overall continuity of biota that is almost unparalleled in Western Europe. It is also large, covering an area of 218 square miles (556 km²). This matters, as small, isolated communities of organisms are always susceptible to local extinction.

Much of the Forest is heathland, but on this walk our mission was to look mostly for fungi, and it is among and upon trees that most can be found. So it was that we kept to the wooded areas as much as possible. We also kept *away* from the ponies. These are the New Forest ponies – beautiful, but plain nasty. Five years ago I saw an elderly lady who tried to shoo a pony away from some birdseed she had put down in the car park. The pony turned around and kicked her sufficiently hard for her to fly two metres through the air. She was quite seriously injured.

Dangerous they may be, but the five thousand ponies that the Forest supports are what make it such a great place to visit and pure heaven for the fungi. They keep the larger areas of grassland short and thus eminently suitable for grassland fungi, and dramatically reduce the amount of undergrowth in the woods. I noticed this recently in a broadly fenced-off area around the 'Knightwood Oak', a historically important tree that found itself gradually disappearing behind a mass of brambles. Where the ponies are free to roam and graze, you can walk for miles, largely untroubled by brambles and ivy. Such open habitats, created and maintained by grazing ponies, provide a huge area in which fungi may fruit without fighting their way upwards. Sadly, most of our woods are ungrazed and overgrown, and any fungi just give up.

DAY ONE

The walk from our hotel in Lyndhurst took us south along Beaulieu Road. It was grey and damp. This is no town road or even hedgerow-bordered country road, but one with grass either side, usually down a small slope. To our left (east) was a small, incongruous but nevertheless natural hill called Bolton's Bench. The Duke of Bolton was a New Forest Master Keeper in the eighteenth century, though why he was so honoured is lost to history. And 'bench'? I am not entirely sure of this either, but there are benches surrounding the group of trees on the top, and maybe they or their predecessors have been there for centuries. I remember coming here in the early 1960s and discovering the fungus known as Cramp Balls, *Daldinia concentrica*, the first fungus I ever identified and the second of the two mushrooms that would direct me to a lifetime interest in mycology. It is rare in the New Forest as it always grows on dead Ash, which is itself a rarity in the Forest.

The Astonishing Valley Mire

The first fungus we found was the **Meadow Puffball**, *Lycoperdon pratense*. It is common and only moderately edible in that it is small, difficult to peel, soft in texture and not of great flavour. Damned completely by faint criticism, I think. Still, it is a pretty thing, slightly oval in outline and with a faint peach blush. The puffball was on the grassy bank that runs down from the roadside (New Forest roads are raised above the surrounding and often wet land), but the flat area at the bottom of the slope was a no-go area for all but the most water-tolerant of fungi, none of which was prepared to brave the day. This is the type of habitat (known as a 'valley mire') that human beings both avoid and disregard, but it is the home to many plants that are found *only* in such conditions. Remarkably, the New Forest is home to ninety out of 120 valley mires that are to be found in the whole of north-west Europe. Here I saw **Marsh Pennywort**, *Hydrocotyle vulgaris*, **Bog Pondweed**, *Potamogeton polygonifolius*, **Bog St John's Wort**, *Hypericum anagalloides*, **Floating Club-Rush**, *Eleogiton fluitans*, and **Common Spike-Rush**, *Eleocharis palustris*. Marsh Pennywort is a considerable revelation for anyone who does not know *it* but does know Navelwort, *Umbilicus rupestris*, as they are superficially identical. The latter is a moderately edible plant (don't bother) of rocky places in the Stonecrop Family. However, Marsh Pennywort is in the Order Apiales and was, until quite recently, in the Apiaceae, the Carrot Family. I should be familiar with such violent deviations from the norm as they are legion, but each one comes as both a surprise and a delight. As to the habitat, this particular valley mire has a National Vegetation Classification: it is M29 Hypericum elodes – Potamogeton polygonifolius soakway. This was almost certainly the rarest ecosystem of all my walks, and the one I was most delighted to see. It is such a pity that it is unknown to nearly everyone, except as a soggy place to walk.

The Fungi of Birch

Our second fungus was growing near one of the many Birch trees at the damp bottom of the grassy slope along the roadside. It was one of the many that are linked to Birch in a mycorrhizal relationship where the vast extent of fine mycelial threads absorb more water and minerals than the fungus can use and which it donates to the tree. The donation is made through a connection with the tree's roots, the so-called Hartig Net, which consists of fungal hyphae that encompass root hairs. In exchange, the tree gives the fungus sugars. The fungus we found was the dark green/brown and large **Ugly Milkcap**, *Lactarius turpis*, for which Birch is the most common host. This is a mushroom I have long considered to be mildly poisonous, owing to its extremely hot flavour. It produces copious quantities of a milky fluid when damaged, and it is worth tasting some of this should you encounter the species.

One of the pleasures of talking to people about fungi on forays or elsewhere is that it is very seldom that I fail to learn something new. It could be a recipe, a bit of folk history, the jolly story of how father managed to poison the entire family and so on. These stories are especially interesting when the person telling them was brought up in another country or culture. It was from a Polish friend that I learned how to cook Ugly Milkcaps to make them palatable – it is just a matter of boiling them and throwing away the water, twice, then frying or pickling in salt (not vinegar). I have not yet tried this and never will because there is an unfortunate and revocatory codicil to this story – the species contains traces of the highly mutagenic compound necatorin. My former position of considering this fungus to be mildly poisonous was wrong: it is, in fact, potentially deadly. I will not be trying *any* method of cooking this species, but if it is one you already eat and are determined to continue eating, I suggest boiling it in watered-down vinegar or lemon juice as a low pH (*ideally* pH 5) degrades most of the troublesome necatorin.

The mushrooms kept coming. Two more Birch-related species were to be seen – the **Birch Bolete**, *Leccinum scabrum*, which is useful only when picked young, dried and powdered for soups etc., and the **Birch Knight**, *Tricholoma fulvum*, which is not useful at all. It had been an unusually bad year for the commonest of Birch species, indeed one of the commonest of all our species of fungi, the **Birch Polypore**, *Fomitopsis betulina*. The specimen we found was much smaller than one would expect for mid-October, it evidently not liking the 2021 weather any more than the rest of us. It is a fungus that I engage my patient foraging companions with for ten minutes or so as there is so much to tell. The large (sometimes over 30 cm wide), kidney-shaped brackets produced by this fungus are annual, forming tiers on the side of dead birch trunks. Old, rotting brackets persist too, and it is not unusual to see a recently fallen birch with new brackets arranged horizontally and parallel to the trunk and old brackets oriented vertically. The fertile layer where the spores are produced is, of course, underneath the brackets, and made up of tens of thousands of tiny pores. How the spores make their way down these tubes without hitting the sides is down to the almost unbelievably precise vertical orientation of the tubes, about which there is more later.

The Birch Polypore is not edible (though one of my more adventurous students did manage to eat a young specimen without ill effect). It does, however, have its uses. First: pulling away the membrane on the underside of the fungus will give you a sterile and slightly antibiotic bandage for any cuts suffered in the absence of a first aid box. Second: I sometimes make a strop for my plane blades and for my chisels from large rectangles cut from the entire fungus, dried, shaped and mounted on a block of wood. With a little burnishing cream it works extremely well, hence the alternative common name of Razor-Strop Fungus. Finally, it is also reputed to be helpful against several diseases, some of them serious. I am not well placed to comment on such matters, and the literature is contradictory. Nevertheless, sliced and made into a tea, it can, at least, do no harm.

It was no surprise to find one of the commonest of the fungi found on autumn walks through woodland and chiefly with Birch. It was the **Brown Rollrim**, *Paxillus involutus*. It is another ugly-looking mushroom, with deeply decurrent gills (the gills running down the stem) and a generally disreputable appearance. Despite its discouraging looks, and the fact that it is considered to be deadly, people do eat it, and most of the time they are fine. However, it contains an unidentified agent that can, eventually, cause death. It is believed that fatalities are restricted to those who have consumed the fungus before. They may be fine once, even twice, perhaps even several times – the final meal, however, results in autoimmune haemolytic anaemia, which destroys red blood cells, causing massive clotting within the vascular system. Nasty.

The Trouble with Parasols

The rain was quite heavy by now, so we walked quickly along the road in the hope of shelter in the woods. Just at the entrance we saw two edible species, a Field Mushroom in the grass and some Parasol mushrooms almost hiding in the scrub. I also found a Field Mushroom in Seil and described it there, but the Parasol is worth a little more attention here. The commonest species by far is *the* Parasol mushroom, *Macrolepiota procera*. It can grow to a considerable size – I have seen them nearly fifteen inches (38 cm) in diameter and almost as tall. It usually grows in rings in permanent grassland, some of these rings being fifty metres or more across. It is first seen as a small, brown, tapering cap nestling in the grass which develops as the stem grows to a drumstick shape and eventually opens out just like a parasol. The patchiness of cap and stem is down to the stretching and subsequent fracturing of their brown skin. It is very good to eat.

I have always suspected that the Parasol mushrooms I have found so frequently in the New Forest are not this common species of open permanent pasture that I know so well, and the group we found that day also gave me considerable pause. There are very few that it might be, with ***Macrolepiota fuliginosa*** being my best guess as it is known to possess a more woolly quality to the cap and is much darker; indeed its specific epithet means 'sooty'. It is also known to grow in woodlands. Fortunately, all *Macrolepiota* (Parasol) species are edible, and it is only the mycologist in me that cares for the specifics. Such difficulties are common with plants and fungi. There will be a handful of species within a genus that appear all the time plus a few that you may never see. Their rarity often makes one suspect that they do not actually exist, but that specimens of one of the common species that looked slightly different was named undeservedly as a new species. I do not, however, think this to be the case here.

Six or seven years ago I spotted a specimen of what I will now call *M. fuliginosa* hiding in the Bracken alongside the car park in the Forest, just as we were setting out on one of my public forays. My guests were slightly ahead, so I decided to pick it and put it in the basket. Unfortunately, it was covered in the type of 'golden dew' routinely produced by mammals. Whether it was a quadruped or biped, I did not wish to consider. The Parasol was otherwise an excellent specimen and destined for the show-and-tell table at the end of the day. So I picked it (carefully) and placed it safely under my pickup truck, on the principle that I did not want it *in* my truck, and no one would want it in the basket. When we returned three hours later, I found it had been stolen, presumably by someone who had taken it home for tea, a tea with extra piquancy, no doubt. Karma.

Before we leave Parasols, if you are determined to eat any, then make sure it is *M. procera*, or, at a stretch, the much more slender *M. mastoidea*. Avoid for now any that bruise pink as they will not be *Macrolepiota* species but *Chlorophyllum* species. Some of these (almost invariably it will be the Shaggy Parasol, *C. rhacodes*) are edible once cooked, but make sure you know what you are doing before proceeding. It is very well worth knowing that a fair percentage of people who eat Shaggy Parasols have to take a day or two off work. And then there are the Dapperlings.

Dapperlings are like diminutive Parasols, equally good-looking, and by luck we found one within 50 m of the Parasol described above. It was the uncommon **Lepiota oreadiformis**. The Dapperlings include several deadly poisonous species, though this was not one of them – not that I would think of eating it. Its specific epithet literally means 'shaped like a variety of fairy', but really likens it to *Marasmius oreades*, the Fairy Ring

Champignon that makes such a mess of people's lawns. It was exactly that, except that the cap was finely scaly and there was a hint of a ring zone on the stem. The Dapperling's small size (though some can reach 10 cm across the cap) means that it is easy enough to distinguish from any of the Parasols that come in at 15 cm or more across. Dapperlings have a ring-zone rather than the distinct and (with some care) movable ring seen in the Parasols.

The subjects of fungal (or plant) identification and Parasols have reminded me of an occasion (one that is increasingly common) when someone tested a mobile phone app on some of the specimens we had found on a fungus foray. He tried it on four species that I had named. Three were spot-on, but one was completely wrong. Frankly, I think a 75 per cent hit rate is almost miraculous, and the writers of the software concerned are all geniuses, but it is nowhere near good enough if the species in question is destined to be your dinner. As it happened, it also misnamed *Macrolepiota fuliginosa* as *Chlorophyllum rhacodes*, which is very similar in a photograph, though the differences between them are much clearer when you have one in your hand and can look more closely. Tempting as they are, I cannot truly recommend them to anyone who wishes to learn about the plants and fungi they find on their walks, as even were an app to be 100 per cent accurate, the user would never learn anything. Perhaps if one was seriously stuck, it might help, but having been provided with an ID, it would be essential to study the organism's characteristics so that any future finds will not require the assistance of a robot. Ultimately, it is cheating, and cheating is no fun at all.

Finally in this small area just inside the woods we found some **Poison Pies** (*Hebeloma* sp.), and a waxcap. The waxcap was ***Hygrocybe cantharellus***, a pretty and slender species which earns its name from the Chanterelle-like gills that similarly run down the stem. As to the *Hebeloma* species, I had no idea, and also no intention of taking a specimen home for ID later. There are about forty species in Britain and, while the larger of these have clear distinguishing characteristics, the rest are just small brown toadstools, nicely matching the 'small brown birds' that so trouble the casual ornithologist. I possess the excellently presented standard work, *The Genus Hebeloma*, by Jan Vesterholt, but seldom the patience to use it. Fatal for the chances of this genus attracting the casual mycologist is that none is edible.

Earthballs and Fungal Forms

One fungus we found that day, one that can nearly always be found in deciduous woodland, was the **Common Earthball**, *Scleroderma citrinum*. Earthballs are quite distinct from Puffballs, even though they are superficially similar, and distinct in more ways than you might think. The latter are generally edible, with varying degrees of tasty; the former are poisonous, though not deadly, ingestion merely involving confinement to very small quarters, and the skin of Earthballs is much thicker. Against all expectations, the similar Puffballs and Earthballs are in different Orders and thus only related in as much as they are both fungi within the Class Agaricomycetes. Class is a higher taxonomic rank, just above Order, the mammals, for example, being in the Class Mammalia, which runs from shrews to whales, respectively in the Order Eulipotyphla and the Order Cetartiodactyla.

This seems reasonable enough: the readily visible differences between Earthballs and Puffballs is about equivalent to that between a rabbit and panda, or a cow and a seal, with each mammal appearing in a different Order within the Class Mammalia. As one might expect, all or most of the animals within a mammalian Order have clear similarities – for example, the Order Eulipotyphla, in addition to shrews, contains hedgehogs and moles. Within the Order Boletales, however, there are Earthballs, Boletes such as the Penny Bun, fungi with gills such as species in the euphonious Hygrophoropsidaceae, which includes the False Chanterelle, various truffle-like species, brown and lumpy above-ground species in the Rhizopogonaceae, earthstars, some bracket fungi that have small teeth hanging below them, a handful of fungi that look like a poorly applied coat of white paint and the jelly-like horror of dry rot, *Serpula lacrymans*. This level of morphological difference is vast, and like finding a stick insect included in with the shrews and hedgehogs.

Such excess is not the result of careless or wilfully playful taxonomy, but a true representation of how things are related on the tree of life. It now gets worse. The Agaricales, taxonomic home of the Puffballs, also include very nearly the same morphological variability as the Boletales: standard mushrooms, small cups, tree-like species, bird's nests, truffle-like, jelly brackets, fungi, puffballs, coats of paint, some brackets and several more. Many of these forms besides the Puffballs have parallels in the Boletales.

These dizzying lists of wildly different forms, many represented in *both* Orders, go against everything we understand about *types*. There is no *typical* member of either Order; they are just a mess of forms. Of course, in normal evolutionary thought where relatedness trumps form every time, both Orders would have an original form from which the rest were descended. Perhaps that would count as the type.

One can only hypothesise that it is the plasticity of fungi that allows such invention. While the underlying mycelium is an amorphous mass of tangled hyphae, fungal fruiting bodies, constructed as they are from yet more hyphal threads, can be formed into any shape imaginable, provided the structure is still functional. The formation of fungal fruiting bodies is, effectively, knitting. By contrast, mammals are rather stuck with their skeletal systems, so they have limited scope for flamboyant variation.

The reappearance of forms in the two lineages is generally a matter of convergent evolution, where the same structure is evolved anew – gilled fungi in both Orders, for example. However, some of these structural convergences might better be termed 'convergent devolution', as they display 'loss of function'. The Boletes, themselves typified as they are with a cap, tubes underneath and a stem (the Penny Bun or Cep, for example), include close relatives that form truffle-like organisms that lack, indeed have lost, the ability to produce the highly functional fruiting body of their brethren, most notably the finely tuned mechanism by which spores are ejected.

For the naturalist or forager such things have little relevance, but they do show how very different closely related species can be. In the field we will judge a species by how much it looks like something we already know; hence the confusion over Earthballs and Puffballs, the former nearer to a Boletus species, the latter nearer to a Field Mushroom. It makes identification just that little bit more difficult, and fun.

Into the Woods

The area of woodland we had just entered is the largest in the Forest. I have explored much of it from various entry points but have always wanted to walk straight across it. It is criss-crossed with rides, broad paths that can accommodate vehicles for wood-land management and riding, and a few less clear and manageable paths. We were in for a three-mile walk, following (or not) these paths. We did not see a single soul for the whole three miles.

We were in an open area of birch and oak, walking along a path much narrower than the rides. There were few fungi to be seen, but the oaks were, or appeared to be (it is not always easy to tell), ancient pollards, the New Forest being one of their last rural bastions. Pollarded trees, kept permanently youthful by the pollarding process, are some of our oldest trees. It is on these and their failing or fallen brethren that so many fungi appear. We were to see one of the most striking of these the following day.

A few Scots Pines came into sight and their commonest fungal companions with them. These were **Saffron Milkcaps**, *Lactarius deliciosus*, which, you will not be surprised to hear, are edible. Whether or not *deliciosus* is overstating it I must leave to you, but I find it pleasant enough, with a flavour halfway between mushrooms and carrots. The specimens that day were in excellent condition – firm, fresh and lacking their particular bane, fungal gnat larvae, better known as maggots. It is easy enough to identify, with its banded markings on top, a tendency to turn green and decurrent, bright orange gills. It produces orange 'milk' when broken, something that is best seen by breaking the stem and printing the milk on the back of your hand. If, after several minutes, it turns red, followed a little later by green, it is *Lactarius semisanguineus*. This too is edible, but bitter. If it is growing with spruce it will be *Lactarius deterimus*, also edible, but *deterimus* means 'of poor quality'.

Fallen timber lies everywhere in the New Forest, none of it collected any more as the commoners' 'right of estover' (literally, the 'right to the necessary') is now fulfilled using plantation timber. A fortune in firewood is thus left to rot and become instead a fortune in natural history. Rotting itself is fascinating and often beautiful. I am always looking out for attractive formations of brown rot and managed to find a nicely presented specimen that day. Brown rot is caused by a variety of fungal agents – Chicken of the Woods, *Laetiporus sulphureus*, and Beefsteak Fungus, *Fistulina hepatica*, usually on oaks, Dyer's Mazegill, *Phaeolus schwienitizii*, on conifers, the Birch Polypore and several more. The fungal mycelium within the trunk first releases hydrogen peroxide, a small molecule able to permeate timber easily. This is, literally, a softening-up exercise which degrades the structural cellulose. The softened cellulose is then slowly digested by the mycelium, in due course causing shrinkage into a multitude of almost cubic blocks.

Difficult Fungi, Easy Fungi

There is a group of fungi, several in fact, which try the patience of every field mycologist. *Mycena* and its related genera are notoriously difficult to identify, with small details counting (as always) for everything and a microscope essential. Some are common, some are exceedingly rare. Fortunately, a respectable number are relatively easy to ID as they have 'tricks' – that is, characteristics that are unique to a single species, or maybe two or three, which is still better than the 150 or so that it could be. Such tricks are: a bloody latex from the broken stem, a white latex, the smell of nitric acid or of raw pastry, being large and pink, having a slippery stem and/or a bright yellow stem, growing on coniferous cones, growing in dense tufts and more. The *Mycena* we found in the wood consisted of forty all clustered together, forming an impressive tuft. It was **Mycena inclinata**, characterised by its tufty nature and warm yellow stem.

While we are on the subject of difficult fungi, the next one was in what most field mycologists will consider to be the most difficult of the genera– it was a *Cortinarius* species, otherwise known as a Webcap. With at least 330 to choose from I was ready, as usual with *Cortinarius* species, to admit defeat. My best guess, however, is **Cortinarius elatior**, because of its conspicuously wrinkled, beige cap and purple gills. All *Cortinarius* species have a ring-zone on the stem, usually as a zone of fibres that are visible due to the rust brown spores that have been caught there. For the forager, the rust-brown spores and ring-zone (the latter being the remnants of a distinct web of fine fibres that radiated from the edge of the young cap to the stem) are all you need to know – it is a *Cortinarius* species and must be left firmly alone. Not *all* are poisonous, but several are utterly deadly, which is all one needs to know.

More cheerful was the **Powdery Brittlegill**, *Russula parazurea,* a Brittlegill that is good to eat and easy to identify, with its bluish green and slightly frosted cap. Unfortunately, it seldom appears in more than ones and twos and is often half eaten by that bane of mushroom hunters, slugs. A better find was a collection of **Millers**, *Clitopilus prunulus*, which nothing seems to eat except the more adventurous variety of foragers. It is a common species, especially in the grassy areas of open oak woods. It is edible and very good but has a serious lookalike in the form of the Fool's Funnel, *Clitocybe rivulosa*, a fungus that can be deadly in quantity. The spore colour, however, is a giveaway – pink in the Miller and white in the Fool's Funnel. To obtain a 'spore print' just leave a fresh cap, gills down, on a sheet of white paper and you will know in an hour or two whether or not this is your prospective Miller. Taking a spore print is the first step after noting the habitat when attempting to identify a mushroom with a cap and gills, so well worth the small effort. The mycelium of the Miller is believed to parasitise that of the Penny Bun, and in finding one species in fruit you can often find the other. Not today, however. It was not a good year for any of the edible Boletes.

We were about level with Denny Wood Campsite at this point, though it was too far to the east of our track to visit. It is one of the best places I know for fungi, as indeed are most well-used campsites. Their plenitude in such situations is, I suspect, down to the short grass, lack of undergrowth and the mild stress of the environment, which encourages the fruiting bodies to appear. There were several houses nestling in the wood, and we passed a couple along a more than usually well-maintained track, the broad grassy verge of which sported one of the best collections I had ever seen of **Fairy Ring Champignon**, *Marasmius oreades*, the damp weather having kept them in prime condition. I was very tempted to pick some, but proximity to habitation stayed my hand.

Rain

The light but persistent rain had relented for an hour or so but returned with a determination that soon became intolerable. The Forest itself was not helping much: the rides were failing to take us in the direction we wanted and the increasing preponderance of coniferous plantation making our short cuts more trouble than they were worth. Looking through my photo collection of the day, I noticed that there were none, save a few smartphone images, after 2.30 p.m. I had forgotten that the rain had made photography impossible, and my expensive bits of kit were packed away. Fortunately, D had kept scrupulous records for posterity. We found a not very sheltered spot and sat down for lunch. I had forgotten the beer.

Slightly miserable as we were on leaving our shelter, we were cheered by a few more fungi, but fungi in general were not the full flush we had hoped for. There is a week or so in most autumns when one simply cannot put foot to floor without treading on a mushroom. This is no exaggeration, I promise. Anyone whose experience of fungi happens to be only or mostly on such days sometimes expects all of every autumn to be similarly productive and is disappointed when it is not. This sometimes leads to the absurd misapprehension that it is because of people picking mushrooms. That the inedible and plain poisonous species, none of which would be picked by a forager, are also missing does not strike them as indicative of any alternative hypothesis. People believe what they want to believe. In the cool year of 2021 that flush did not materialise, at least not in southern England; nor did the complaints, though I suspect people had other things to worry about.

Despite us not seeing fungi everywhere, we were covering a lot of ground and soon had a respectable list. I will not trouble you with everything we found in that area, just two. The best-looking was another Dapperling, called, I am willing to wager without resort to a microscope, *Lepiota magnispora*. The group consisted of seven specimens at various stages of growth, something that is always helpful in identification.

Cheering the day were several groups of **Blushers**, *Amanita rubescens*, all in good condition. Despite being edible and excellent, like a barrister whose brother is serving time for GBH, it has some unfortunate relatives. These include the Death Cap, the Destroying Angel and the Panther Cap, all of which are in the genus *Amanita*. This has deterred many people from eating Blushers, and cautious forager that I am, it was a long, long time before I felt confident enough to consume any on toast. It is, nevertheless, easily identified, most particularly from its invariable characteristic of bruising pink. It is well worth the effort to learn; after all, you will not suffer much competition.

Standing Hat

We passed a dozen fungi, merely noting their names, and eventually joined a long, wide drive which would bring us out at Standing Hat, to the north-east of Brockenhurst. The drive was fairly bare of fungi, with only the odd **False Death Cap**, *Amanita citrina*, and several **Slippery Jacks**, *Suillus luteus*, to brighten the walk. Standing Hat is familiar territory for us both, as it is where we hold some of my public fungus forays. It is a productive mix of ancient grassland, ancient woodland and coniferous plantation.

We had seen enough of these last two habitats that day, so explored instead a little of the grassland. There were several groups of **Snowy Waxcaps**, *Cuphophyllus virgineus*, in the grass. It is small, slightly translucent-white and does not look remotely pleasant to eat. However, it is one of the best of the edible fungi and common in permanent grassland, including lawns. There were also two *Agaricus* species, *A. arvensis* and *A. porphyrhizon*. The first of these is the **Horse Mushroom** and common everywhere; the second is known as the **Lilac Mushroom**, a name well deserved as it has an unusual lilac flush. Back in the early 1980s I struggled to identify this species as there were almost no books on British fungi forty years ago, something that is difficult to believe when I now own more than 120. The two or three books I owned then did not trouble to mention so rare a fungus. Although rare in Britain, I have found it to be among the most common of its genus in the New Forest. It is not considered to be edible, in part at least because it is rare; however, I tried one once and it was excellent.

The Pub

We walked the mile to Brockenhurst and went into a pub – but only after a great deal of disrobing as we both looked as though we had recently been dragged out of a lake. We found a quiet corner where no one could see us, and downed a couple of beers for me and two large glasses of Pinot Grigio for D. Not long before we left, I disappeared to the small room for two or three minutes. When I returned, D told me of an encounter she had just suffered with a gentleman who had been secretly listening to our mycological conversation. He had berated her about the picking of mushrooms, telling her that picking them in the New Forest was banned and that we should not do it. He had disappeared by then, and I wanted to chase after him to, er, explain things (that he should not berate my wife being one of them), but D told me to leave it.

The memory of this sour end to a wet day is with me as I write, so I will leave the explanations I had in mind until the next day, when we walked the middle section of our mycological journey.

DAY TWO

Millyford Bridge

We were well practised in taxi management by now, our taxi driver of the previous night having performed admirably considering how very wet and slightly tipsy we were. Today we were not so lucky. It is difficult to explain precisely where you want to go to a taxi driver when there is no address or even a vague postcode. I said we would like to go to Millyford Bridge, and he said that, sure, sure, he knew it, but was much more concerned that we had cash to pay for the ride. Unfortunately, he did *not* know where Millyford Bridge was, and managed to turn a two-mile journey into a seven-mile journey. When we arrived, I told him about the 'short cut' back and gave him a tip; I have no idea why.

Millyford Bridge, a place I have visited for fungus forays on at least thirty occasions, is my second-favourite place in the Forest. It is a small piece of heaven on Earth and heaven itself for the mycologist. And no, I am not going to tell you where number one is: find your own. On a good day, when there is one of those 'flushes' I mentioned earlier, we can spend two hours just walking around the tiny car park.

Millyford Bridge was not quite as giving that day as it has been in the past, but still there were plenty of fungi. The grassland and grassy bank alongside the road have always been among my most treasured spots, and so it was that day. The Snowy Waxcap was there, a small cluster of yellow club fungi known as **Clavulinopsis luteoalba** and the stunning **Parrot Waxcap**, *Gliophorus psittacinus*. The last of these is a real beauty and common in such mature grassland. Its 'parroty' names come from the multitude of colours it employs (for no particular reason that I can see), very much like a parrot, and with green dominating. When it is young, it is *entirely* green and almost impossible to spot in the grass. It is also almost impossible to pick because of the slime that covers every surface except the gills. Its generic name makes a failed attempt to reflect this, *Gliophorus* meaning 'covered in glue'. All of the Waxcaps were once in the genus *Hygrocybe* and many still are, but they have now been redistributed into about eight European genera. This has resulted in field mycologists having to learn about forty new Latin names. They were hard enough to learn the first time.

Oyster Mushrooms and Maggots

Every forager has his *spots* and a mental map of where they are. I estimate that I have around a thousand tucked away in my head and am able to tell you (not that I will) nearly every location where I have found Penny Buns, truffles, Sea Beet, Marsh Samphire, Pacific Oysters and many more edible species. At and around Millyford Bridge there are a dozen such species with their accompanying locations fixed in my mind. Most of them that day were unproductive, but the fallen Beech that has been manufacturing Oyster Mushrooms for the last ten years was covered in them. There are a few mushrooms that go by the name Oyster Mushroom, the most familiar being *Pleurotus ostreatus*. At Millyford Bridge they are *P. pulmonarius*, the **Pale Oyster**; at least I *think* they are. The reason for this hesitation is that the two species are not well defined, and it is believed that they can hybridise. For the forager this matters not a jot; they are all edible.

One thing to look out for with Oyster Mushrooms is maggots, for which they have a particular appeal. The collection I saw that day did not look promising as there was a dense cloud of tiny flies swirling around them. I split a couple apart and found no maggots, so presumably any eggs that had been laid there had not yet hatched. No one minds eating gnat eggs.

Maggots, however, are not to everyone's taste. It is not so much the maggots, which are generally a pleasant enough source of protein; it is the mess they make of any species of mushroom they might be consuming. This is a very anthropocentric view, of course, as those maggots will be the larvae of any number of invertebrate species, mostly flies or beetles. Of these hundreds of fungivorous species, most of them are flies known as fungus gnats (*Mycetophilidae*), of which there are an astounding 480 species in Britain. Most invertebrates and all fungus gnats rely entirely on fungal fruiting bodies for their livelihood.' Many are limited generalists, inhabiting a large but still restricted range of soft fruitbodies such as Boletes, Brittlegills and *Agaricus* species. Sometimes, most often with the beetles, a bracket fungus is colonised, and some species will insist on only one species of bracket.

Despite my playful and covert warning about eating gnat eggs, with most fungal gnat species the adult will lay her eggs in the soil and the emergent larvae will eat the fungus from the inside. (I am not sure about Oyster Mushrooms, as they grow on hard wood.) Being eaten from the inside does not sound too good for the fungus, but it has a negligible effect on spore production and dispersal. Other larvae, however, are 'spore-grazers', which obviously does have an effect. Tiny ecosystems such as this inevitably invite freeloaders, represented here by predatory species of beetle, for example, the tachyporine staphylinid, *Lordithon lunulatus*. It is a common predatory beetle in Europe, with black and orange bandings, and is usually found in bracket and other firm fungi consuming fungivorous invertebrates. While ephemeral fruiting bodies such as Oyster Mushrooms do not support the entire lifecycle of associated invertebrates, pupation occurring in the soil beneath the soon-to-disappear fungus, the more robust and long-lived bracket fungi certainly can, with pupae forming within them.

The picking of mushrooms is a natural part of the life of hunter–gatherers, but with our impact on ecosystems we need to take more care than our forebears, for whom hunting and gathering were all. When collecting fungi for the table, I always consider that other organisms depend on them too, and that frequently they depend on them entirely.

* Peter Chandler, *Fungus Gnats (Diptera: Mycetophilidae, Mycetophilinae)*, vol. 9, part 8 of *RES Handbook for the Identification of British Insects* (London, 2022).

Fungal gnats still swirling around my head, I turned my attention to the other fungi on the fallen Beech. Quite a few fungi are extremely rubbery, and what adaptations they underwent to change the more familiar textures of fragile, soft and fibrous into that of a tap washer I cannot say. I found one common species here with a rubbery disposition, the **Beech Jelly Disc**, much more respectably called *Neobulgaria pura* var. *pura*. I was pleased to see it because we had not seen anything so far but Basidiomycetes. *N. pura* var. *pura* is an Ascomycete. If you find a Beech Jelly Disc, you are likely to find a hundred, and a hundred it was that day, maybe more. Its status as a variety is indicated by the repetition of its specific name of the 'original' form, that is, the first that acquired the name. *N. pura* var. *foliacea* is darker, more convoluted and relatively rare. A rubbery texture, incidentally, is not confined to the Ascomycetes, as an Elder tree we found that day near the stream bore some very rubbery **Wood Ears**, *A. auricula-judae*, a Basidiomycete and edible, if a little chewy.

The Gee-Whiz Science of Ballistospory

One of the most impressive sights in a mature beechwood is that of the enormous bracket fungi that grace dead or dying trunks. At Millyford Bridge I visited a Beech stump whose fortunes I have been following for several years. Over that time a succession of Beech saprotrophs (including Oyster Mushrooms) having taken up residence and duly fruited. Dominant through most of those years has been a specimen of a now huge bracket fungus known as the **Southern Bracket**, *Ganoderma australe*. Several large 'plates' have formed, and it is possible even to shelter under it with a bit of wiggling through the Bracken. Incidentally, *australe* simply means 'southern'.

A few years ago I was there on a bright, windless day and could see the cloud of brown spores cascading from the white fertile layer on the underside. The top surface is a matt brown and coarsely wrinkled. These cascading spores form in and fall from thousands of tiny pores. These pores are the openings to tubes about 1 cm long that are arranged vertically to within a fraction of a degree. A broken bracket will usually reveal layers of such tubes from previous years. Ganoderma and a few other bracket genera have acquired this ability to produce perennial fruiting bodies, an unusual practice considering how ephemeral most fruiting bodies are.

The spores of *Ganoderma* and thousands of other species, all in the Basidiomycetes, are produced on the end of structures embedded in the walls of the tubes or gill or spines or plain flat surfaces from which they marginally project. These structures are known as 'basidia' and are common in one form or another in most of the fungi that you are likely to see. So fundamental are they that the entire Division (the highest Class below a Kingdom) in which they are found is called the Basidiomycetes. The other Division that forms fruiting bodies that are commonly visible to the naked eye, the Ascomycetes, are similarly named for their base reproductive structure, the ascus, a long, sausage-shape tube containing eight spores (usually) which are shot into the air courtesy of hydrostatic pressure – they are 'squirted'.

Basidia and their usual method of spore dispersal are micro-machines of considerable complexity. This is one step up from the 'nano-machines' that work at the level of proteins. My favourite, everyone's favourite, bit of biological nano-tech is the near-ubiquitous system that moves material from one part of a cell to another. Here the eye-wateringly complex protein kinesin latches on to whatever is being carried and quite literally walks along one of the intra-cellular highways made of the protein-complex tubulin. I promise you that it is worth looking up an animation of this by typing 'kinesin animation' into a search engine.

Basidia are much, much larger, but still invisible from a human perspective – typically 14–20 microns in length, meaning that fifty, end to end, will mark 1 mm. They are roughly club-shaped, with (usually) four prongs at the end which project horizontally from the internal surface of the pores or gills. These prongs are called 'sterigma', plural 'sterigmata'. The basidia, complete with their sterigma, are packed almost side to side on the inner surface of a tube, with sterile 'packing' cells between them to reduce overcrowding. The basidia, packing cells and their underlying plumbing system of hyphae make up what is called the 'fertile layer' or, more technically, the 'hymenium'.

After a certain amount of highly complex genetic activity with which I will not trouble you, one haploid nucleus (one set of chromosomes) is moved to the tip of each sterigma. The remaining spore structures are created around these nuclei, and in time four spores are formed on each basidium. They average out over many species at 8 microns in diameter.

They now face the problem of releasing themselves into the air. The sterigmata that are holding them in place could wither, perhaps, but spores are 'sticky' and would simply stay put. They need to shoot outwards (horizontally) by a few microns to avoid this terminal fate, but not so far that they would then stick to the other side of the pore (or to another gill, in the case of gilled mushrooms). Enter the 'surface tension catapult'. Once the spore is almost ready to set off on its journey, a small deposit of the sugars mannitol and hexose form on (mostly) one side of the spore and also on a small projection (the 'hilar appendage') that forms on the spore near its attachment to the sterigma. The sugars are hydrophilic, meaning they attract water, and will condense water from the air to form a thin, lens-shaped layer on the sugary area

on the side of the spore and a large droplet on the hilar appendage. The droplet has been dubbed 'Buller's drop', after the mycologist A. H. R. Buller, who first described it. Once they have
reached the appropriate size, the two drops will come into con-
tact and coalesce in a fraction of a second, the larger, spherical
droplet flowing onto the lenticular drop on the side of the spore.
This results in a transfer of the potential energy held as surface
tension to kinetic energy from the movement of the larger droplet, thus shooting the spore horizontally from the hymenium.
Buller discovered his drop about a hundred years ago, but it was
not until 1991 that this mechanism was described (or at least, proposed) – by Professor John Webster from Exeter University. I
have one of his books on my shelves and still think very fondly
of the day I spent in his erudite and charming company looking
for fungi in the woods of Devon. This is a mycological form of
name-dropping, for which I apologise.

Spores will accelerate at a frankly silly rate – 25,000 times that
of the acceleration provided by Earth's gravity and within an
order of magnitude of the acceleration of a bullet from its car-
tridge. Fortunately, they do not travel far as they are impeded in
their motion by the air in the tubes, which at this scale is effectively thicker than porridge. Each species will have finely tuned
its shooting capabilities to how far the spore can travel without
hitting anything. Some species in the Basidiomycetes have a flat,
cupped or otherwise exposed hymenium, and there is no limit as
there is nothing to hit, and with gilled fungi there is anything up
to 4 mm between gills. With *Ganoderma* species the internal diameter of the pores is about 0.2 mm, 200 microns, and the spores
are shot about 20 microns. After this very short journey they fall
at the rate of 1 mm per second until they exit the tube.

For fungi with gills or tubes, keeping their hymenium layers absolutely vertical is essential for spore dispersal. Almost any

gilled fungus that is disturbed sufficiently to tilt its gills away from the vertical will do one of two things. It will either bend its stem, starting from the top until the cap is level, or change the orientation of the gills until they are vertical. The first technique is preferable as moving the gills but not the cap will cause a narrowing of the gap between them, and for fruiting bodies with tubes the orientation of the tubes relative to the supporting cap is fixed, so rotating the entire cap is the only method that works. Sensory mechanisms not unlike the otoliths in our ears tell the individual parts of a mushroom which way is up, and which correct their attitude by growing more on one side than the other. None of this has any relevance to the forager, except that it dismisses the notion that using an open-weave basket so that you can scatter spores through the forest as you prance along as being as absurd as it sounds. Mushrooms are not pepper pots.

Picking Mushrooms

We walked eastwards across a tiny road bridge and turned to the south to a very different environment, damp grassland with its tussocks grazed to small bumps and a plant that I am always pleased to see because it can be used to make beer. **Sweet Gale**, also known as Bog Myrtle, goes by the Latin name of *Myrica gale*. It is rare in England, or at least confined to the west and southwest and scattered elsewhere. It was once an ingredient of ales before hops were adopted. It possesses a powerful aromatic smell, not entirely unlike pine. The best part is the immature flower heads. I sometimes make 'pine-candle' toffee, and while writing this I began to wonder if Sweet Gale toffee might work too.

The ground was becoming impassably wet and mossy, this landscape being known as a 'sphagnum acid flush', so we crossed back to the drier grass on the north side of the road and walked towards a wood edge behind some isolated standard oaks. Individual trees and wood edges are often productive of fungi, so hopes were high. The **Penny Bun**, *Boletus edulis*, is one of the most highly prized of all the fungi and often the only one people bother to collect. We had seen none the day before, but there were half a dozen slightly slug-nibbled specimens beneath these oaks. Two years previously, in what everyone interested in such things called a 'Cep year', they were everywhere. Over the eight days I spent there that autumn I must have seen a thousand.

A fair proportion of that thousand were in the back of a car, collected by someone who insisted against all the evidence that they were 'for personal consumption'. Commercial collection is illegal, but, rightly or wrongly, I did not report what I saw, even though (entirely by coincidence) the same person appeared doing the same thing on four of those eight days and in four separate locations. My reluctance was down to consideration for my guests. The last thing anyone wants on a jolly public foray is the police turning up. Many people become very agitated about such reports, myself included, but this was only the second time I had seen this so flagrantly in forty-two years.

Until recently people would appear in the Forest with their baskets and pick a few mushrooms, then go home. This is just what happens all over Europe and has done for millennia; indeed it is from Europe that most of the Penny Buns you find in expensive restaurants and markets are picked.

Foragers are not quite the peaceable folk one might imagine, and if, while drinking our morning stiffener prior to a foray, my guests and I see someone coming out of the woods with a basket of mushrooms, the instinct (and I believe it really is an instinct, and a visceral one at that) was always to mug them. We never did.

No such qualms were felt by a woman three years ago who berated (that word again) my guests for picking mushrooms. They passed her 'enquiries' on to me, and no amount of polite explanation about it being an educational foray, my status as a writer and Fellow of the Linnean Society, written proof that I had permission or an appealing smile would placate her – she was apoplectic and determined to stay that way. She phoned the emergency line, and twenty minutes later a Ranger duly turned up, greeting me with a cheery 'Hello, John, how's it going?'

The difference between what I do and the person with a car-full of perfect Ceps is vast. On my forays we collect one or two specimens of whatever we find (unless it is rare or potentially rare, in which case I make a note of it and take a photograph instead and leave the mushroom in peace) and arrange them on a show-and-tell table with their Latin and common names underneath. We also collect a few of the very common edible species for a fry-up, so that people learn what they taste like. None of this will have any effect on the populations of any of the species; it is, after all, the fruiting bodies that we collect, not the entire fungus.

I have used the same procedure for many years but have still managed to find myself in trouble every now and then. Usually, it is like the man in the pub from the previous night or the unpleasant woman I have just mentioned. Sometimes, however, matters go to a higher authority and I end up in the newspaper or giving radio interviews. What the self-righteous complainants never seem to be interested in is what I actually do. They already know, or think they know, that I am a despoiler of the earth – so why ask?

Infected by the extreme views of the permanently discontented on the collecting of fungi, some local natural history societies and fungus groups seldom pick anything at all.

Instead, they peer at a specimen and comically use a dentist's mirror to see what the gills and stem look like. This is reasonable if you are doing a rough survey (and are skilled at identifying a species from so casual an examination), but people new to the interest will never learn much. To identify an unfamiliar fungus, moss, flowering plant or a myriad of other organisms, to get to really know it, you need to get up close and personal – look at the minute features with a loupe, feel its textures, learn its smell.

My friend Thomas, who forages and teaches the subject in Denmark, where foraging for mushrooms is a way of life, can barely believe the stories I tell him about the over-precious response to foraging in general, and mushroom collecting in particular. He considers the Brits to be barking mad.

Fungi on Trees

More exciting than the underwhelming Penny Buns was a bracket fungus on one of the birches. It was one I have barely seen before, the **Giant Elm Bracket**, *Rigidoporus ulmarius*. This was a first-class specimen, lacking most of the green algae that habitually colonise its upper surface.

We wandered back to the other side of the road, where I spotted something fascinating. Fascinating to me, at least. It was yet another large fallen Beech, but one that was at a very advanced stage of decomposition. I have written about the phenomenon of pseudosclerotial plates (PSPs) briefly in the London chapter and more extensively in my *Spotter's Guide to Countryside Mysteries*, but this showed me its ultimate fate. PSPs are tough, thin membranes within wood that has been infected by any of a small number of rot fungi. The commonest cause here is Brittle Cinder, *Kretzschmaria deusta*, a fungus that produces fruiting bodies that appear as white, then black, brittle and irregular plates on the bark of infected Beech.

Fungal colonies do not cohabit with any enthusiasm, so they build walls around and between them, forming any number of colonies completely enclosed within the trees by PSPs. Although they are created by fungi, they are, of necessity, immune from fungal attack. Once the wood in a Beech tree has rotted away completely, all that is left is a honeycomb of these PSPs, and that is what I was delighted to see that day.

Of less fascination, but at least a little more photogenic, was the common, pale orange and rubbery **Jelly Rot**, *Phlebia tremellosa*. It is impressive both from a distance and close up. Its upper surface is irregular and surprisingly hairy for anything that is otherwise rubbery. Underneath the fertile layer was a mass of orange wrinkles.

Just next to the Beech with the Jelly Rot was the common sight of autumn leaves scattered among thousands of tiny mounds of the moss. Such a scene is a lovely and common sight in the Forest, the moss concerned being ***Leucobryum juniperoideum***. Frequently this same moss will cover a fallen tree completely, the bright shroud of its decay. Occasionally a piece of moss will be dislodged, enabling it to grow fronds over its entire surface and looking like a green flying saucer.

Mosses are a perennial feature of the New Forest, best seen, I think, in the autumn, when their growth is stimulated by the rains and when the bright, warm colours of those fallen leaves make such a striking picture. Inevitably, autumn is my favourite season because of the fungi. I love the Forest in all seasons, but a winter walk has only a stark beauty, and one in summer can be dusty-dry and crowded.

A Great Treasure

It was after these musings that we discovered the glittering star of our visit to the Forest. Growing on an old oak, it was the **Tiered Tooth**, *Hericium cirrhatum*. I have seen this species only three or four times, usually in much less than perfect condition. This one, however, was a beauty in the prime of its youth, and I spent half an hour taking its portrait. Its riotous form is beyond description, but I can say that the irregularly tiered, cap-like structures were flaky on top with white spines underneath, the entirety a near virginal white with a hint of cream.

It is a rare fungus, but the commonest of three British *Hericium* species, and is listed on the Red List of Fungi for Great Britain as 'vulnerable', three steps down from 'critically endangered'. Its cousin, *H. erinaceus*, is one of only four British fungi to gain protection as a Schedule 8 species of the Wildlife and Countryside Act 1981, the 'schedule' itself being merely a list of all the species of plants, fungi and animals for which a prosecution can be undertaken against someone who is thought to have damaged them. A few years ago, I saw (and photographed) this latter species not far from where we were that day. All British *Hericium* species are, unfortunately, edible, and it is not unknown for people to steal them ('steal' is the only word) in contravention of a deeply held understanding among foragers and just about everyone else, that it is criminal to remove so rare a fungus, even if not all *Hericium* species come under the law. I did not even touch that Tiered Tooth, though I did sniff it. It smelt fungusy.

Of the many things to look out for when trying to identify a fungus, texture is one of the most helpful. Some are almost rock hard, many are fibrous, some leathery, some rubbery and some fragile. Such textures are reflections of the underlying micro-structures, and visible under a microscope. To the naked eye,

Hericium species, with their pale colour and thousands of spines hanging downwards, look very much like Hedgehog mushrooms in the Genus *Hydnum*. However, *Hydnum* is in the Order Cantharellales, along with Chanterelles, sharing their tough and flexible texture. The extremely fragile *Hericium* species, however, are in the Russulales, along with the otherwise physiologically different *Russula* species the Brittlegills. This is a clear case of texture triumphing over form.

Hericium cirrhatum was an impossible act to follow and, indeed, only three of the dozen further finds that day are worth relating. Two were pleasantly edible, and one was edible but with an acquired taste and a high toleration of slime. The **Amethyst Deceiver**, *Laccaria amethystina*, and the **Trumpet Chanterelle**, *Cantharellus tubaeformis*, are both good to eat, and attractive – the first purple, the second yellow-stemmed and brown-capped. Both are small and common. The latter species is the better tasting and a reliable stand-by in pine, spruce and beechwoods. A frequent foraging phenomenon is to wander around a woodland finding nothing, then stop for a moment only to see one, then three, then a hundred of them at your feet. They are very well camouflaged.

The third species was the **Slimy Beech-Tuft** or Porcelain Fungus, *Oudemansiella mucida*, the specific epithet saying it all. They can sometimes cover the entire side of a dead Beech tree (always Beech) with their shiny, white, hemispherical caps.

I often bump into someone I know in the Forest, and so it was that day. It was my friend Peter, who lives there, a fellow forager and member of the amiable group of eccentrics that make up the Association of Foragers. Like a couple of elderly patients in a doctor's waiting room talking about their ailments, most of our conversation consisted of us taking turns at telling stories of persecution from those who do not like what they think we do.

It was completely dark by the time we were back at our car in Lyndhurst. We were satisfied enough with the day, but both felt there could be more to find in a week's time.

DAY THREE

Three Common Fungi

Although late in the year, the day promised better than we had endured a week or so previously. It was certainly brighter, and warm for late October. D had decided not to join me, which meant that I had lost my taker of notes and carrier of tripod. With nothing but a collection of photographs and a poor memory to record proceedings, it is all a bit vague. This was not helped by the necessity of parking my pickup at Millyford Bridge (the end point) and walking to the start point a mile away while trying not to look at any fungi. Unfortunately, I am incapable of walking past a fungus, so precisely where and when I found anything remains a blur.

First up was the **Sheathed Woodtuft**, *Kuehneromyces mutabilis*, growing, as ever, as a dense tuft on a deciduous tree stump. This is a slightly tricky fungus in that it is reputedly edible and good but has a doppelgänger in the worrying form of the Funeral Bell, *Galerina marginata*. This latter species is as deadly as it sounds and one that I see two or three times a year. Both species grow in tufts on wood; both are brown; both have a ring on the stem. Yes, there are differences, and I know both species very well to the point that I can tell them apart 99.9 per cent of the time. But 99.9 per cent is, obviously, *nowhere near* enough for anyone planning their supper.

306

At least there is no such temptation with the **Shaggy Scalycap**, *Pholiota squarrosa*, which is mildly poisonous and looks nothing like anything edible. Anyway, it produces rust-brown spores, something almost unknown among edible fungi. Edibility, of course, is not an essential qualification for admiration, and their good looks are enough for me. These form dense rubbery tufts on dead tree trunks. They are as shaggy as their name suggests, with dry, orange/brown scales on a yellow cap.

The third was the honey fungus. It was and is common everywhere, a pest for the gardener and forester alike. Many years ago it was thought that there was only one species, and the appearance of its fruiting body anywhere on or near a tree spelled doom to the tree and very likely its neighbours. The doom could come from the fungus, which is an aggressive parasite, or from the chainsaw used to cut the tree down in the misplaced hope of banishing the fungus from the garden. However, many perfectly healthy trees may have succumbed unnecessarily as there are six species in Britain, only two of which are routinely and virulently pathogenic. The bad guys are the honey fungus, *Armillaria mellea* and *A. ostoyae*, with the rest opportunist parasites or mere saprotrophs, living only on material that is already dead. It was an immature specimen of one of the 'rest' that I saw that day, the **Bulbous Honey Fungus**, *A. gallica*. A neat-looking fungus, it is usually seen in ones and twos on the forest floor with its distinctive swollen base. The honey fungus, by contrast, grows in dense tufts at the base of dead or soon-to-be dead trees and has confluent, tapering stems. Honey fungi in general are edible to some people but, it seems, poisonous to others. It is generally thought that under-cooking is the problem, so ten minutes in the pan should count as a minimum. I consider them rather sickly in flavour, so you are missing nothing.

Mycena species are, as I mentioned earlier, difficult to identify, except for those with a helpful 'knock-down' characteristic. ***Mycena pelianthina*** is a common fungus of leaf litter, and close physically to the even more common, relatively large and very pink *M. pura* and *M. rosea*. It is smaller and not so brightly coloured but shares the same raw-potato smell. The knock-down character here, however, is a distinct dark edge to the gills. An hour later I was to find one of the most appealing of the *Mycena* species, ***Mycena rorida***. '*Rorida*' means 'dew', nicely reflecting the stem which is, unusually, covered in a sheath of clear mucus. It has one more distinctive trick, though not visible that day (or any *day*, really), in that it is one of the several species that glows in the dark. Writing this has inspired me to venture a night-time fungus foray next year.

The Worst

I mention in the Introduction that everyone loves a bad boy, your author included, and my next find was exceptionally lovable. It was a group of red-brown toadstools (I hesitate to follow my self-imposed convention of using 'mushroom' here), all in perfect condition. I could tell from twenty paces that they were a *Cortinarius* species (Webcaps), with a vague idea of which one.

Having taken no samples, I cannot be completely certain of the name of my specimen, just 99 per cent. It was the **Fool's Webcap**, *Cortinarius orellanus*, and deadly. It is similar in appearance to its equally deadly cousin, the Deadly Webcap, *C. rubellus*, which has famously caused disasters wherever it grows, including in Britain. It differs from *C. orellanus* in its more pointed cap and its insistence on growing with conifers.

The Pond

Almost the last thing I found on that walk was unconnected to anything fungal – it was a pond. About five metres across, it was just alongside the road. This, I thought, would be an appropriate place to end the adventure. With a childhood interest in rockets and anything technical I always wanted to be a rocket scientist – literally – or any career in technology, electronics, perhaps. But at the age of fourteen or so, not too long before I became interested in fungi, I went ponding with a young lady. We brought our jam jars back to her home and emptied them into a large glass bowl. There were so many things to see – Daphne species, Caddis Fly larvae, a Hydra perhaps (it was a long time ago), plus lots of green bits (algae) floating about. It was this that sparked an interest in the natural world that has stayed with me ever since and become more intense with the years.

The walks I took with dear D parallel the journey I have made through life as an observer of natural things both commonplace and plain weird. I would not have missed either, as this examination, this consideration, is the very essence of life to me. I hope that you will now continue your own walks and find that joy in what you observe. With observation comes understanding, and an understanding of the natural world leads to what I can only call love. I took a sample of the pond water from the Forest and looked at it under my microscope at home. Immediately, I was taken back to that pond, over half a century ago, where that love was first kindled, a love that has taken over and enriched my life.

Acknowledgements

First, I would like to thank my dear D for her tireless support throughout the writing of this book. She was my constant companion on the walks, my recorder, researcher and, of course, observer.

Thank you to my good and knowledgeable friend Miles King who kindly agreed to read through a draft of the book to spot any errors. He had a busy time of it, it seems. He also made many useful suggestions. Similarly, and as always, my gratitude is due to Bryan Edwards who was my final arbiter on some tricky identifications.

Eddie Bailey has been invaluable in answering all my questions on the geology of the various places D and I visited, albeit at enormous length. Thanks Ed. My daughter, Lily Wright, an adopted Londoner who is better attuned to the times than her father, was very helpful in editing my mini essay on the 'alien species controversy'. She may have saved me from a grim fate, so thank you Lily!

My editor, Louisa Dunnigan at Profile Books, is well practised in showing patience with my books but had to up her game with this one. Thank you, Louisa, for putting up with me, but also for your welcome and accurate direction; you are a saint. Managing editor Georgina Difford, designer James Alexander, copyeditor Matthew Taylor, proof-readers Charlotte Webb and

Patrick Taylor, and indexer, Ben Murphy, have turned an error-riddled manuscript into a 'proper' book. They have done this with great skill, and not a little charm. Thank you all.

A book needs a cover, and I have once again been fortunate in having Clare Curtis provide the superb artwork, while Pete Dyer designed the jacket. The dustjacket spread is a work of art, guys. I am grateful also to Kate McQuaid who has done sterling work as my publicist.

Finally, and again as always, many thanks to my agent, Gordon Wise of Curtis Brown.

Further Reading

Note: Most of these books deal with British and Irish species. However, they will also be useful in the broader north-west of Europe.

Plants

Tom Cope and Alan Gray, *Grasses of the British Isles*, BSBI Handbook no. 13 (London, 2009)

Simon Harrap, *Harrap's Wild Flowers: A Field Guide to the Wild Flowers of Britain & Ireland* (London, 2018)

Owen Johnson and David More, *Collins Tree Guide: The Most Complete Field Guide to the Trees of Britain and Europe* (London, 2006)

James Merryweather, *Britain's Ferns: A Field Guide to the Clubmosses, Quillworts, Horsetails and Ferns of Great Britain and Ireland* (Princeton, NJ, 2020)

John Poland and Eric Clement, *The Vegetative Key to the British Flora* (Southampton, 2020)

Francis Rose, *Colour Identification Guide to the Grasses, Sedges, Rushes and Ferns of the British Isles and North-Western Europe* (London, 1999)

Clive Stace, *New Flora of the British Isles*, 4th edn (Stowmarket, 2019)

Bob Watson, *Trees: Their Use, Management, Cultivation and Biology* (Ramsbury, 2007)

Fungi

M. B. Ellis and J. Pamela Ellis, *Microfungi on Land Plants: An Identification Handbook* (Slough, 2017)

Thomas Laessoe and Jens H. Petersen, *Fungi of Temperate Europe* (Princeton, NJ, 2019) [relatively easy to use, but be warned that it comes in two enormous volumes]

Paul Sterry and Barry Hughes, *Collins Complete Guide to British Mushrooms and Toadstools: The Essential Photograph Guide to Britain's Fungi* (London, 2009)

Lichens

Frank S. Dobson, *Lichens: An Illustrated Guide to the British and Irish Species* (Slough, 2011)

Invertebrates

Peter C. Barnard, *The Royal Entomological Society Book of British Insects* (Chichester, 2011)

Laurence Bee, Geoff Oxford and Helen Smith, *Britain's Spiders: A Field Guide* (Princeton, NJ, 2020)

Paul D. Brock, *Britain's Insects: A Field Guide to the Insects of Great Britain and Ireland* (Princeton, NJ, 2021)

Peter Chandler, *Fungus Gnats (Diptera: Mycetophilidae, Mycetophilinae)*, RES Handbook, vol. 9, part 8 (London, 2022) [a masterpiece, but not for the beginner, including your author]

Peter Eeles, *Life Cycles of British & Irish Butterflies* (Newbury, 2019) [butterflies depicted in all their life stages]

Steven Falk, *Field Guide to the Bees of Great Britain and Ireland* (London, 2018)

Francis S. Gilbert, *Hoverflies* (Exeter, 2015) [just one of the scores of books produced by Naturalists' Handbooks that enable the identification of various groups of invertebrates]

Barry Henwood and Phil Sterling, *Field Guide to the Caterpillars of Great Britain and Ireland* (London, 2020)

Dave Hubble, *Leaf Beetles* (Exeter, 2017)

David T. Salt, *Insects on Dock Plants* (Slough, 1999)

Phil Sterling and Mark Parsons, *Field Guide to the Micromoths of Great Britain & Ireland* (London, 2018)

Paul Waring, Martin Townsend and Richard Lewington (illus.), *Field Guide to the Moths of Great Britain and Ireland* (London, 2018)

Ecology

Ben Averis, *Plants and Habitats: An Introduction to Common Plants and Their Habitats in Britain and Ireland* (East Linton, 2020)

Sophie Lake, Durwyn Liley, Robert Still and Andy Swash, *Britain's Habitats: A Guide to the Wildlife Habitats of Britain and Ireland* (Princeton, NJ, 2020)

Anwar Maun, *The Biology of Coastal Sand Dunes* (Oxford, 2009)

E. Pollard, M. D. Hooper and N. W. Moore, *Hedges* (London, 1977)

J. S. Rodwell (ed.), *Woodlands and Scrub*, vol. 1 of *British Plant Communities*, 5 vols (Cambridge, 2005–6):
vol. 1, *Woodlands and Scrub*
vol. 2, *Mires and Heath*
vol. 3, *Grasslands and Montane Communities*

vol. 4, *Aquatic Communities, Swamps and Tall-Herb Fens*

vol. 5, *Maritime Communities and Vegetation of Open Habitats*

Peter A. Stroh, Kevin Walker, Stuart Smith, Richard Jefferson, Clare Pinches, Tim Blackstock and George F. Peterken, *Grassland Plants of the British and Irish Lowlands* (Bristol, 2019)

Miscellaneous

H. Godwin, *The History of the British Flora* (Cambridge, 2010)

Geoffrey Grigson, *The Englishman's Flora* (London, 1996)

Richard Ingrams, *The Life and Adventures of William Cobbett* (London, 2006)

Brian Moss, *Ponds and Small Lakes: Microorganisms and Freshwater Ecology* (Exeter, 2017)

Margaret Redfern and Peter Shirley, *British Plant Galls* (Shrewsbury, 2011)

John Wright, *The Naming of the Shrew: A Curious History of Latin Names* (London, 2015)

Index

Index

Wild Angelica (*Angelica sylvestris*)
256–7
Wildlife and Countryside Act
(1981) 185–6, 304
Wild Strawberry (*Fragaria vesca*)
181
Wild Thyme (*Thymus drucei*) 214,
235
William Cobbett, The 192–3
Willow Brackets (*Phellinus
igniarius*) 173
Winkles (*Littorina littorea*) 60
Wireweed (*Sargassum muticum*) 82
Wistman's Wood 247–8
Witch's Butter (*Tremella
mesenterica*) 242
Wood Avens (*Geum urbanum*) 68,
182
Wood Ear (*A. auriculajudae*) 295
Wood Forget-Me-Not (*Myosotis
sylvatica*) 162, 265–6
Woodruff (*Galium odoratum*)
265–6
Wood Sorrel (*Oxalis acetosella*) 90,
230, 265–6
Wood Spurge (*Euphorbia
amygdaloides*) 190–1
Woolly Fringe-Moss (*Racomitrium
lanuginosum*) 268
Wormwood (*Artemisia absinthium*)
61

Y
Yarrow (*Achillea millefolium*) 31, 99
Yellow-Flag Iris (*Iris pseudacorus*)
254
Yellow-Horned Poppy (*Glaucium
flavum*) 25, 27
Yellow Iris (*Iris pseudacorus*) 144
Yorkshire Fog (*Holcus lanatus*) 236

Z
Zetland Arms 93–4
Zostera 56–7, 59

X
Xanthoria parietina 23